AF381195

KONNY STEDING
NOTHING

FSC
www.fsc.org
MIXTE
Papier issu
de sources
responsables
Paper from
responsible sources
FSC® C105338

Preface

I don't know what I am doing. It is changing all the time. But it always comes back to similar things. I come back to simple paintings. Sometimes it's hard, sometimes it isn't. I paint mostly the same thing every day and I want to do a lot. Painting the same picture is pleasure. My painting is direct. I usually paint on the wall, sometimes on the floor. I like to paint big paintings with big brushes. I feel more at home in a big area. I want to express my feelings with paint and brush. I try to see what the painting offers.

Parcours

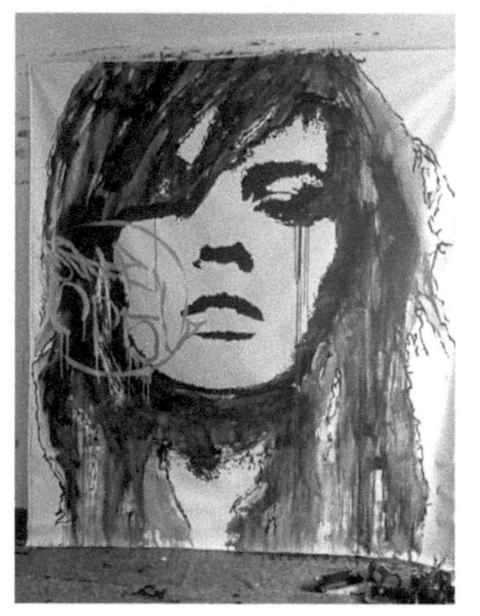

May 12, 2012

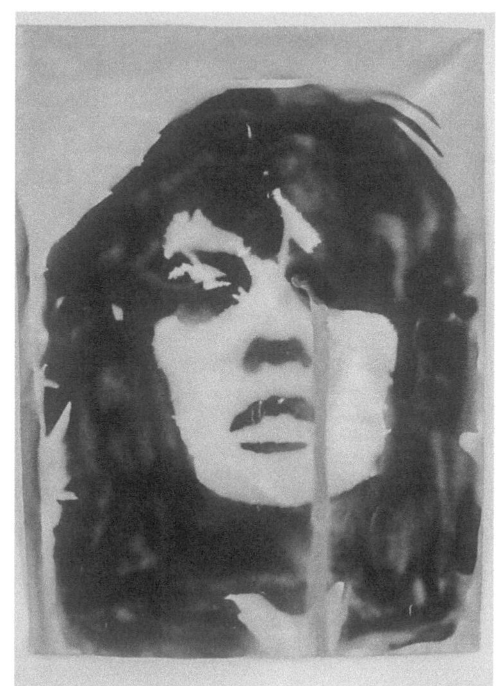

November 22, 2011

2016

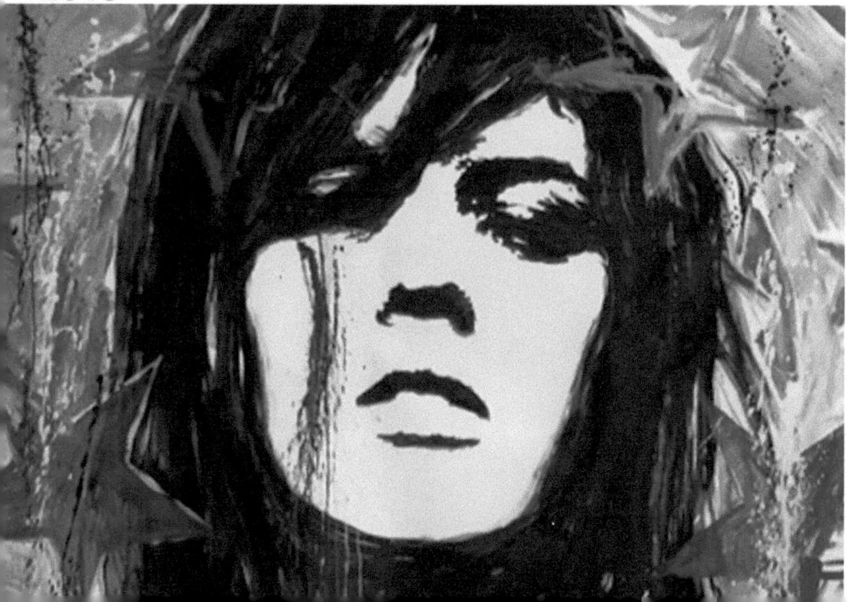

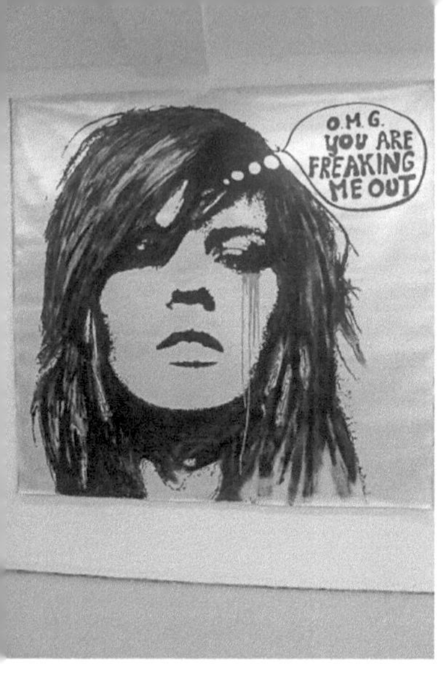

O.M.G.
YOU ARE
FREAKING
ME OUT

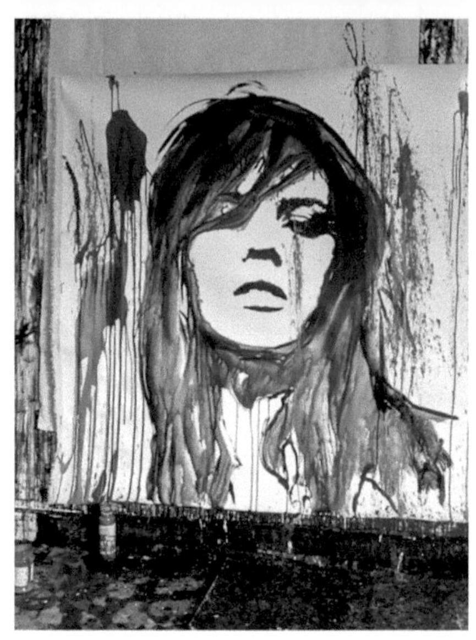

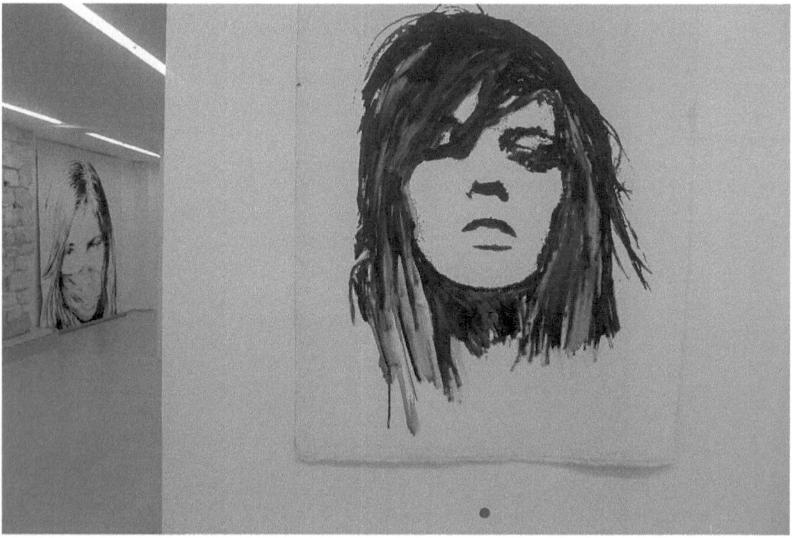

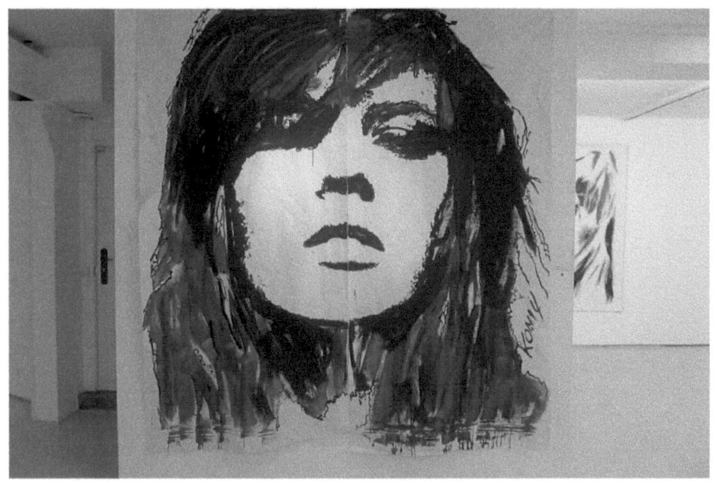

Exposition, Galerie Moretti&Moretti, November 22, 2011

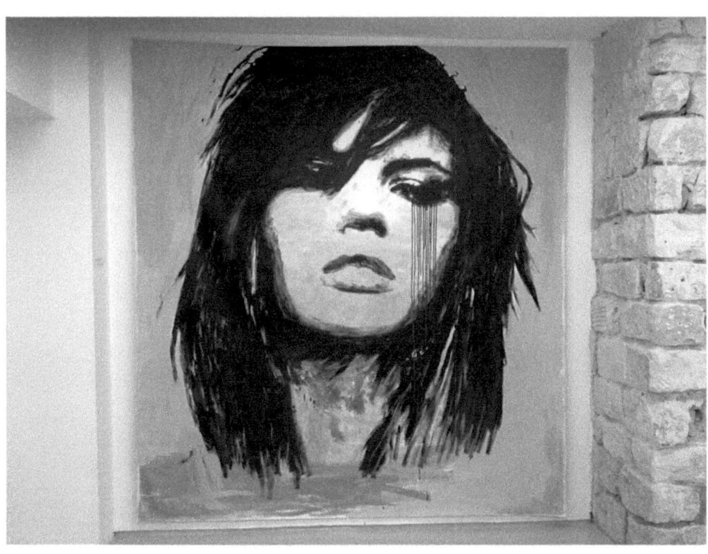

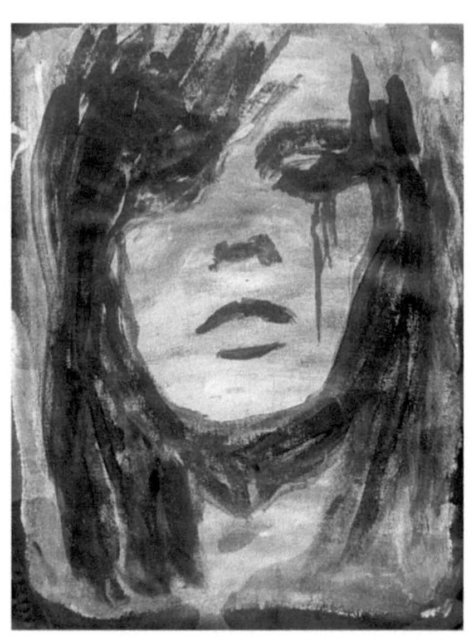

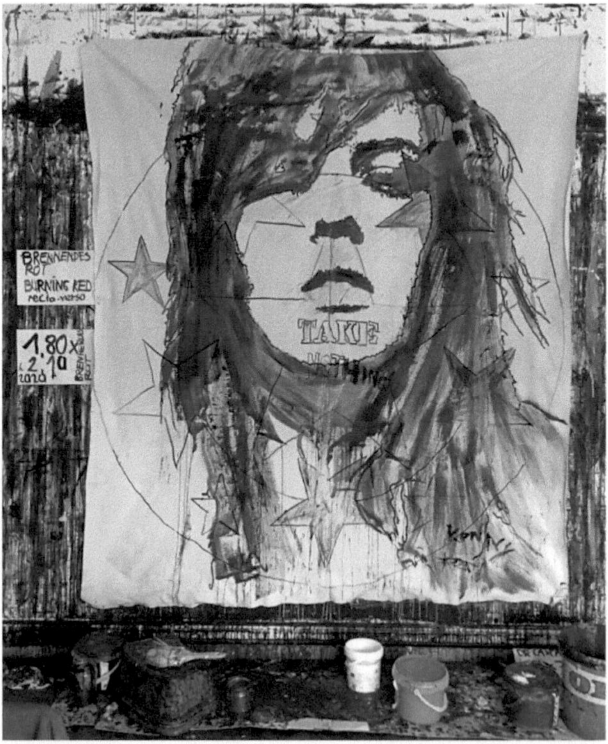

BRENNENDES
ROT
BURNING RED
recto-verso
1.80 x
2.10
2020
BRENNENDES
ROT
TAKE
Konar

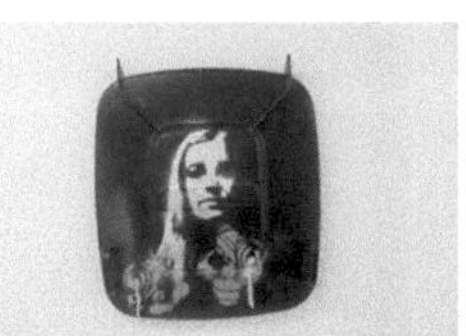
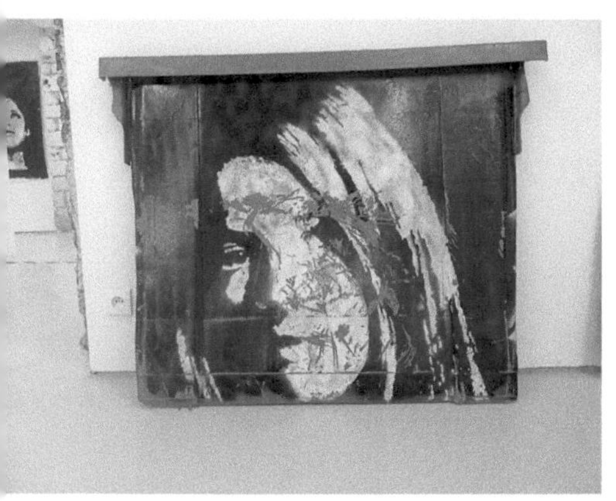
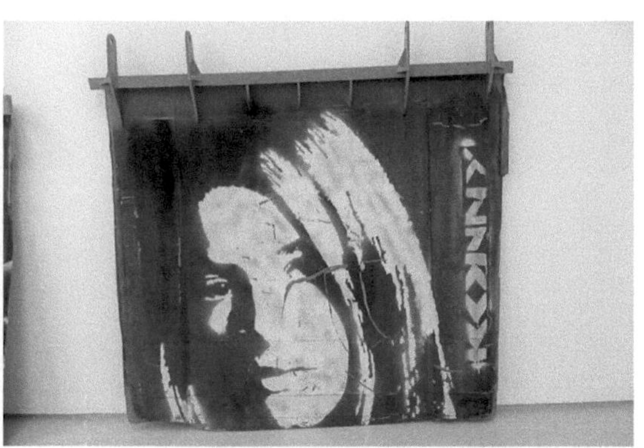
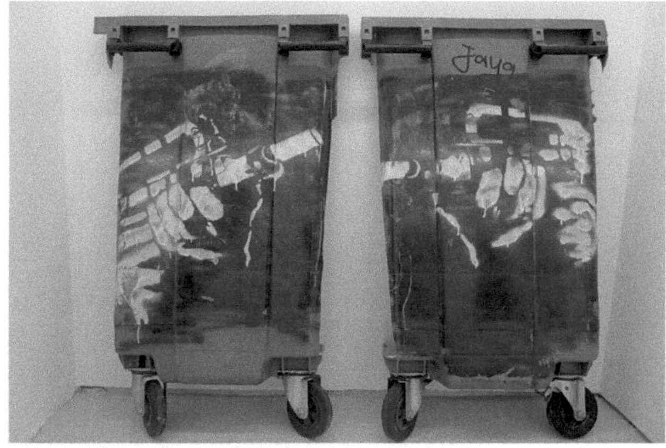

Garbage container

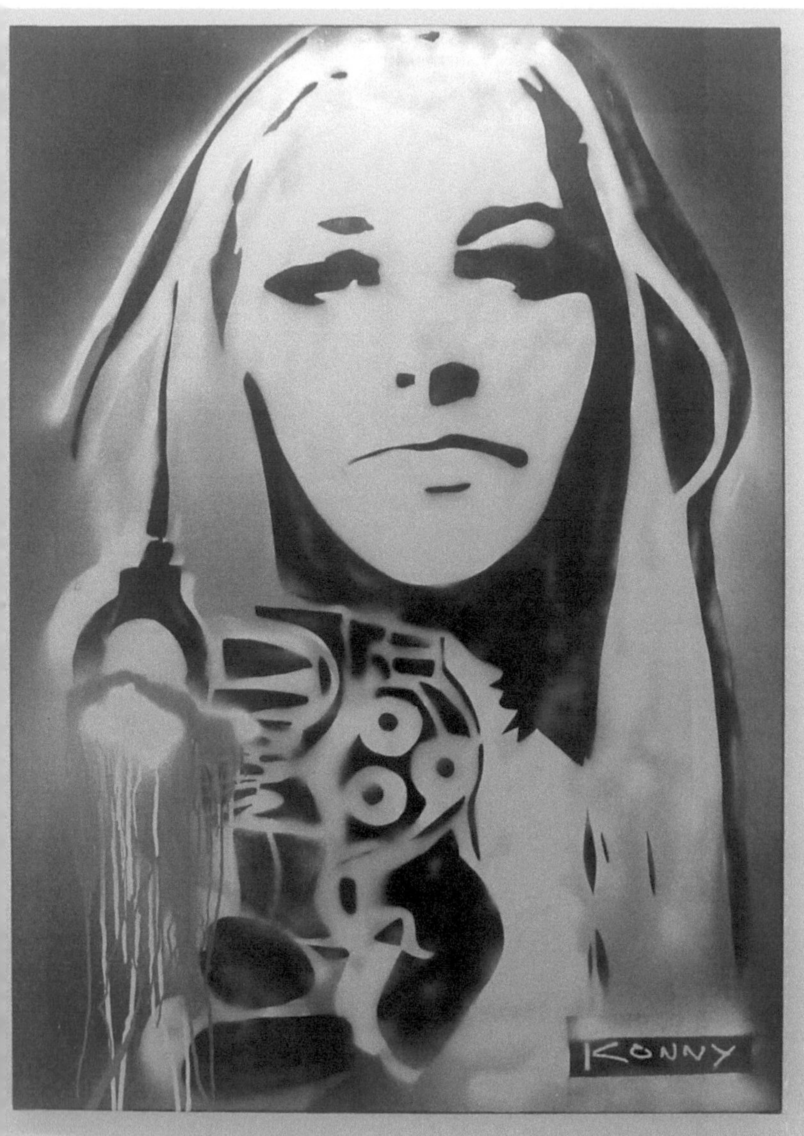

self portrait

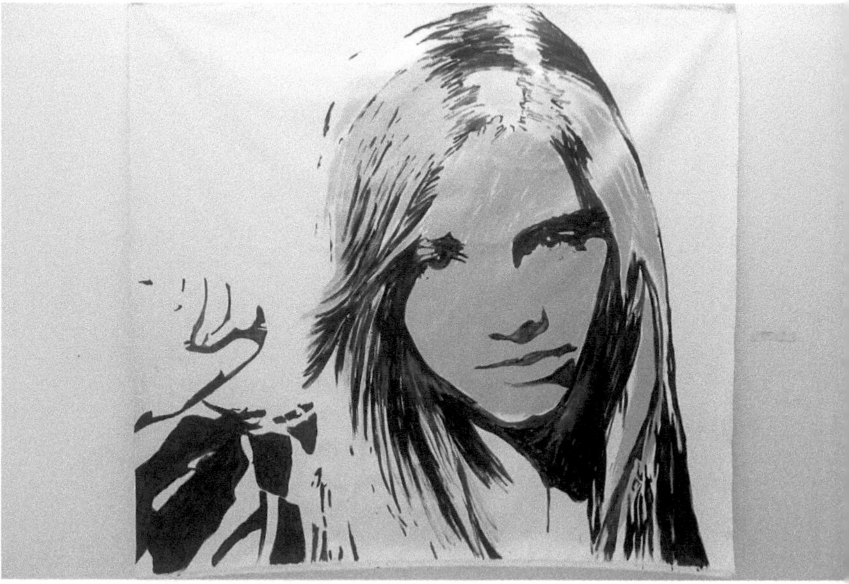

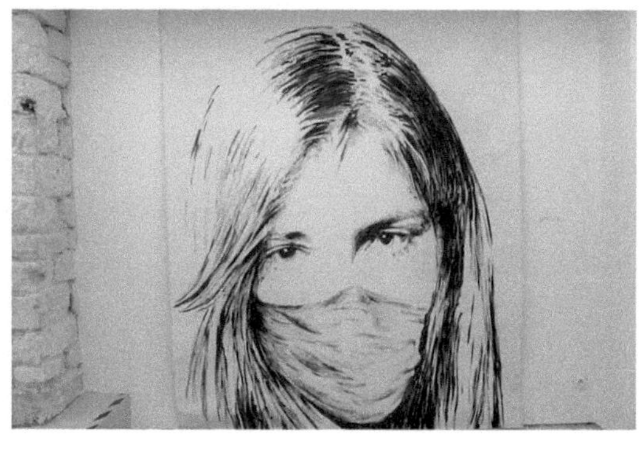

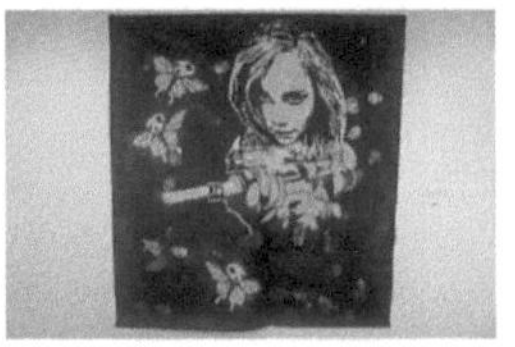

Karoline

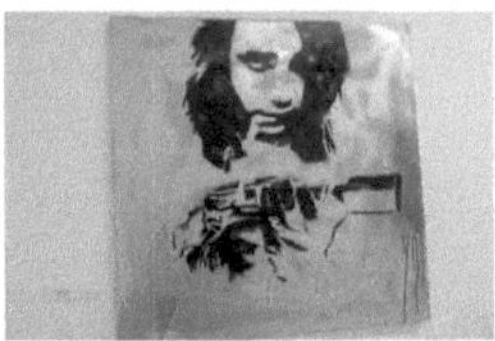

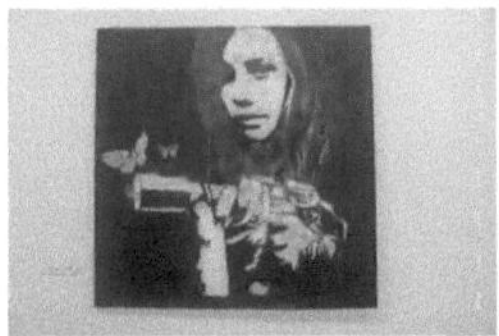

**Holding
a Butterfly**

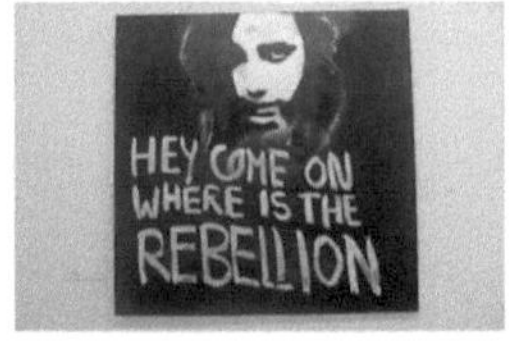

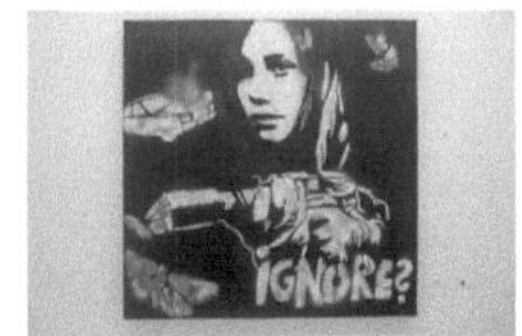

Hey come on

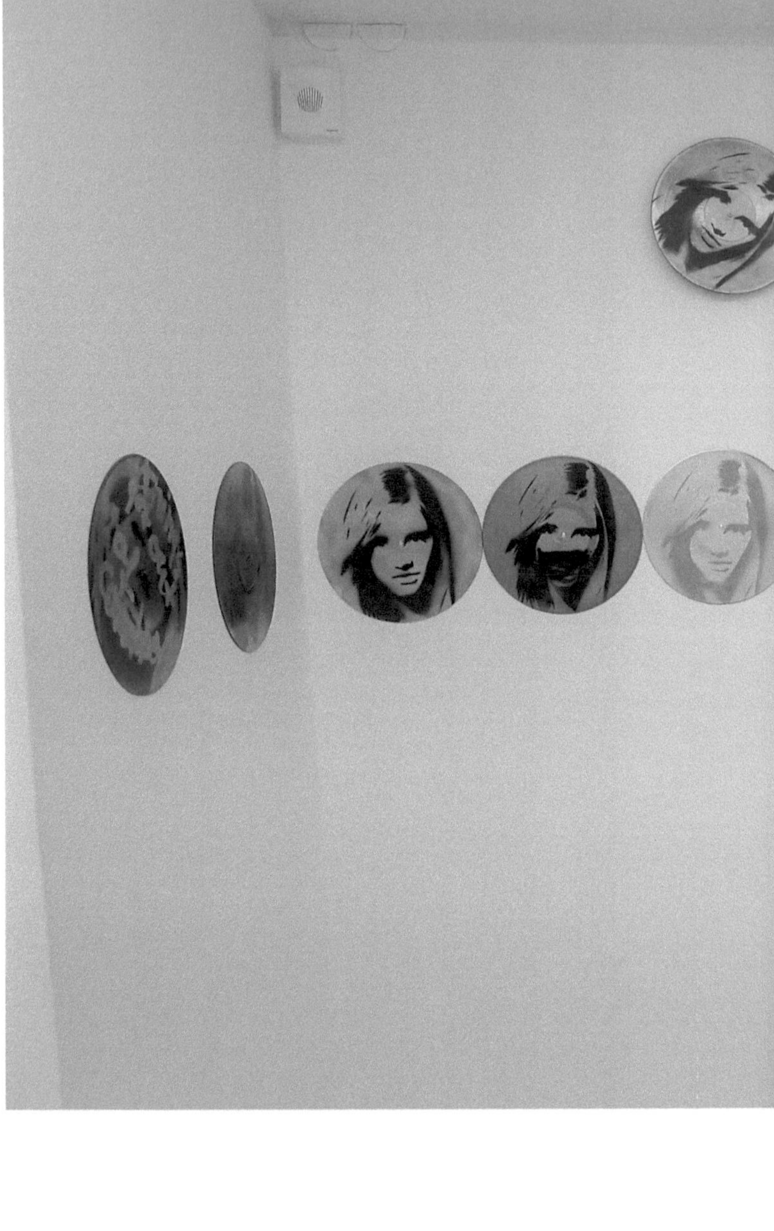

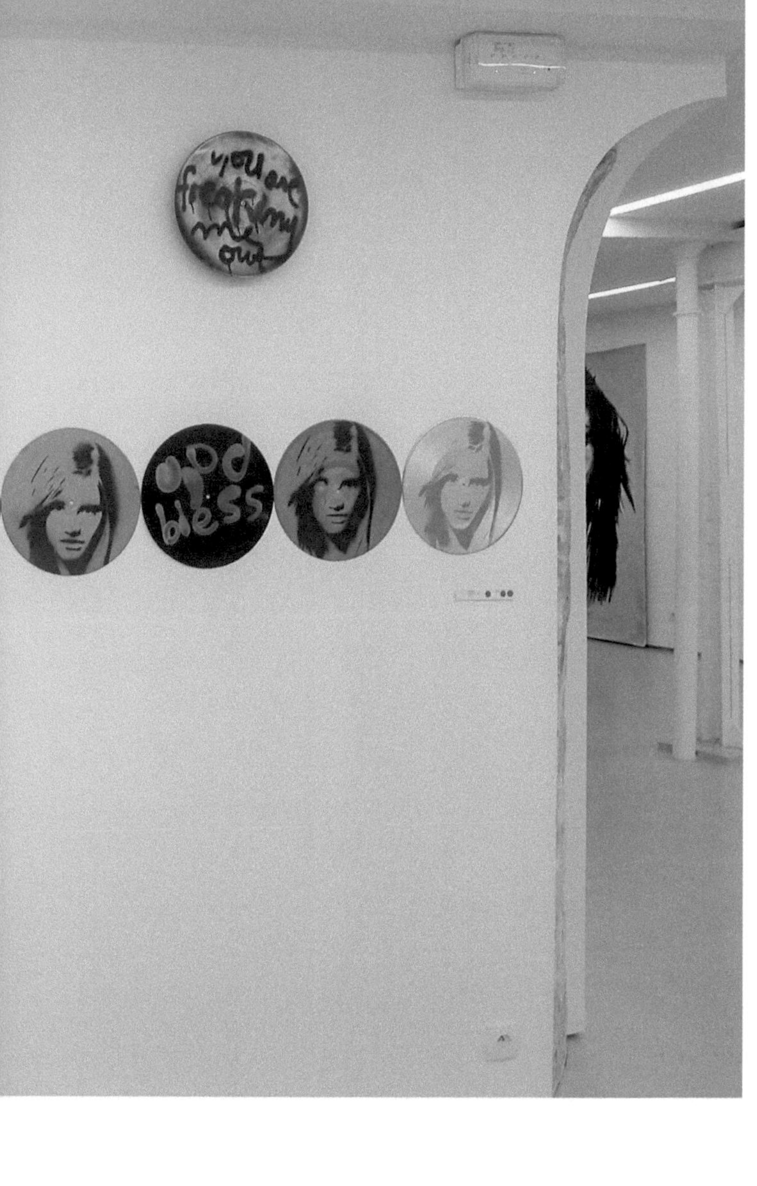

Lost Painting

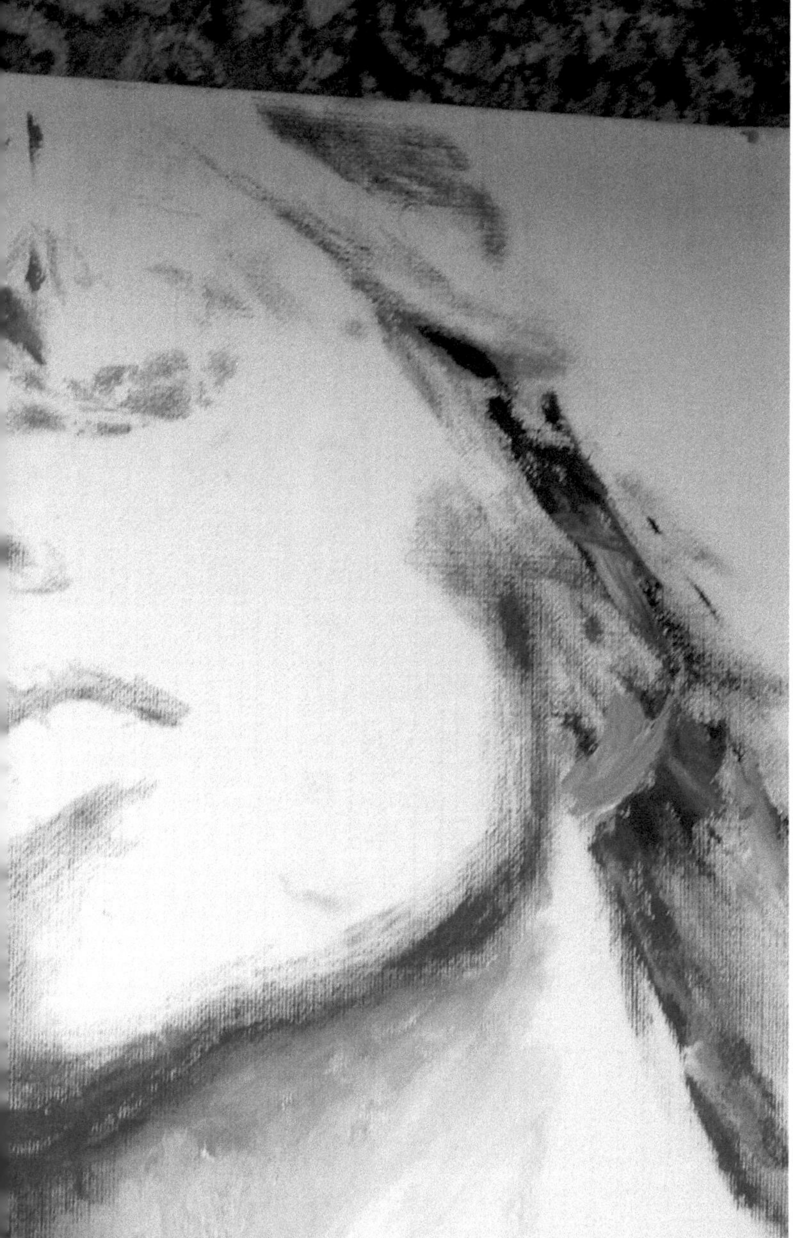

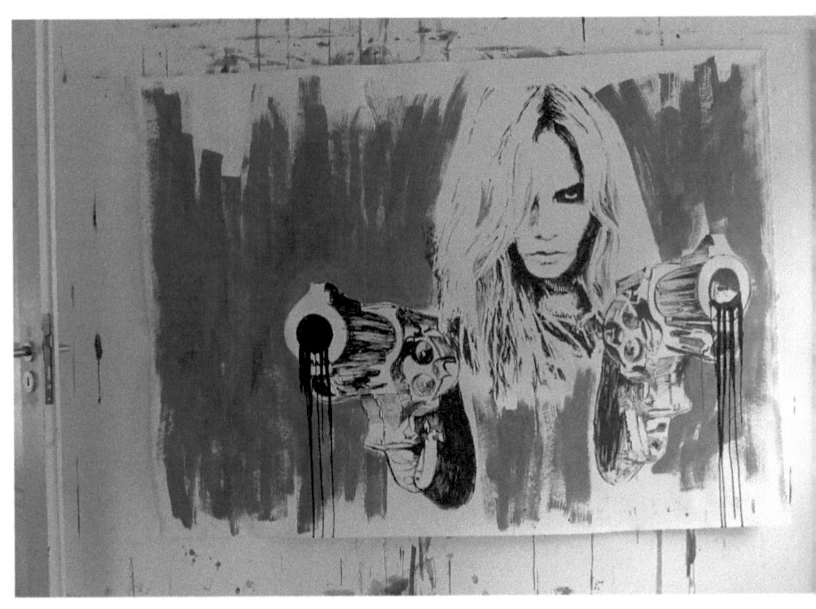

Dinner party

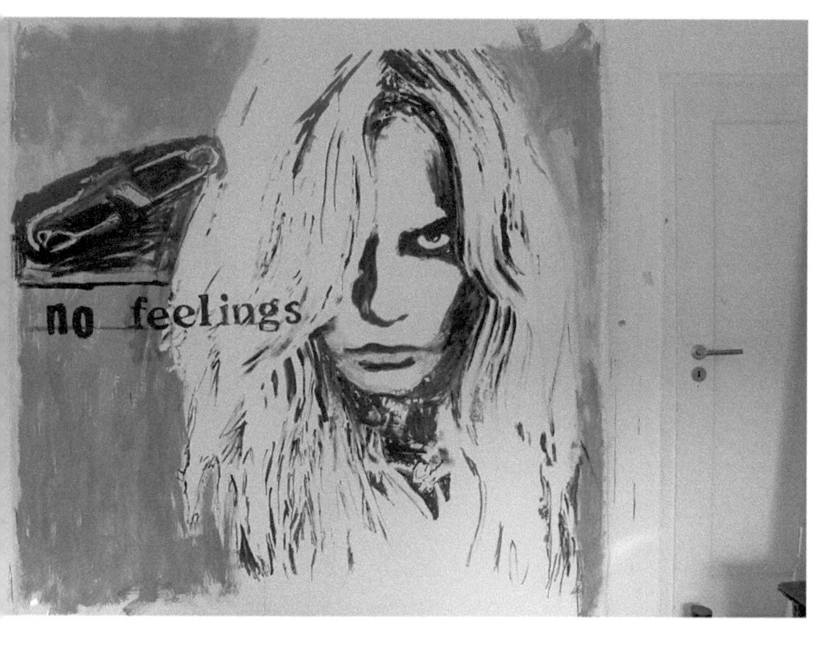
no feelings

After a Party. Director Jean Pierre Moretti,
2011

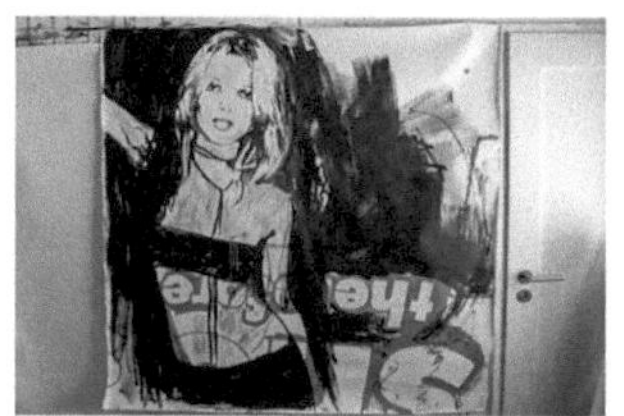

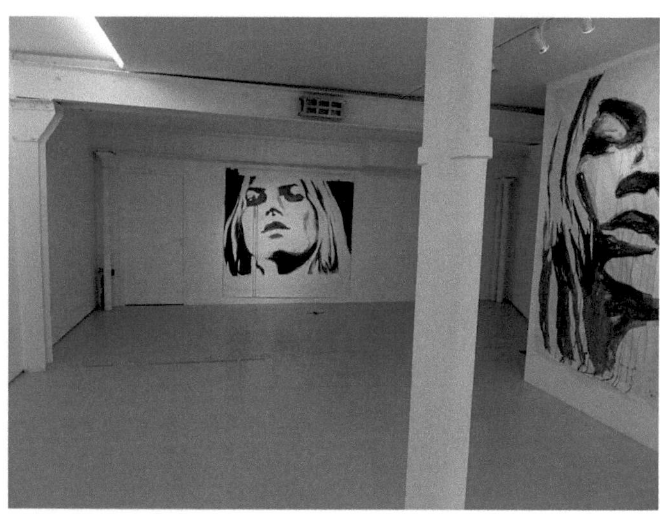

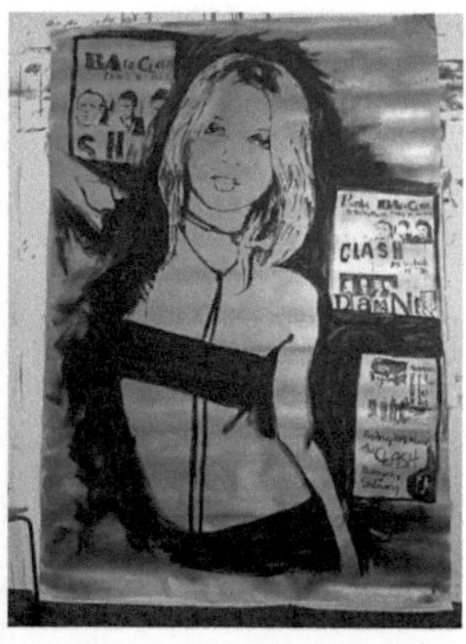

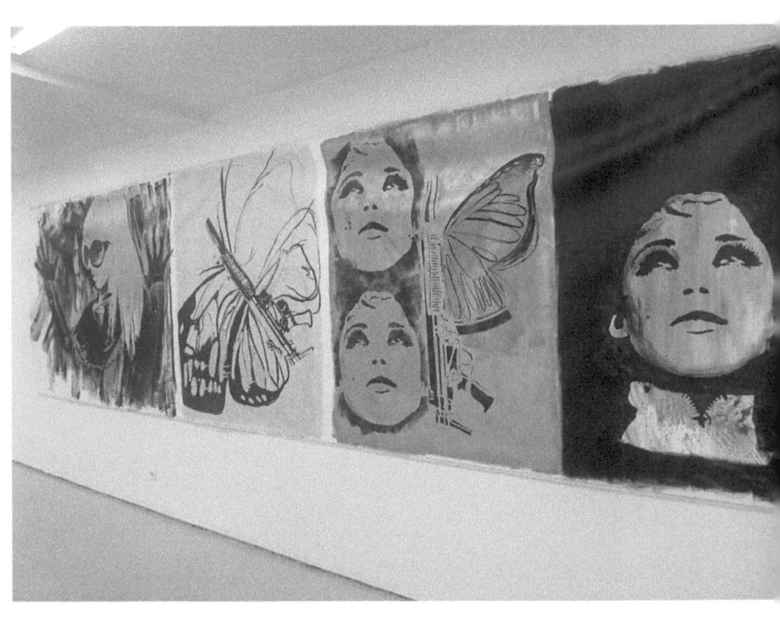

**You toss it, they transform it 1, Galerie
Moretti&Moretti, 2011**

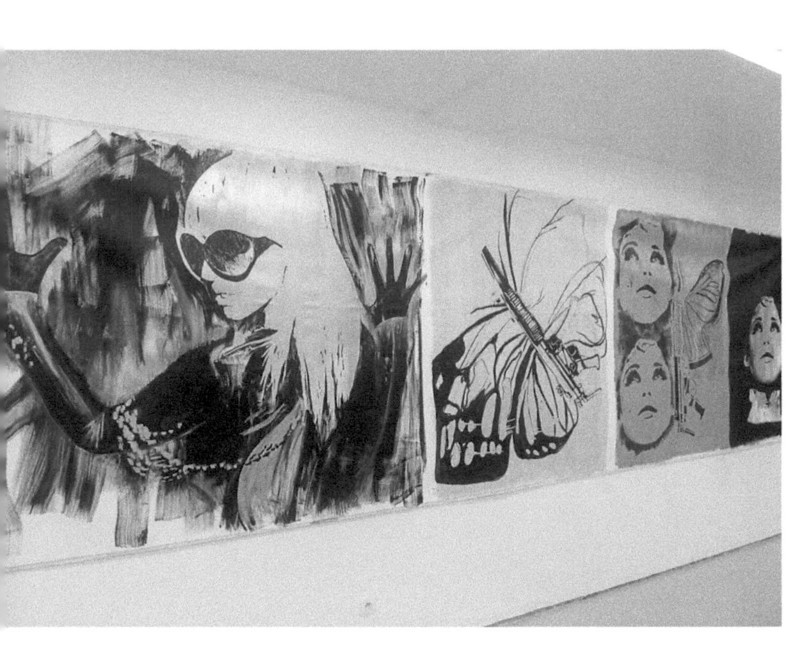

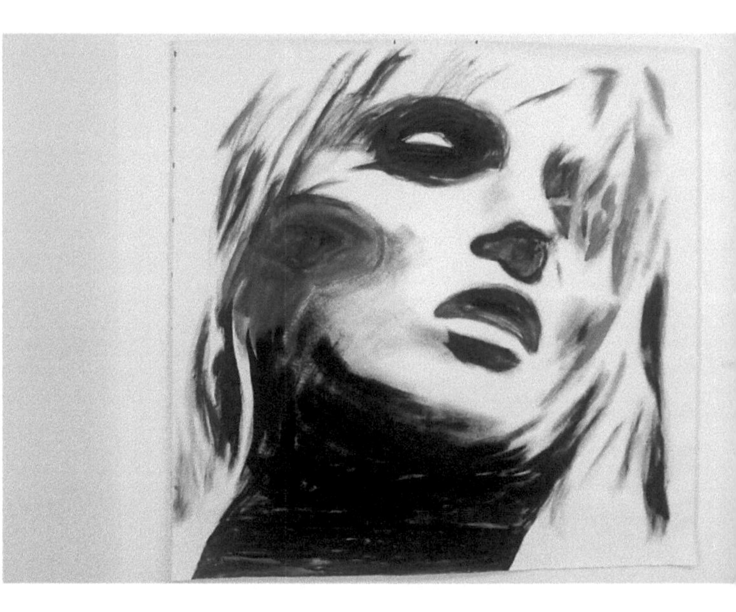

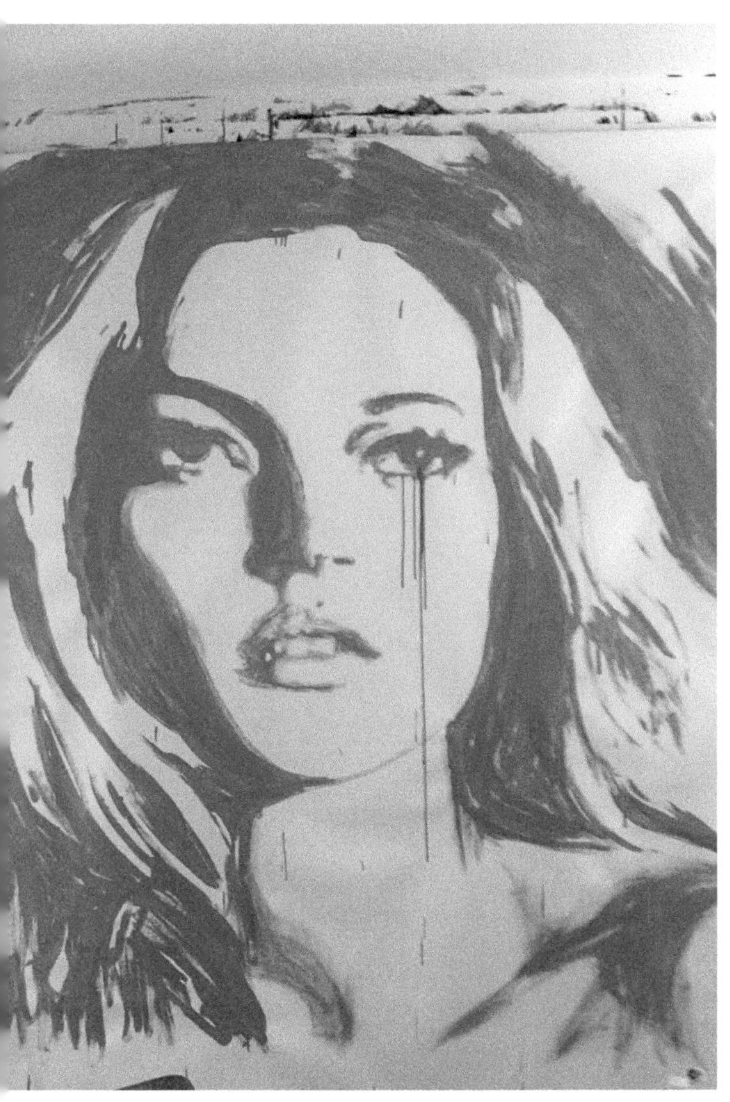

You toss it they transform it 2

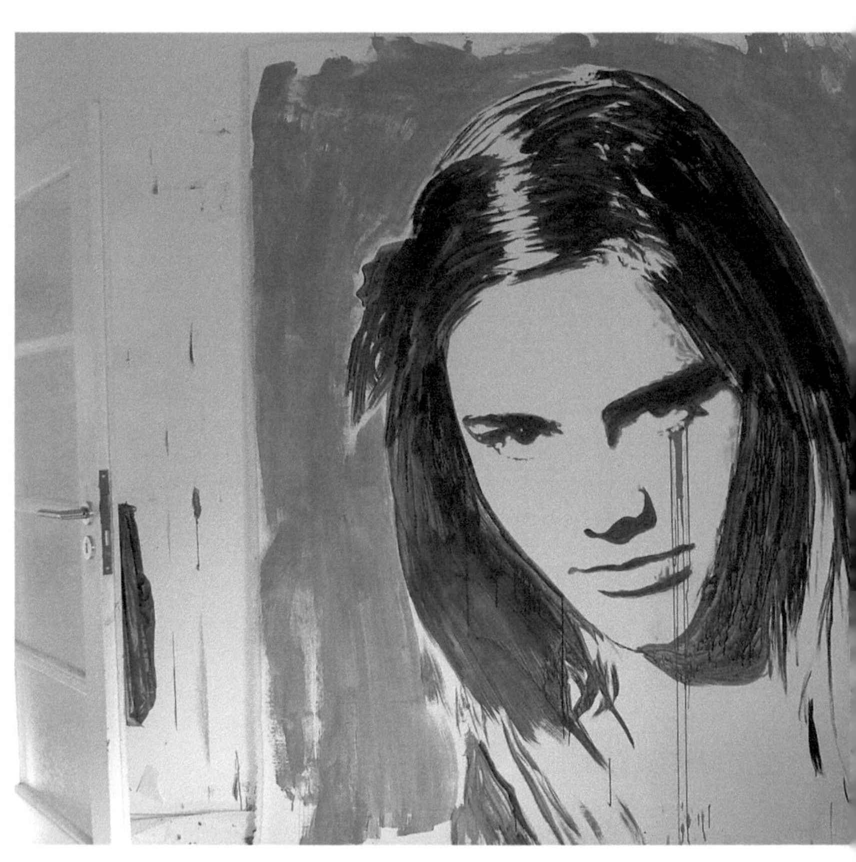

Nothing is real

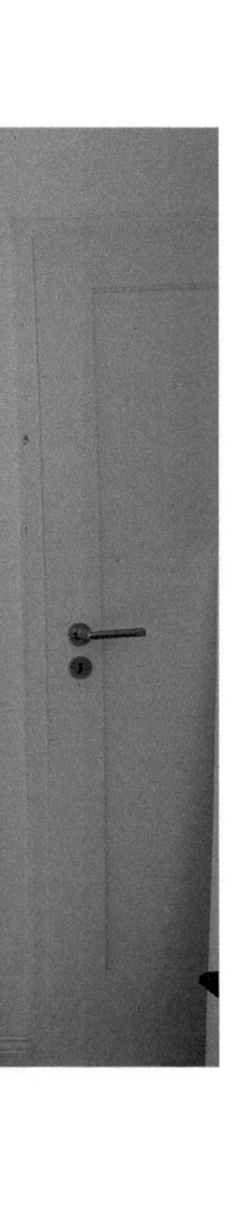

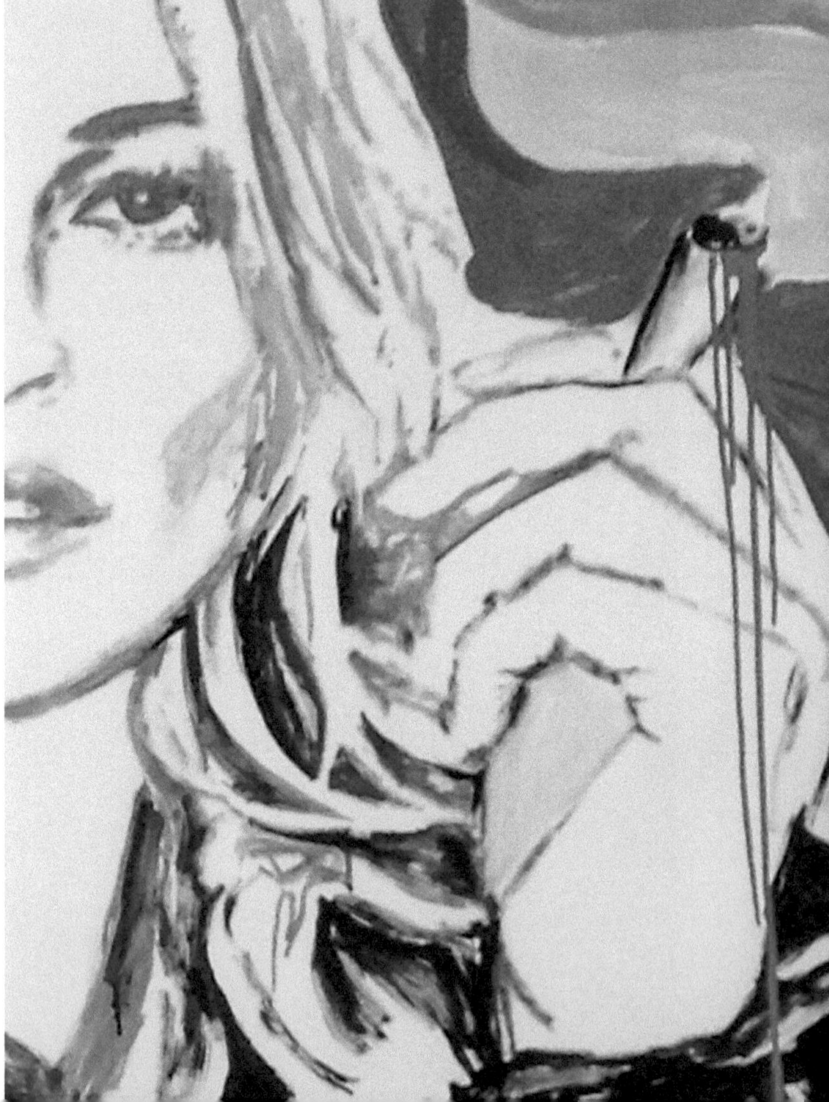

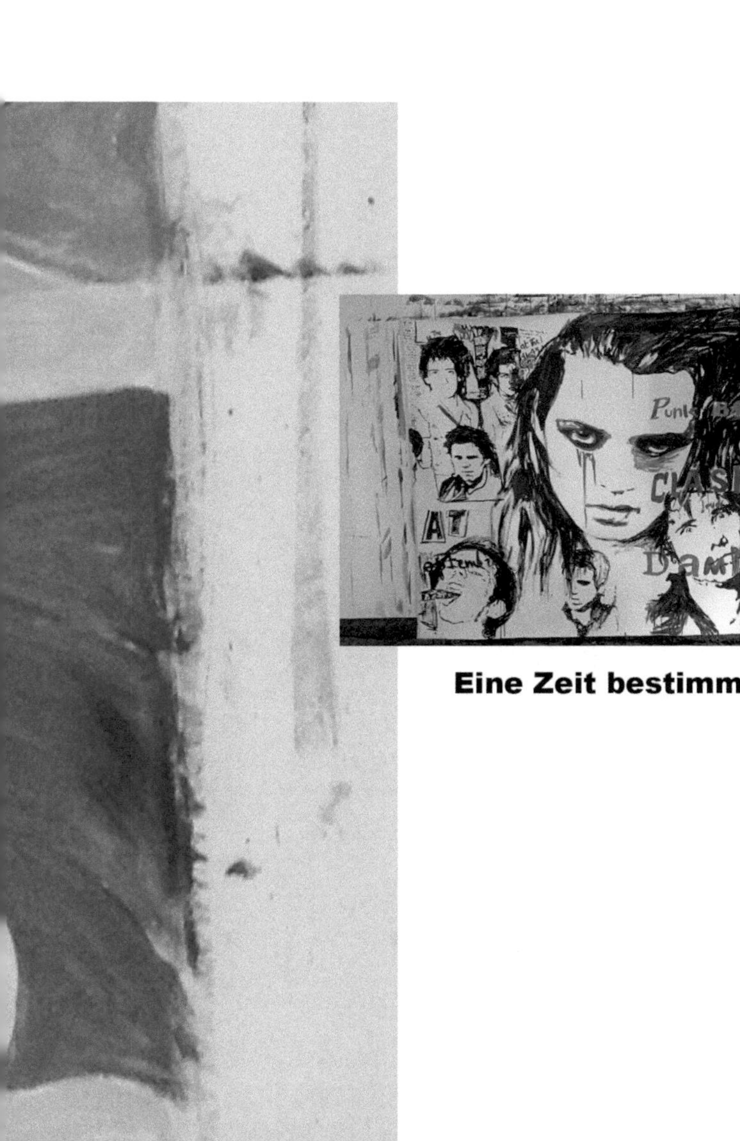

Eine Zeit bestimmen

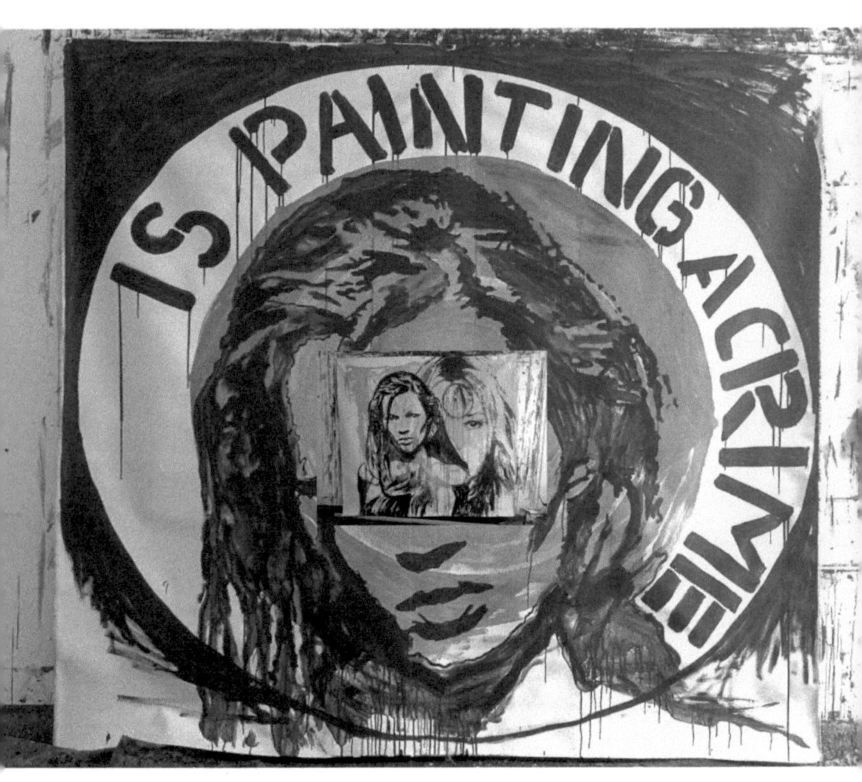

in der Welt

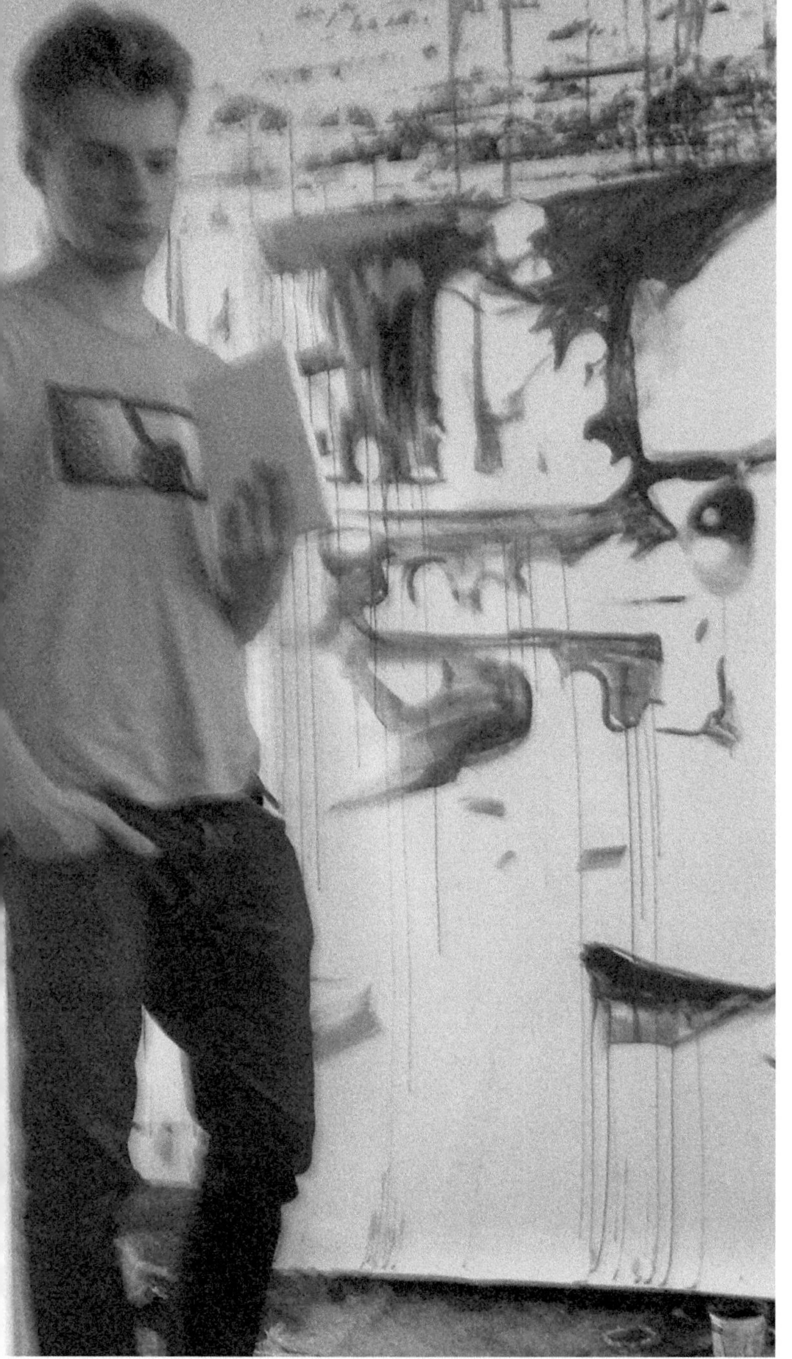

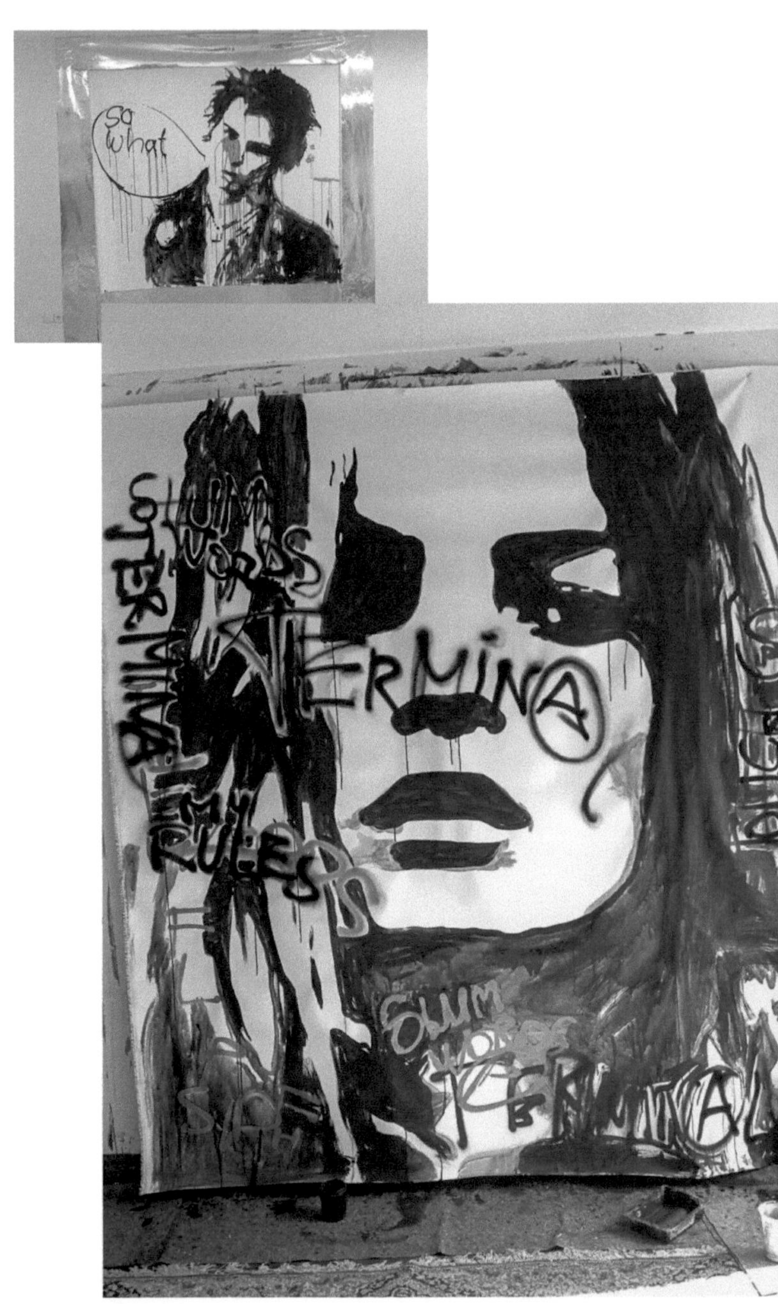

so what
DUMB
WORDS
DETERMINA
TERMINA
MY
RULES
DUM
WORDS
TERMINAL

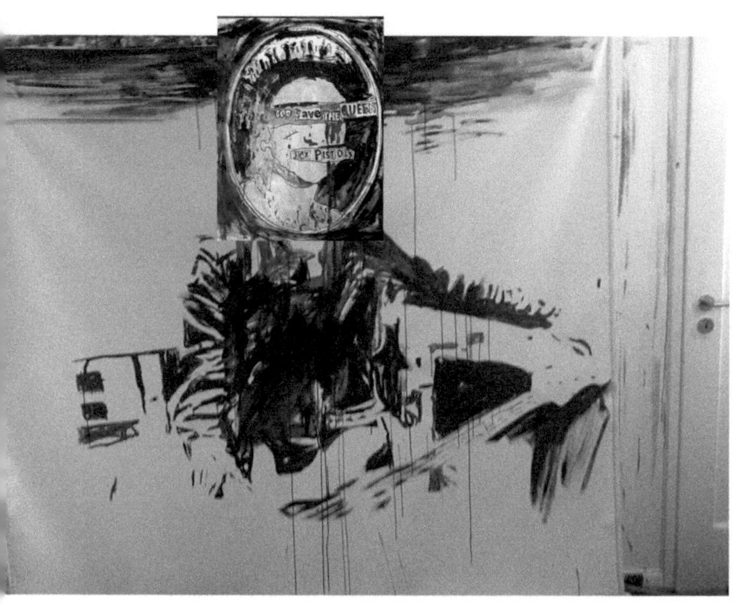

yesterday in allen Museen und Galerien.

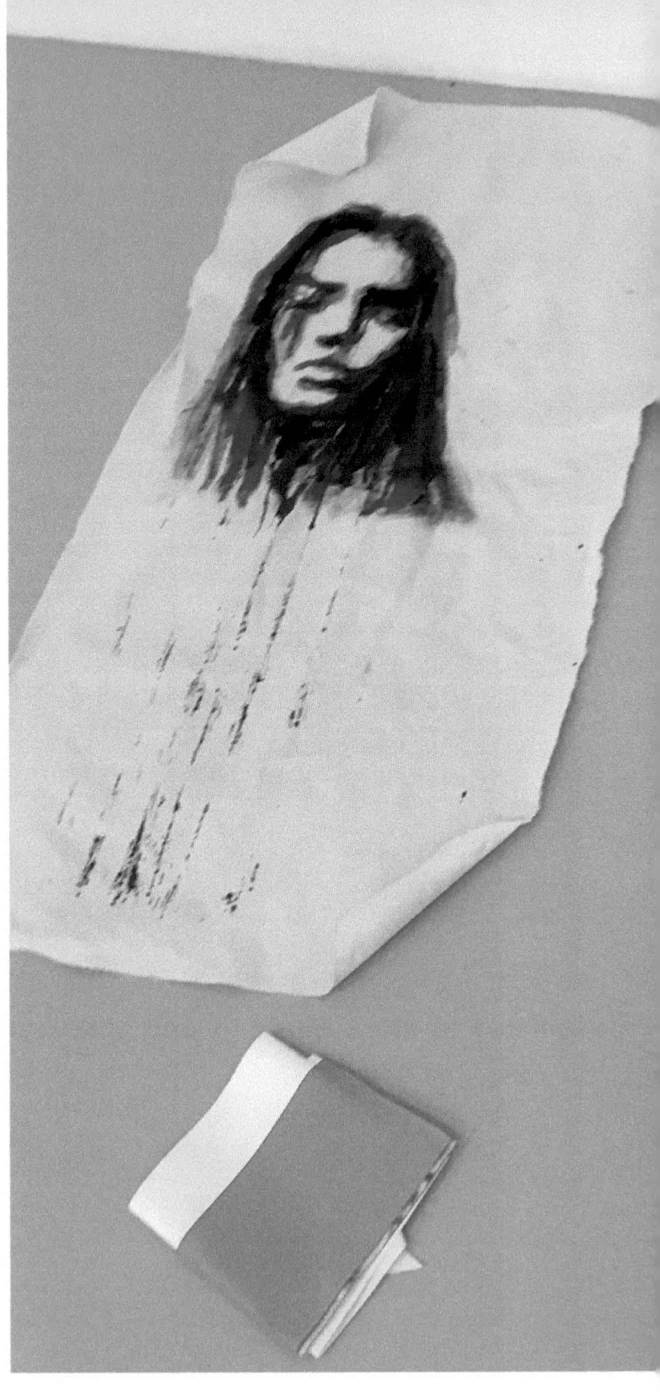

Paintings lost 2018?

JE SUIS PAS
STREET ART.
JE SUIS UN
PEINTRE

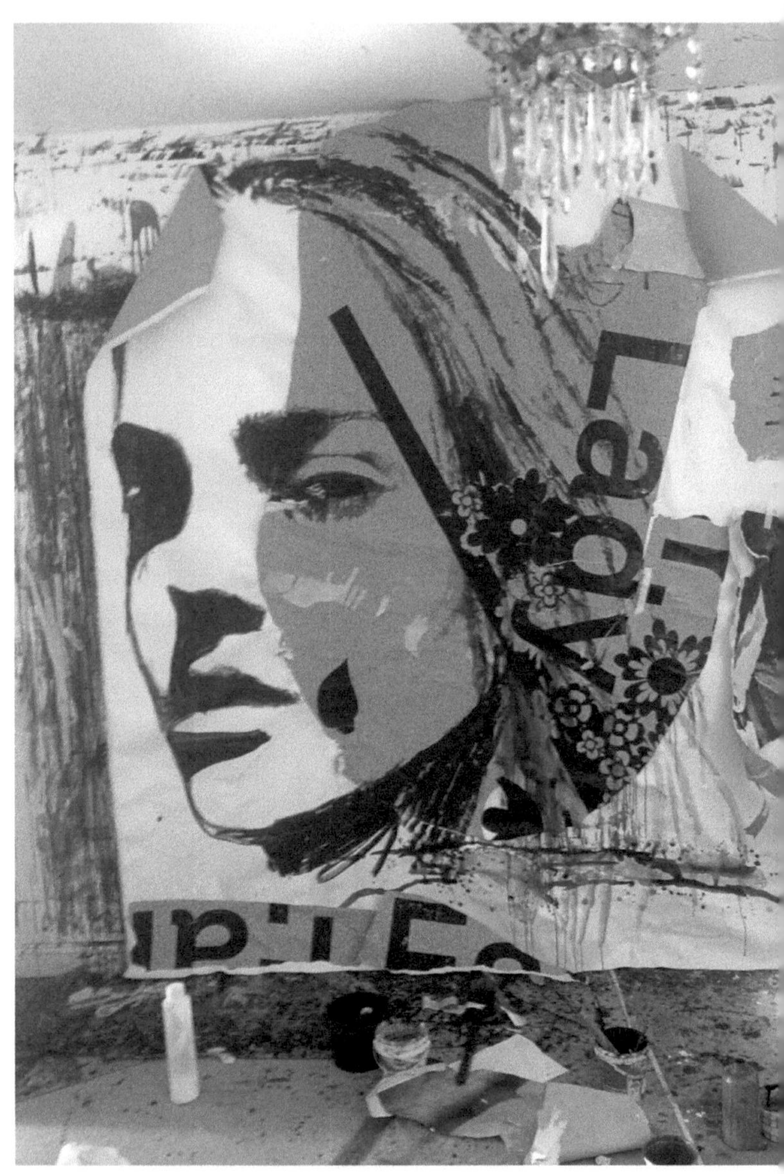

Paintings rediscovered in a garbage container 2018?

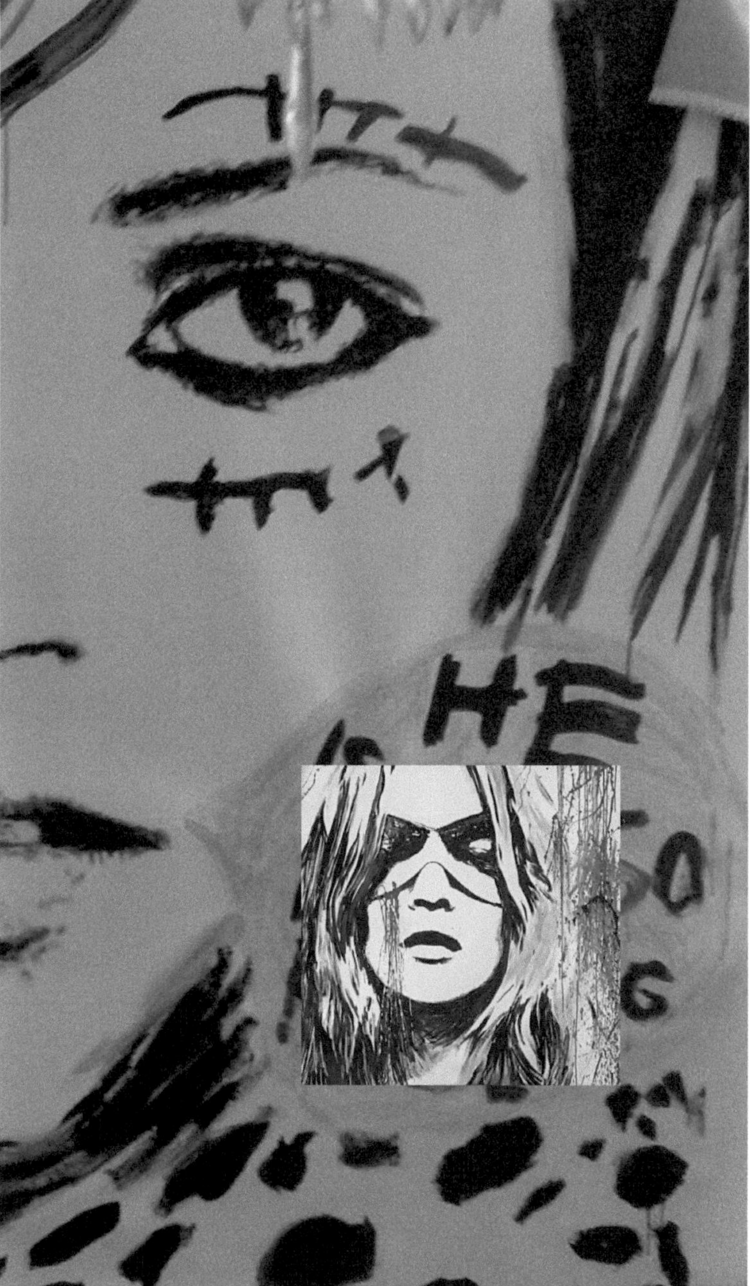
HE
O
G

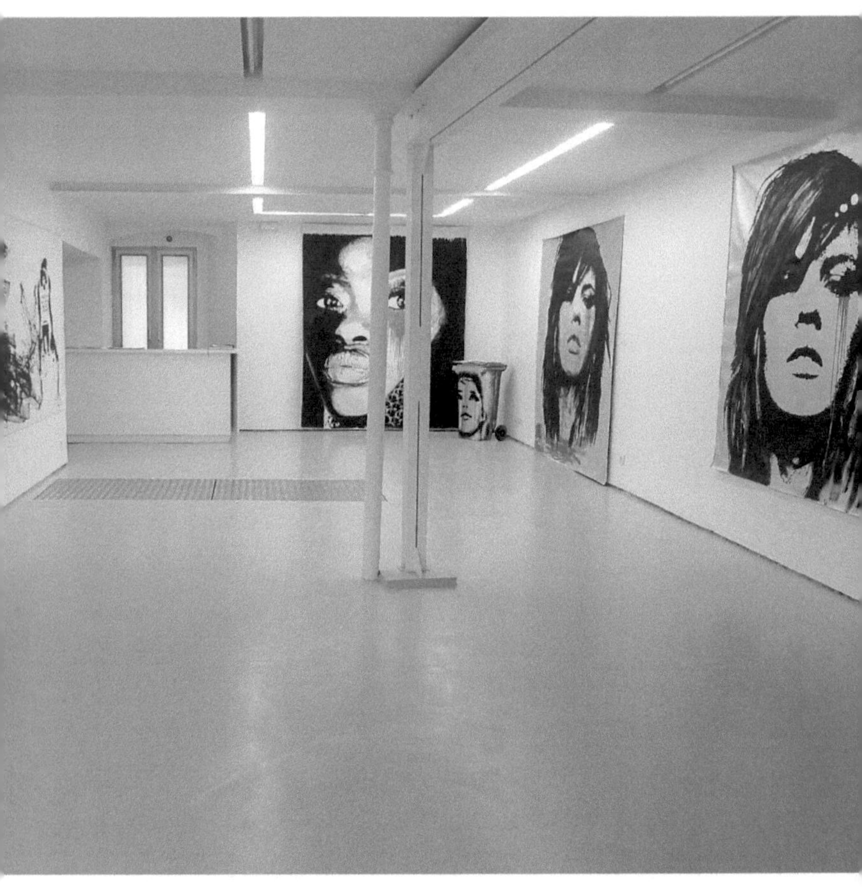

Wild exposition Galerie Moretti &Moretti, 2011

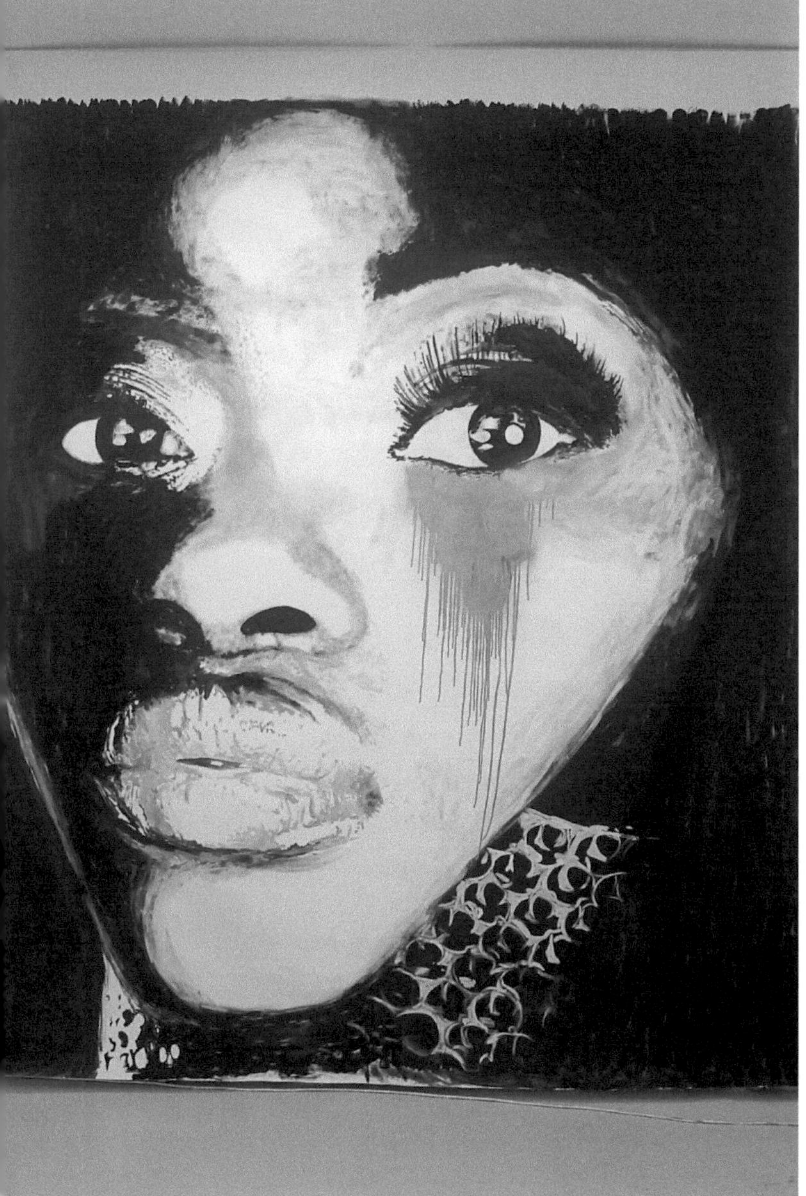

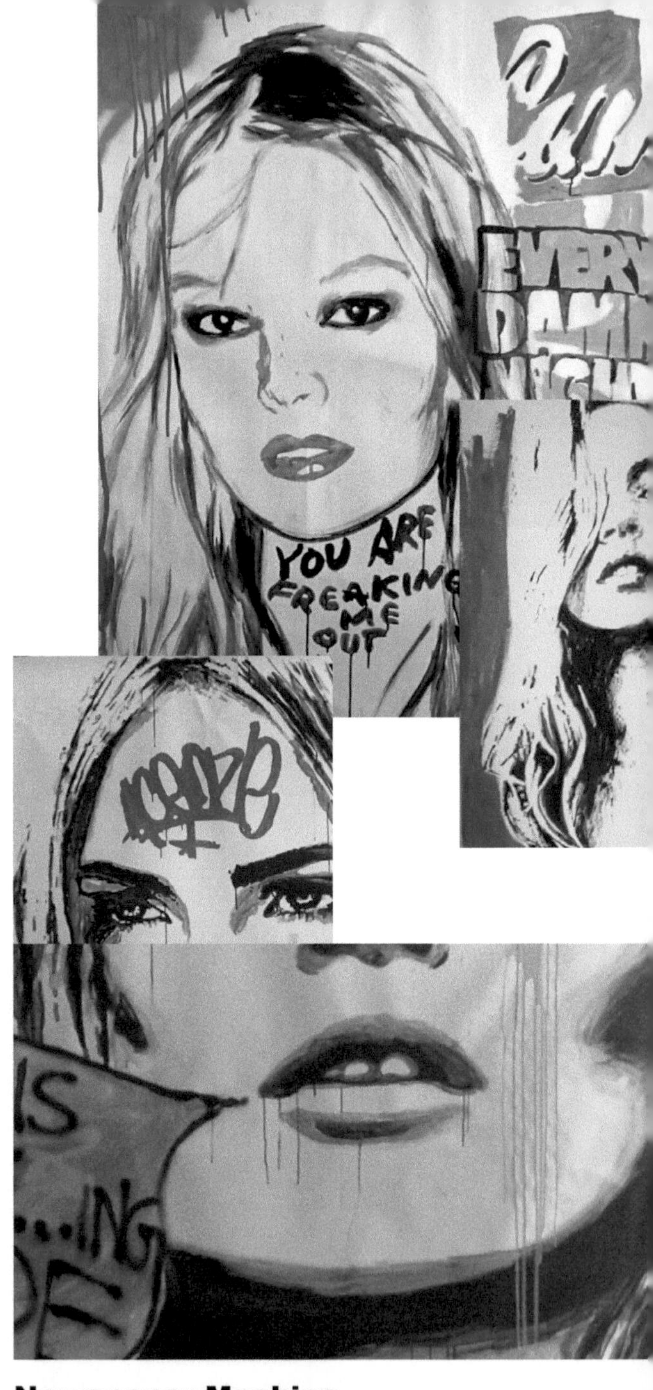

Newspaper Machine

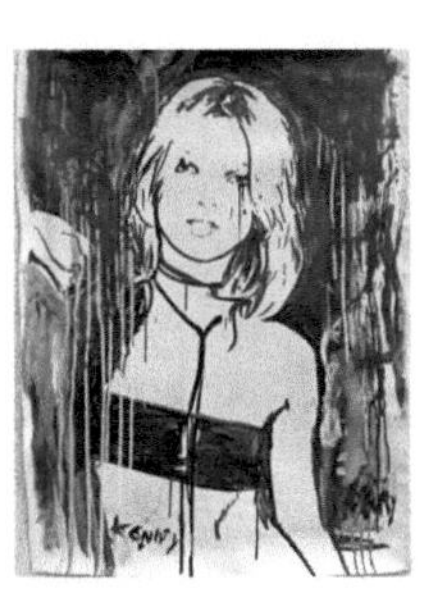

intersection

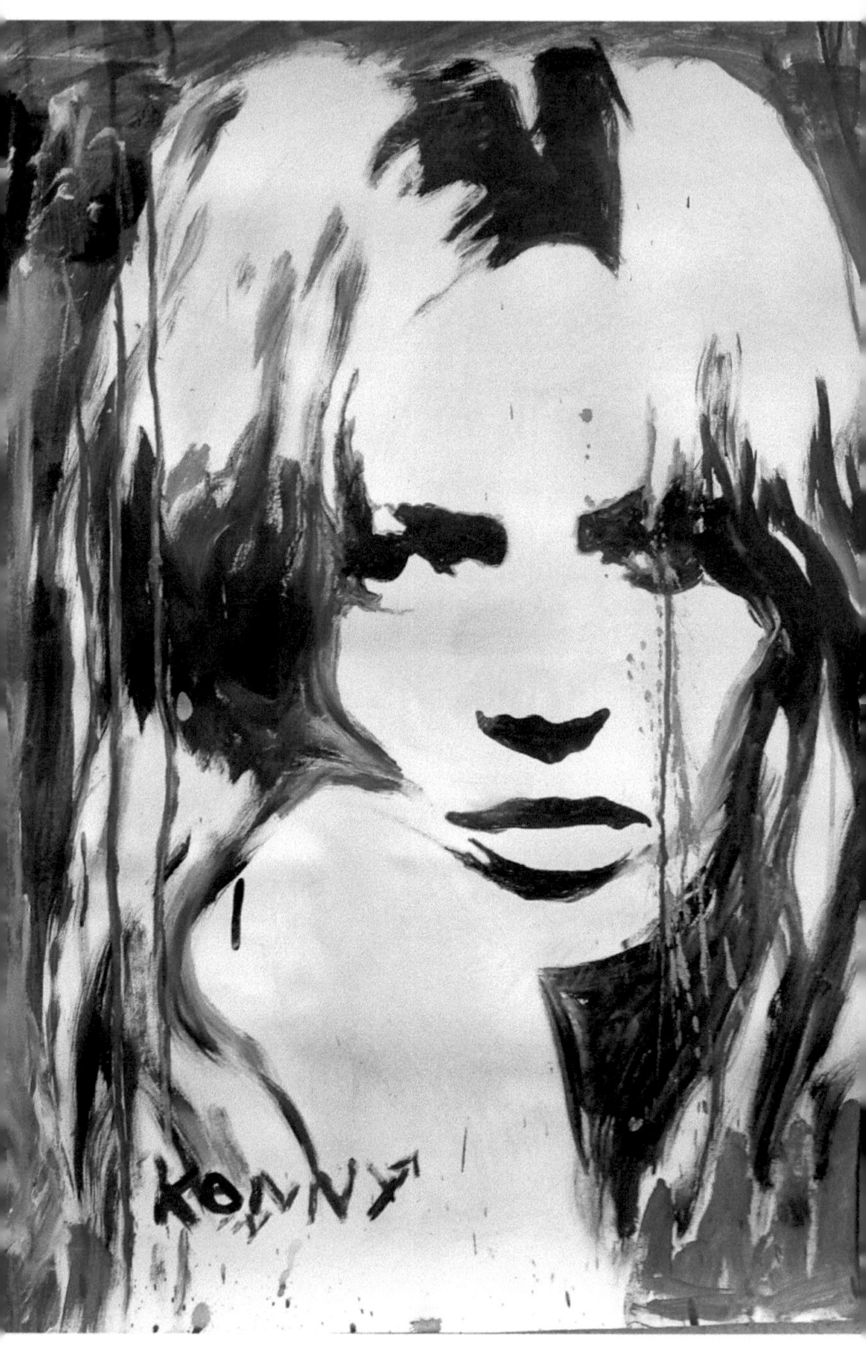

people on the street

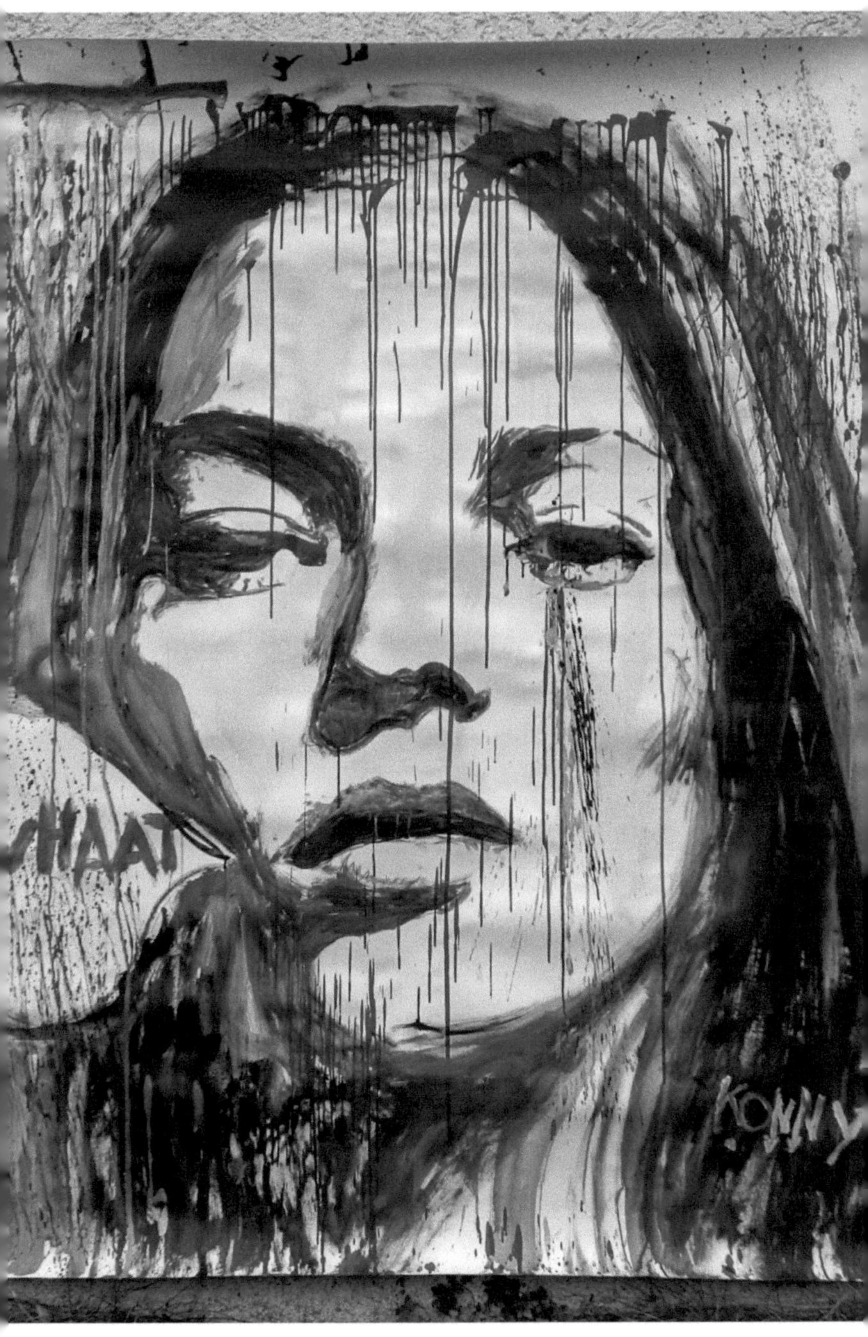
SHAA
KONNY

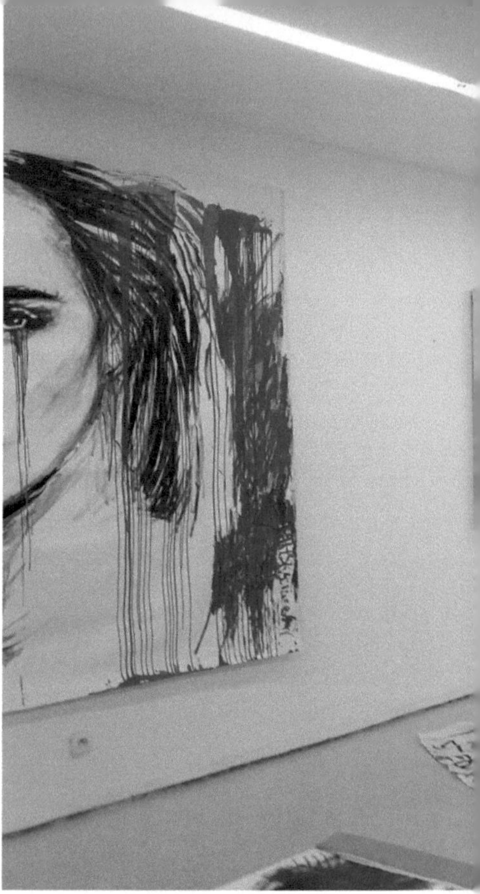

September 11, 2015

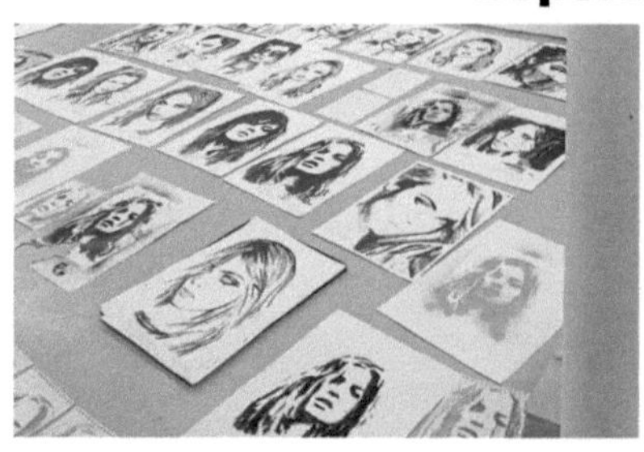

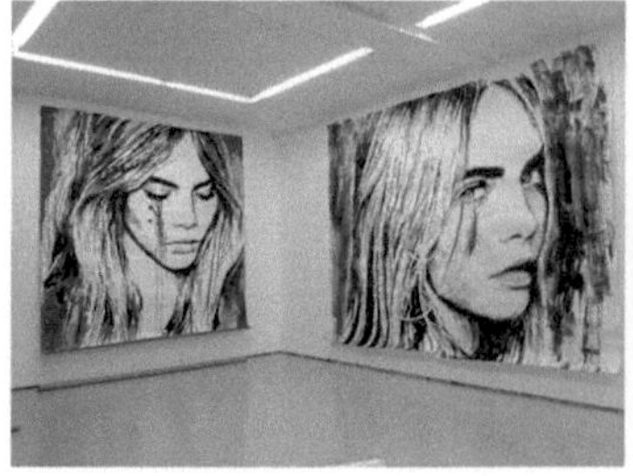

December 05, 2014

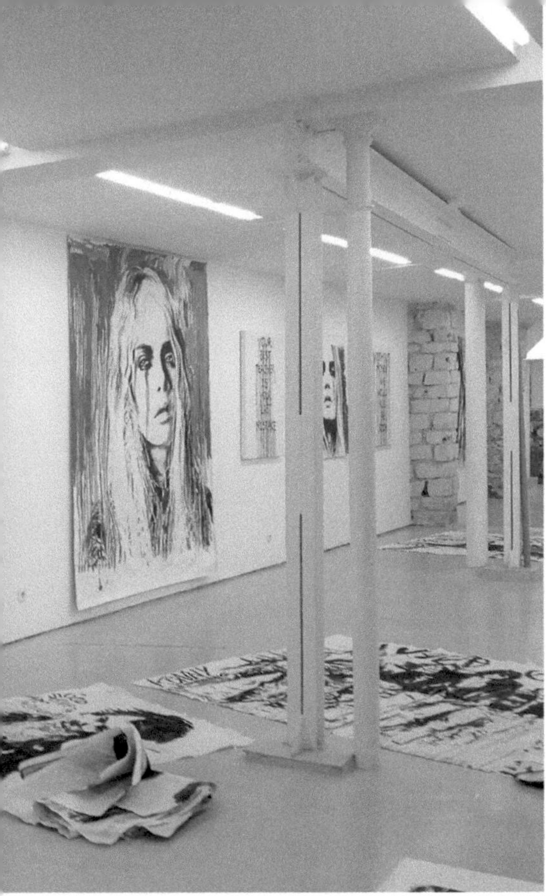

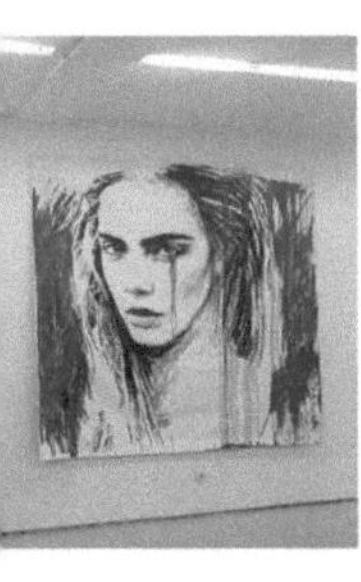

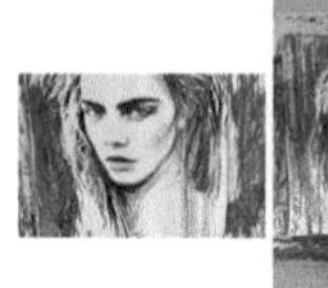
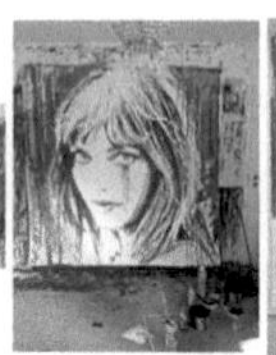
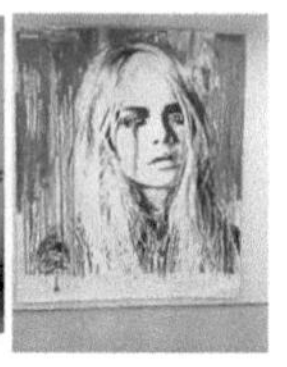
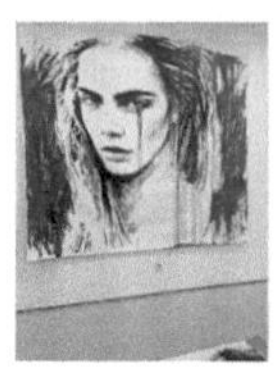
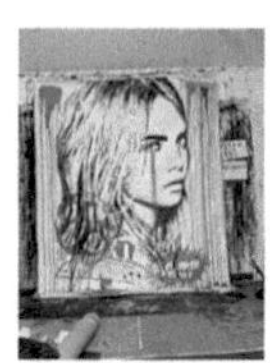
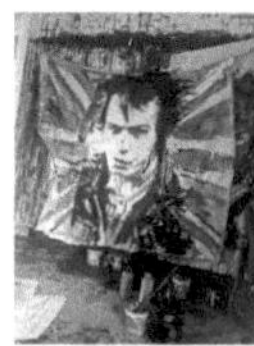
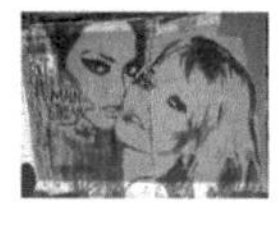
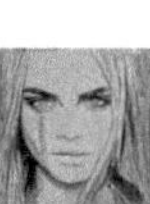
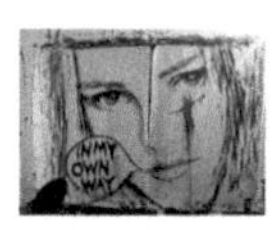
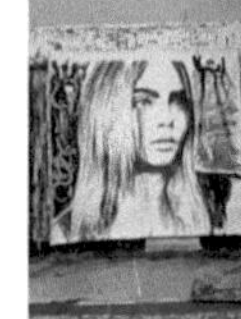
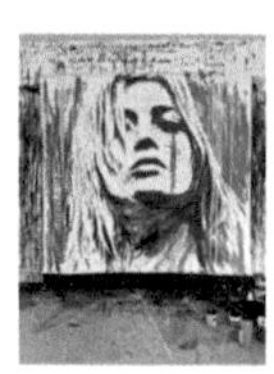
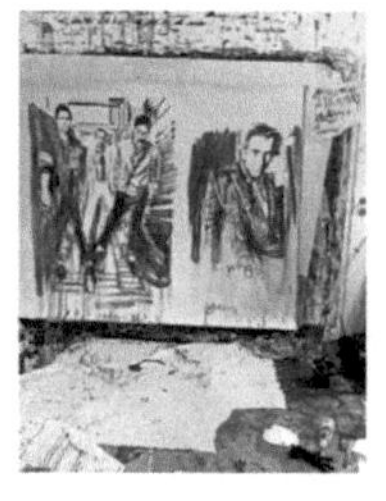
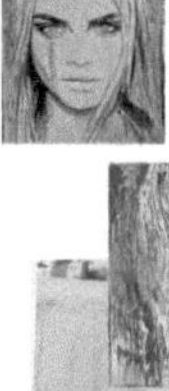
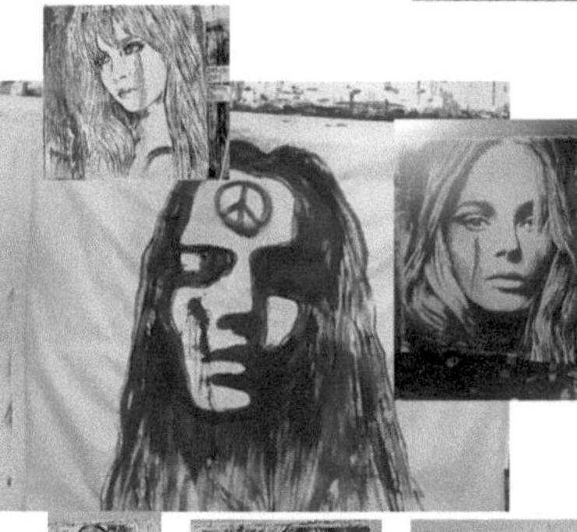
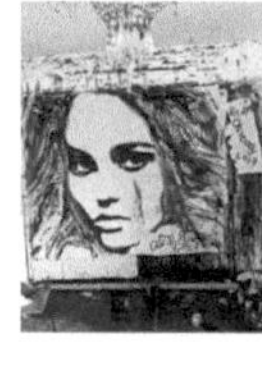
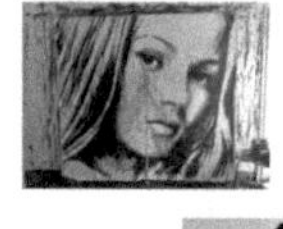
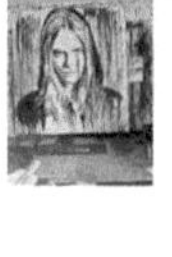
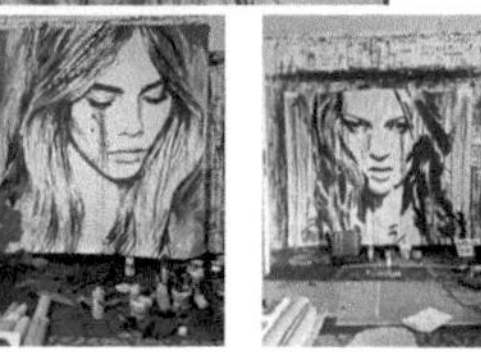
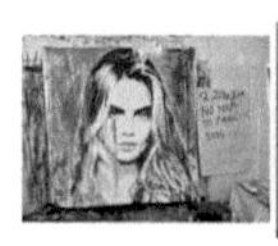
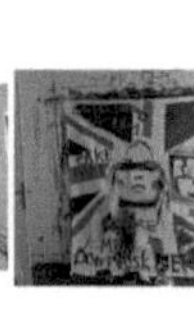
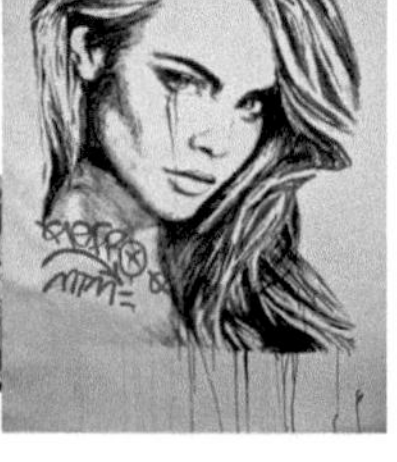
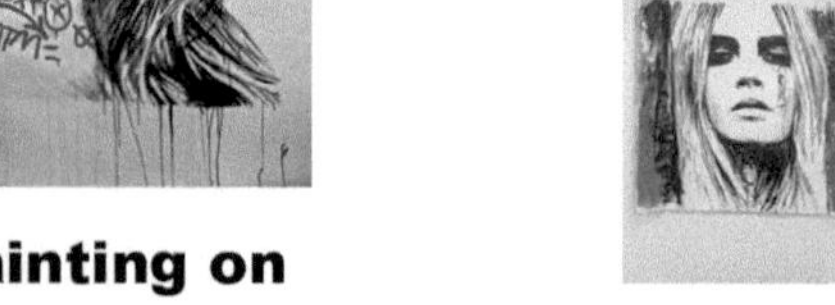
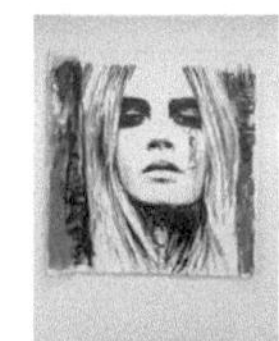
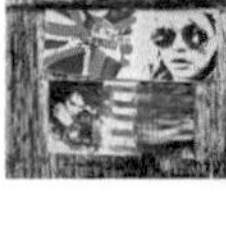

painting on canvas

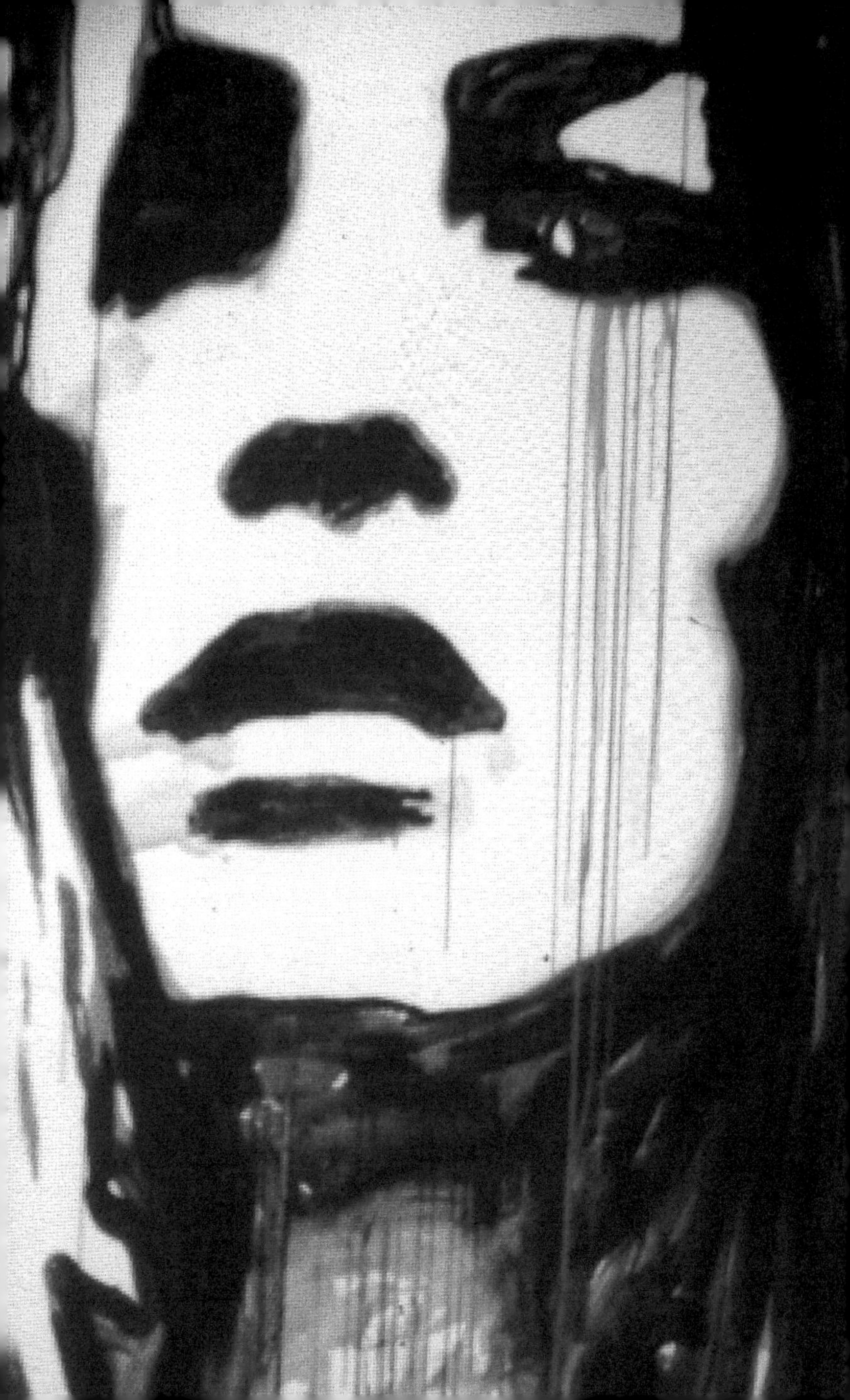

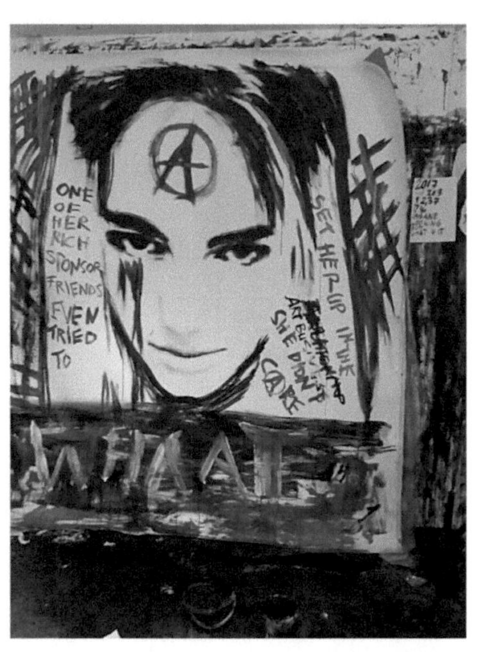
ONE
OF
HER
RICH
SPONSOR
FRIENDS
EVEN
TRIED
TO
SET HER UP
IN THE
ART BUSINESS
SHE DIDN'T
CARE
WHAT

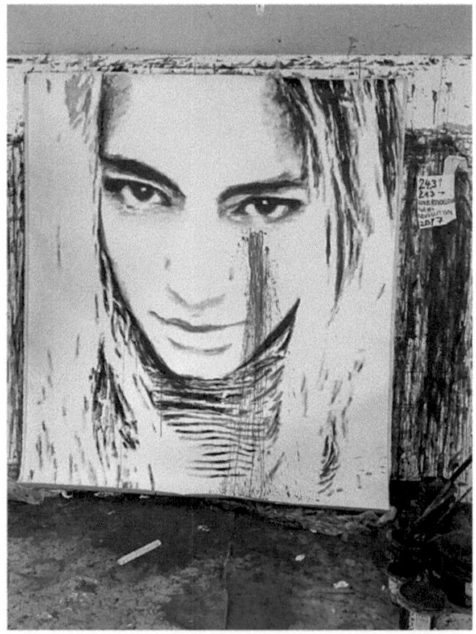

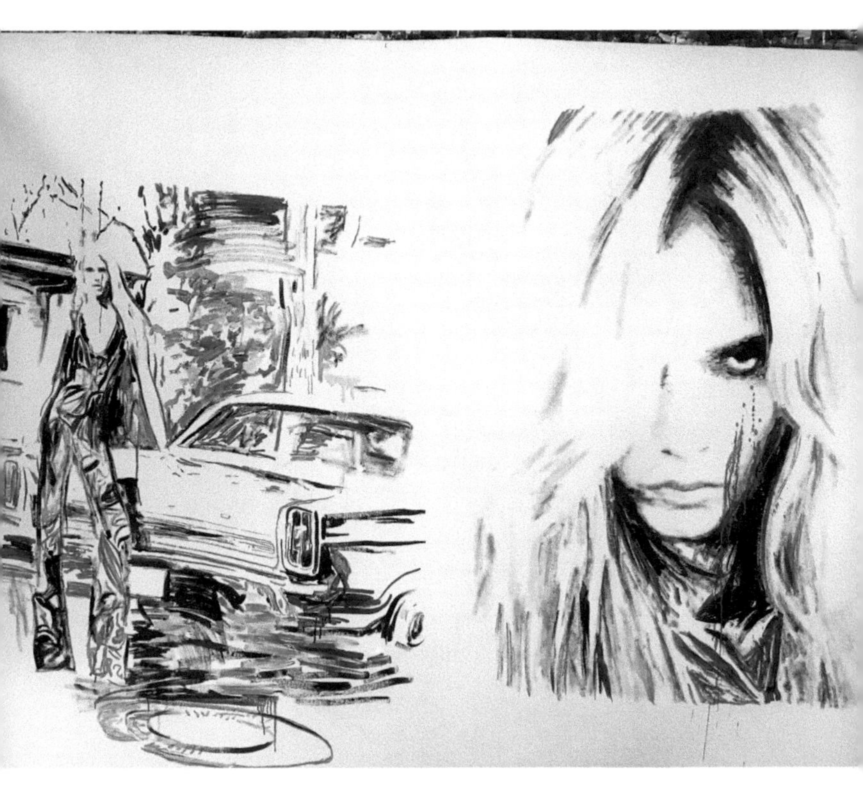

February 28, 2017

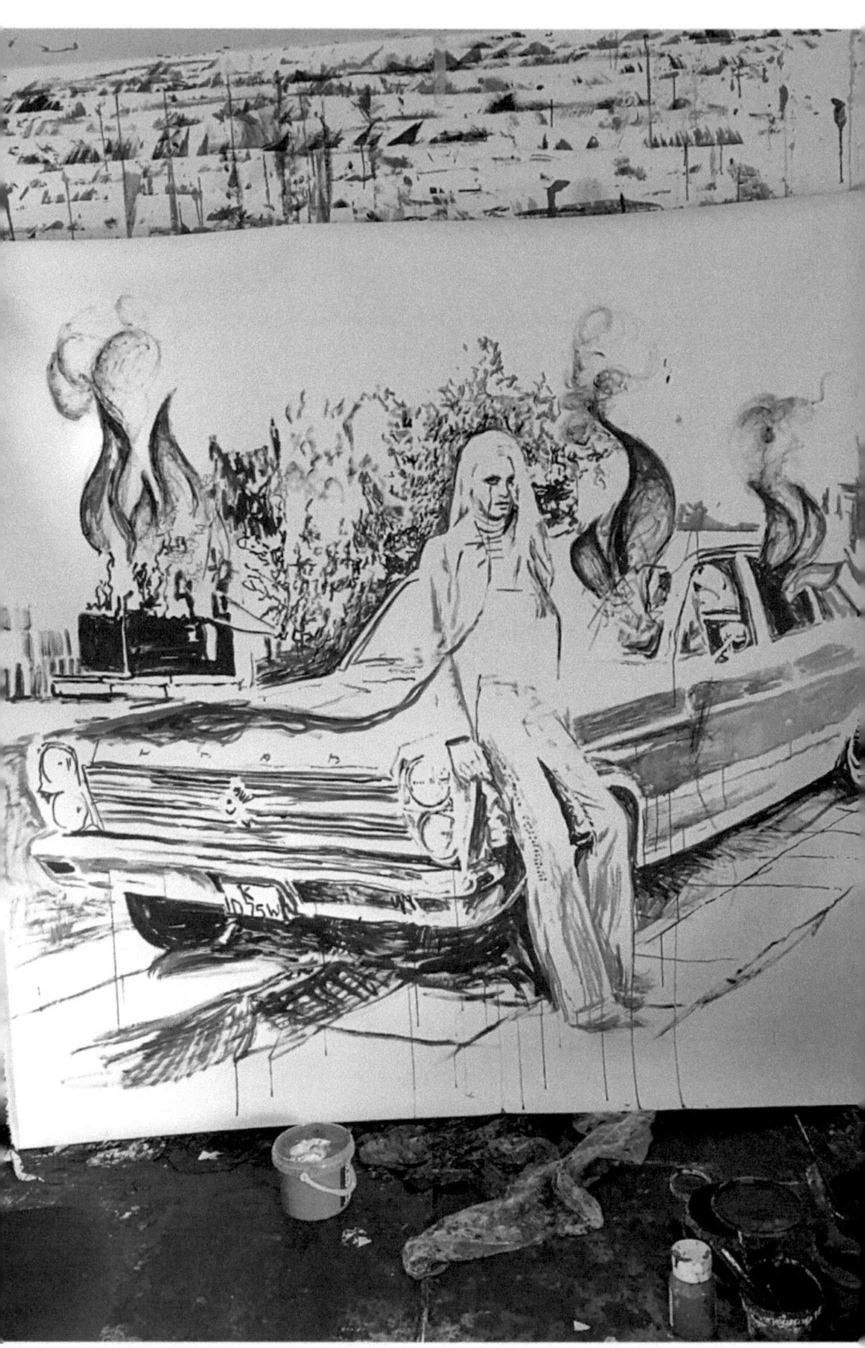

**burning cars Paris

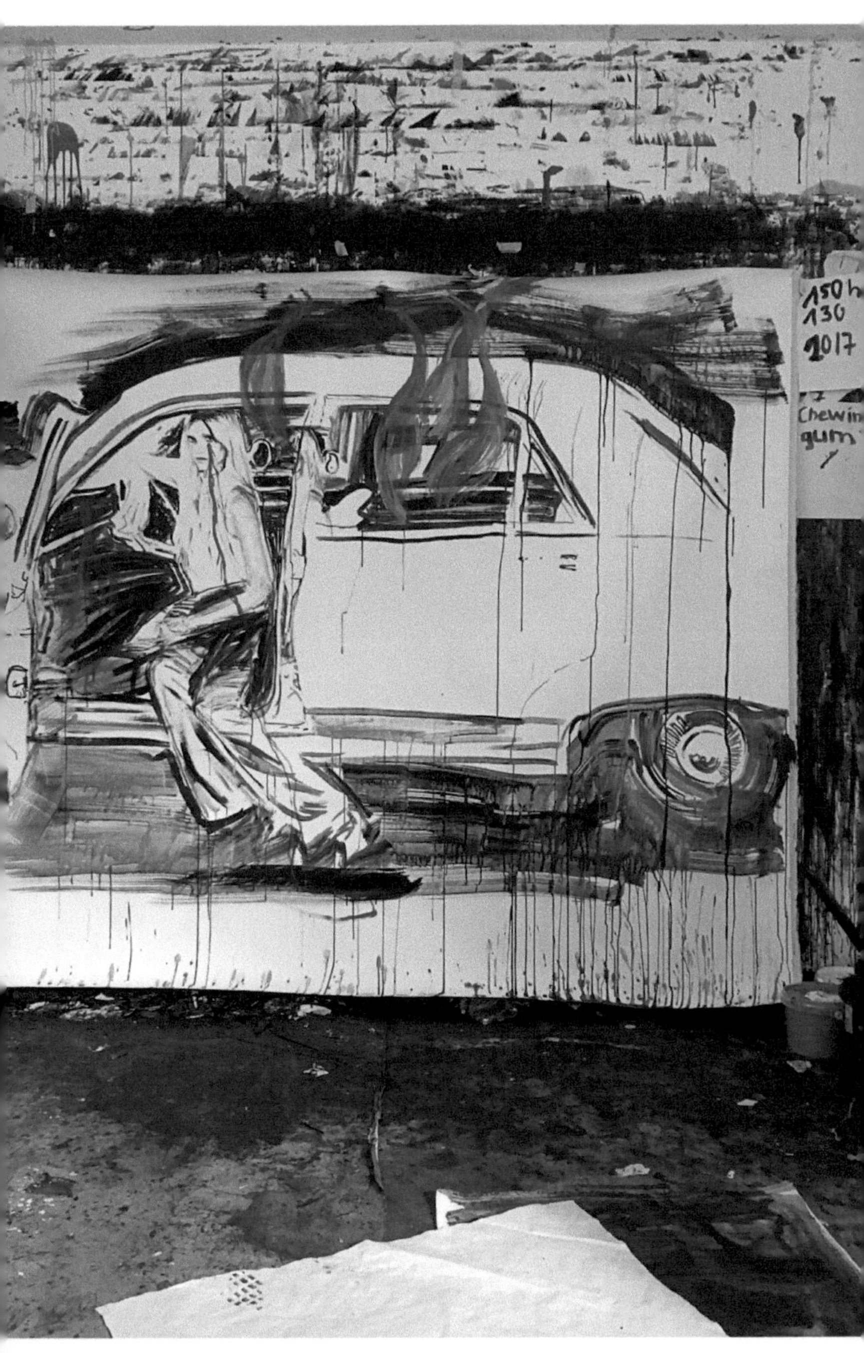

150 h
130
2017
Chewin
gum

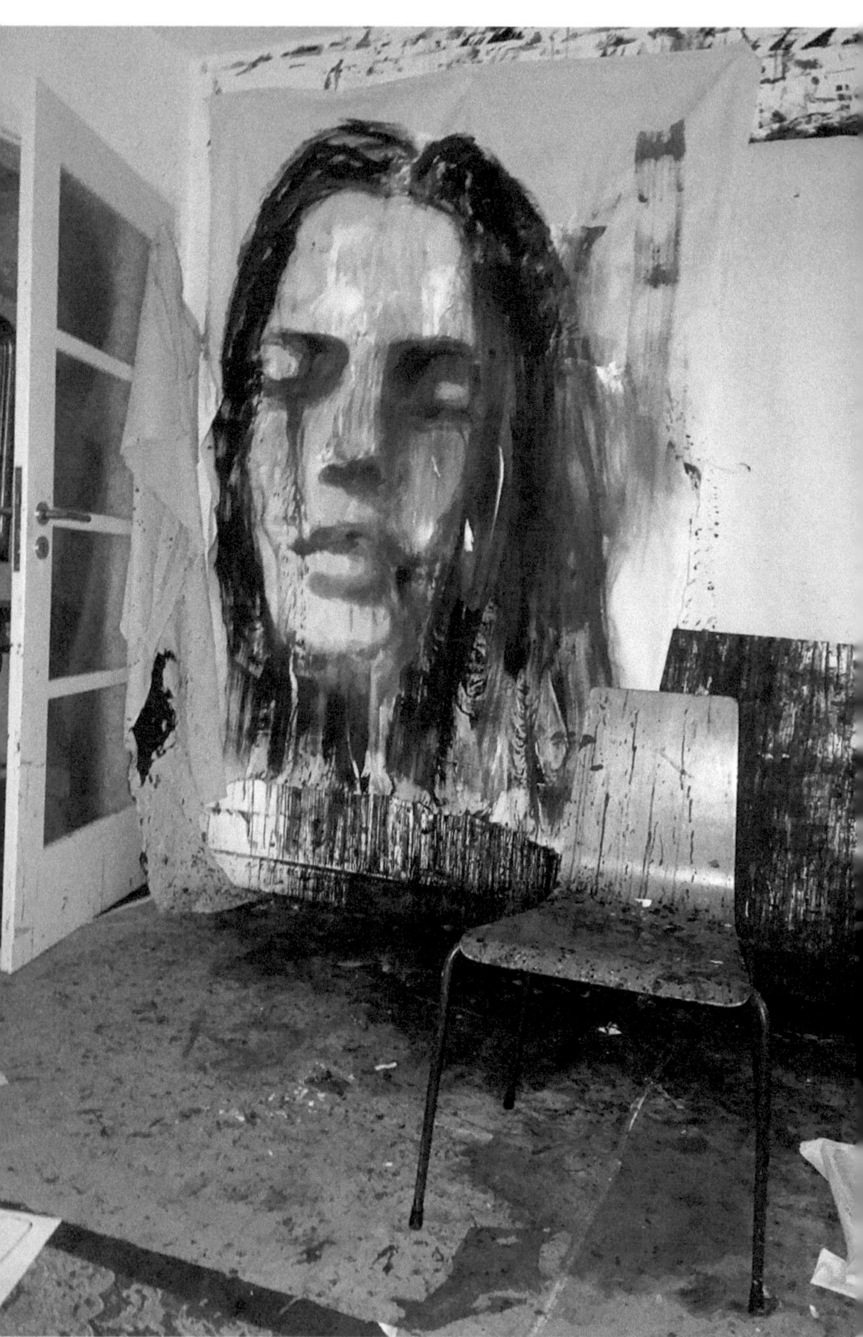

sad faces

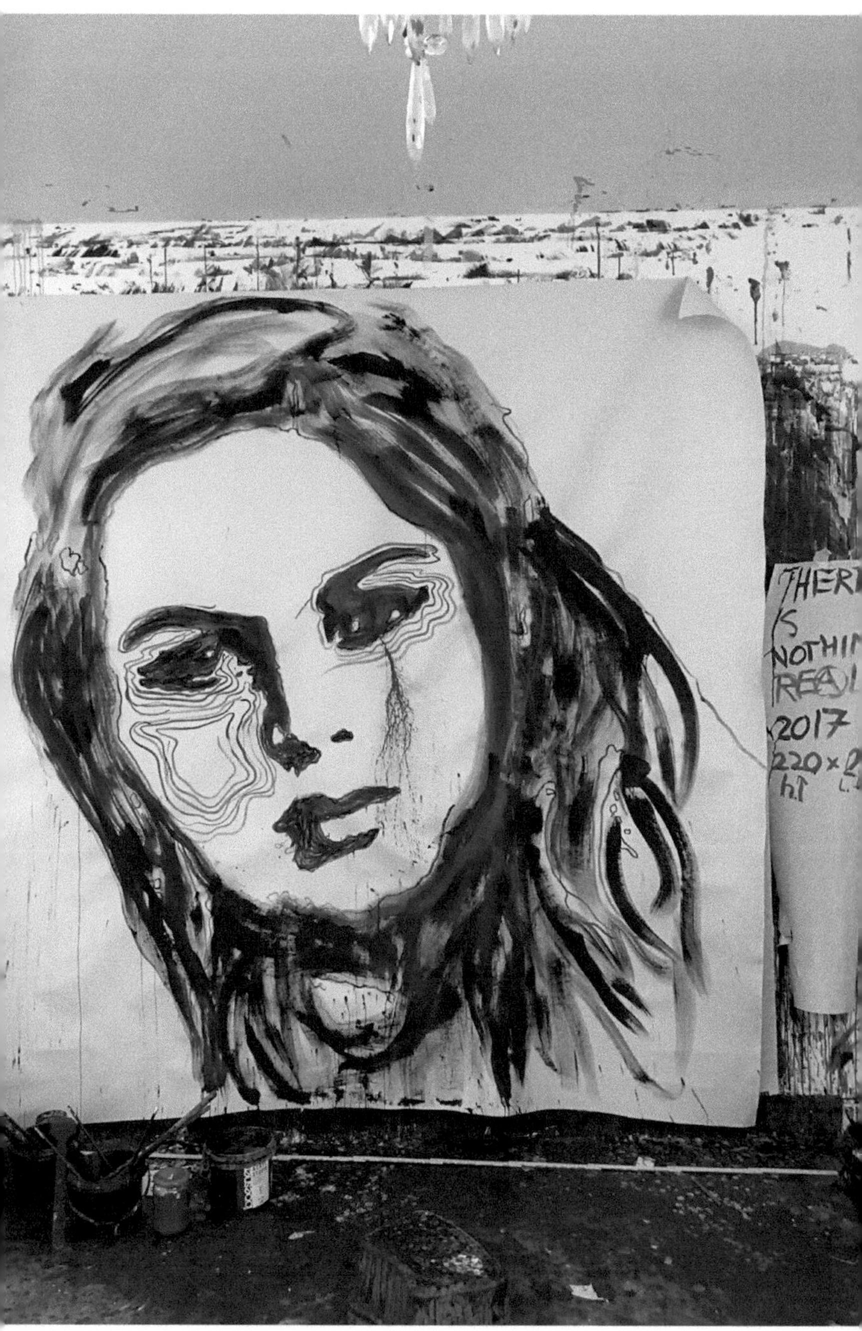
THER
IS
NOTHIN
REAL
2017
220 x 2
h.t

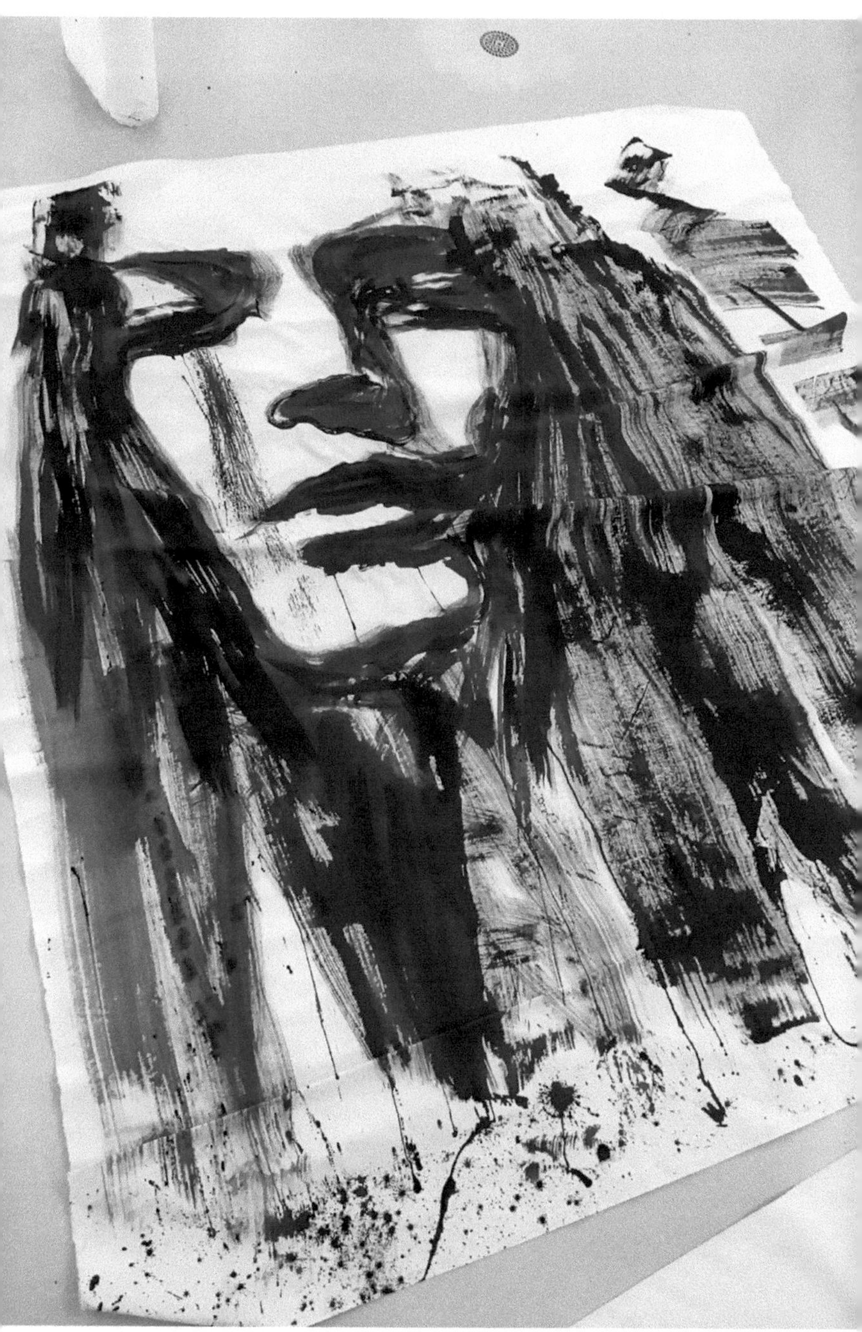

Traurige Gesichter

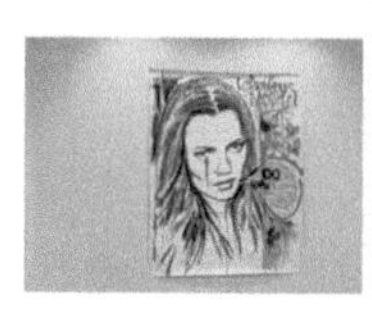
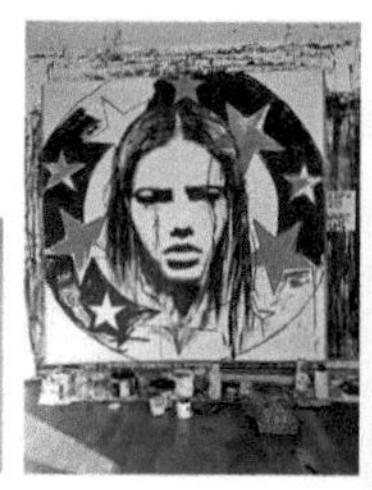
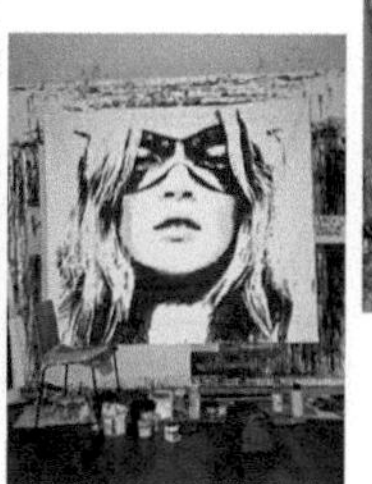
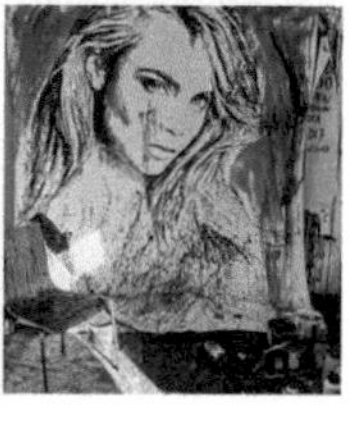
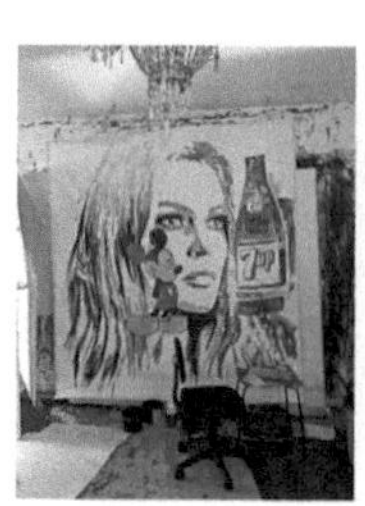
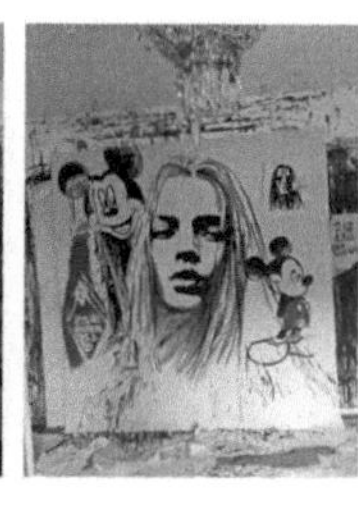
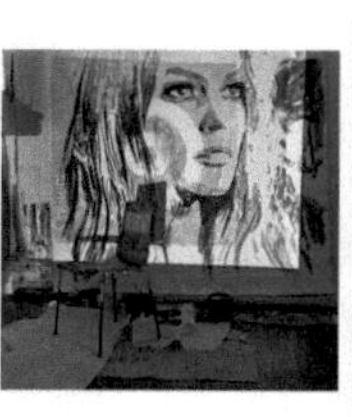
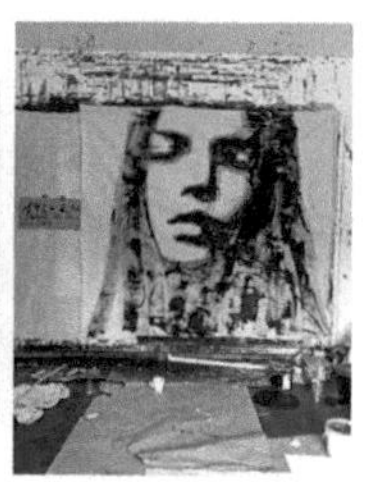
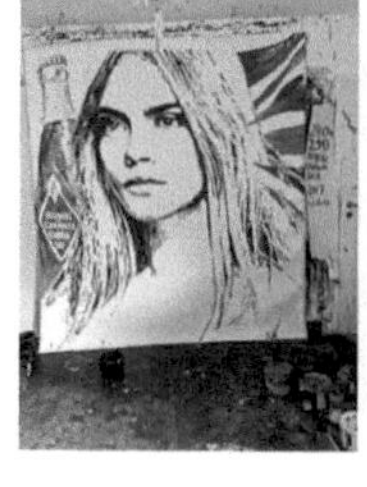
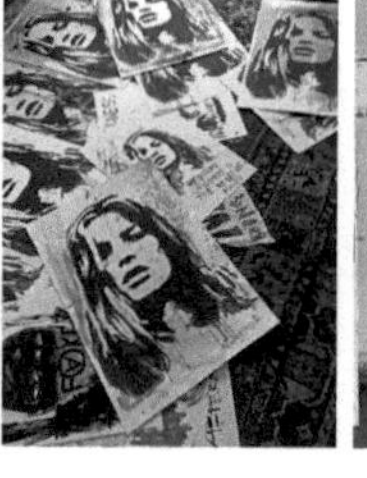
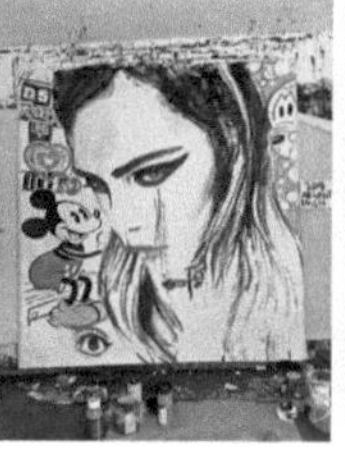
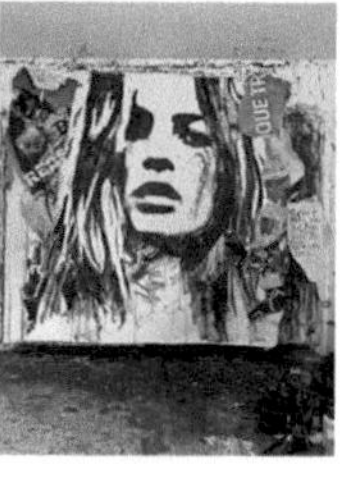
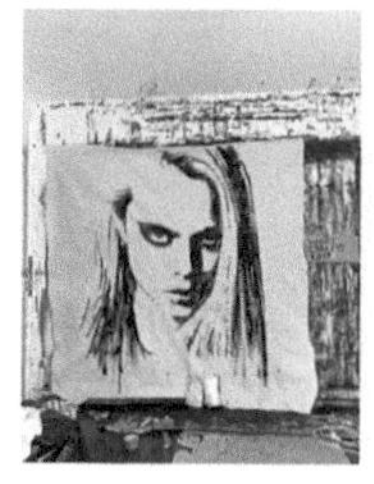
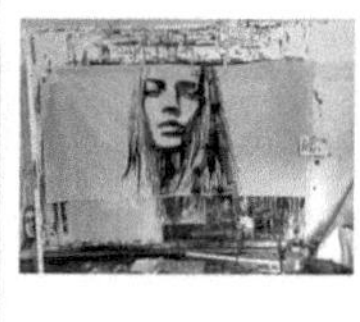
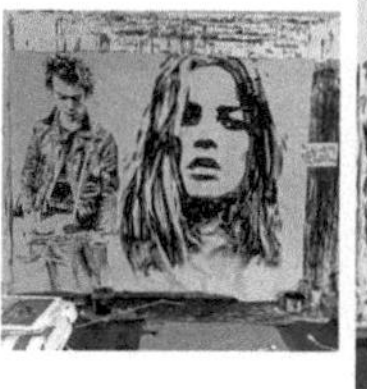
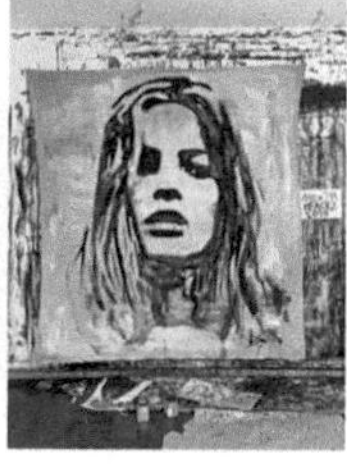

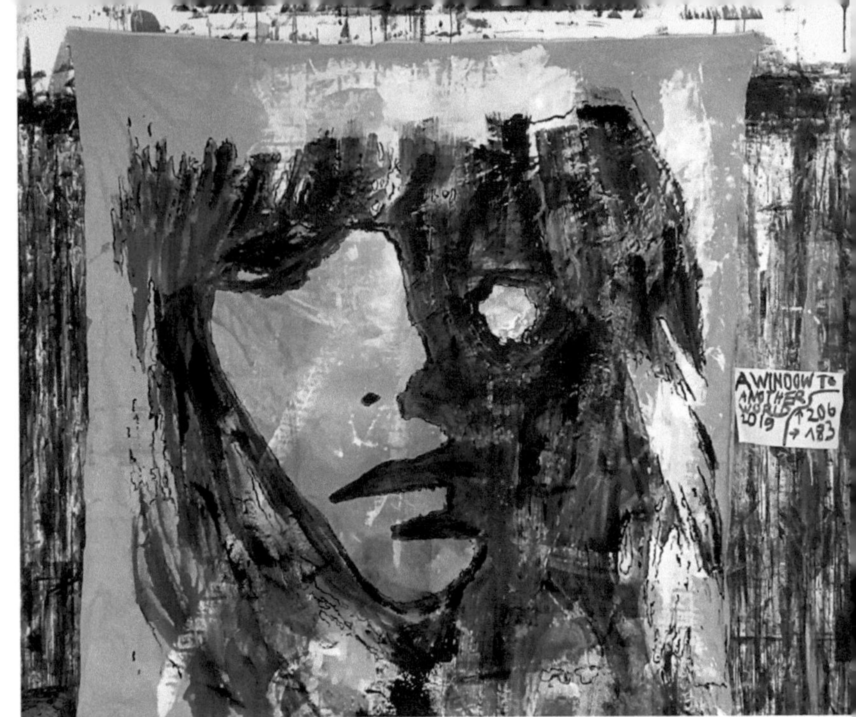

peace and Love

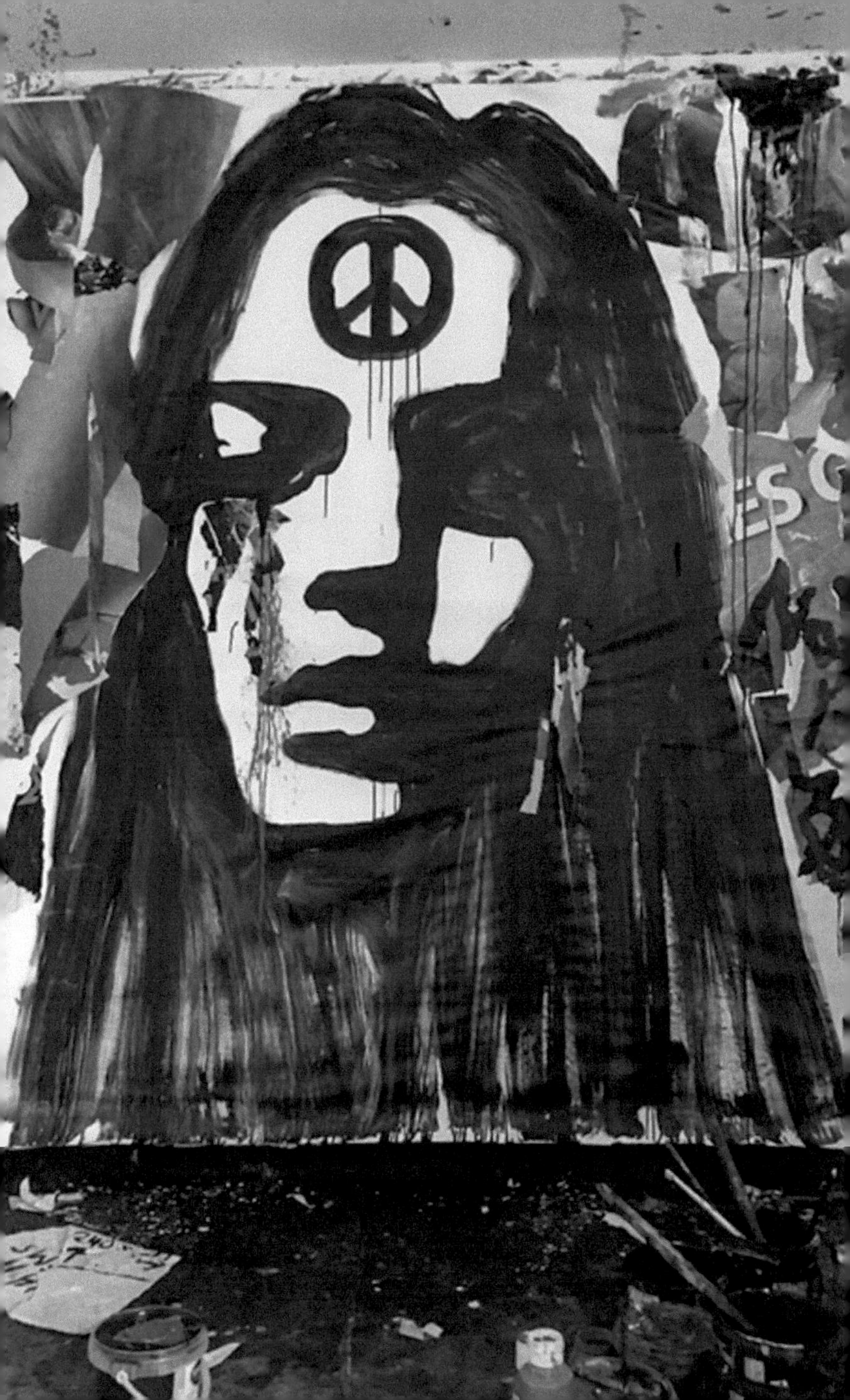

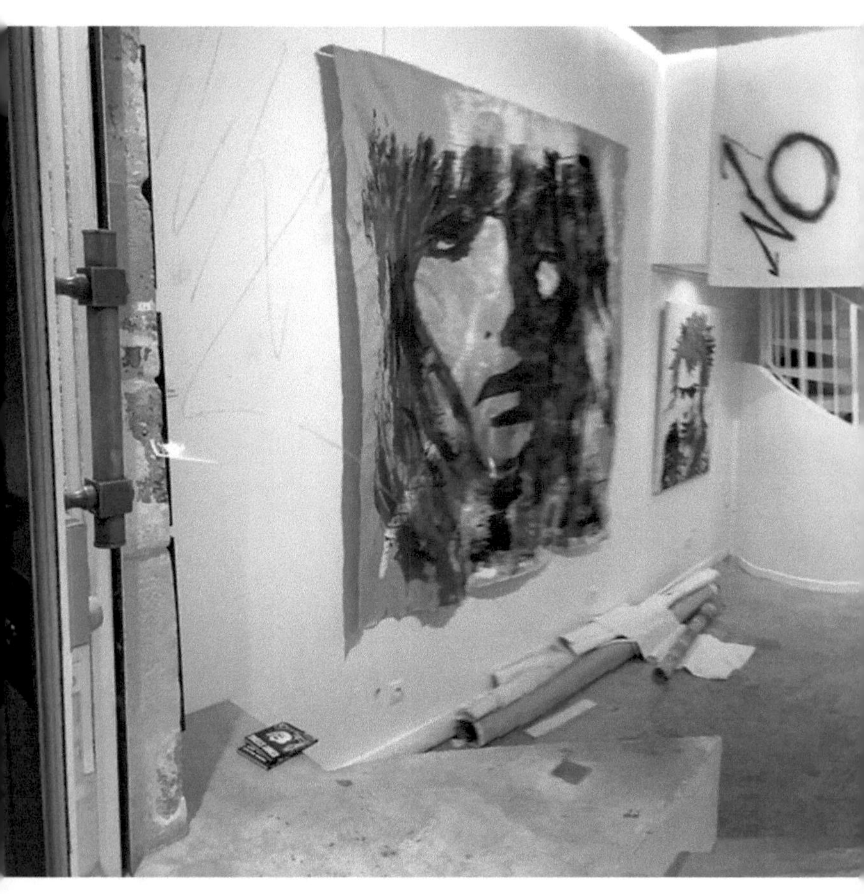

Exposition Galerie de la Clé, 2019

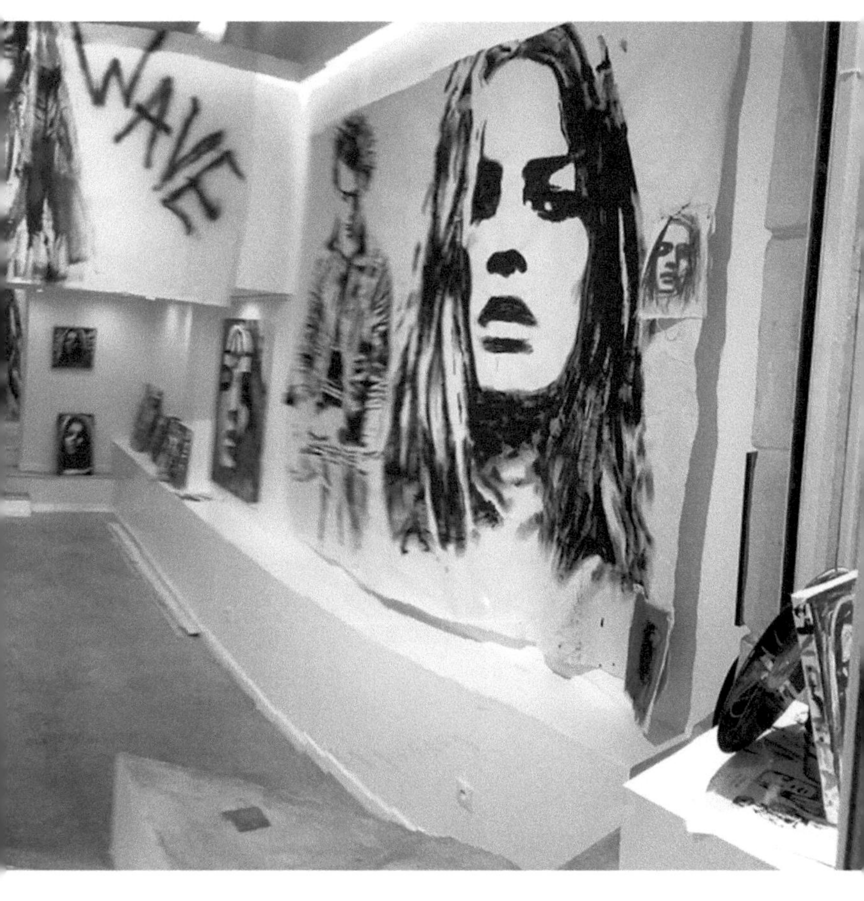

D'ailleurs.....

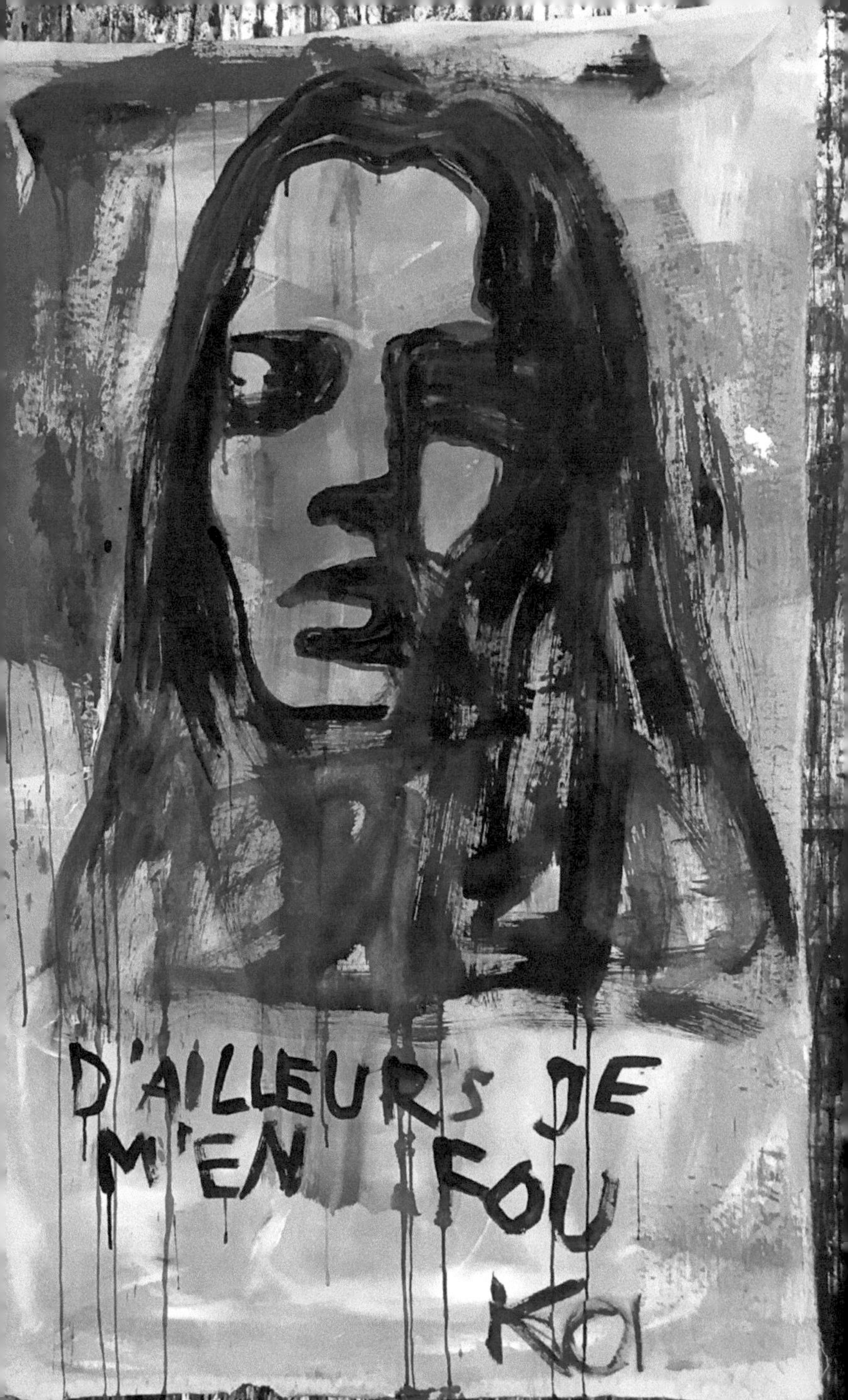
D'AILLEURS JE
M'EN FOU
KOI

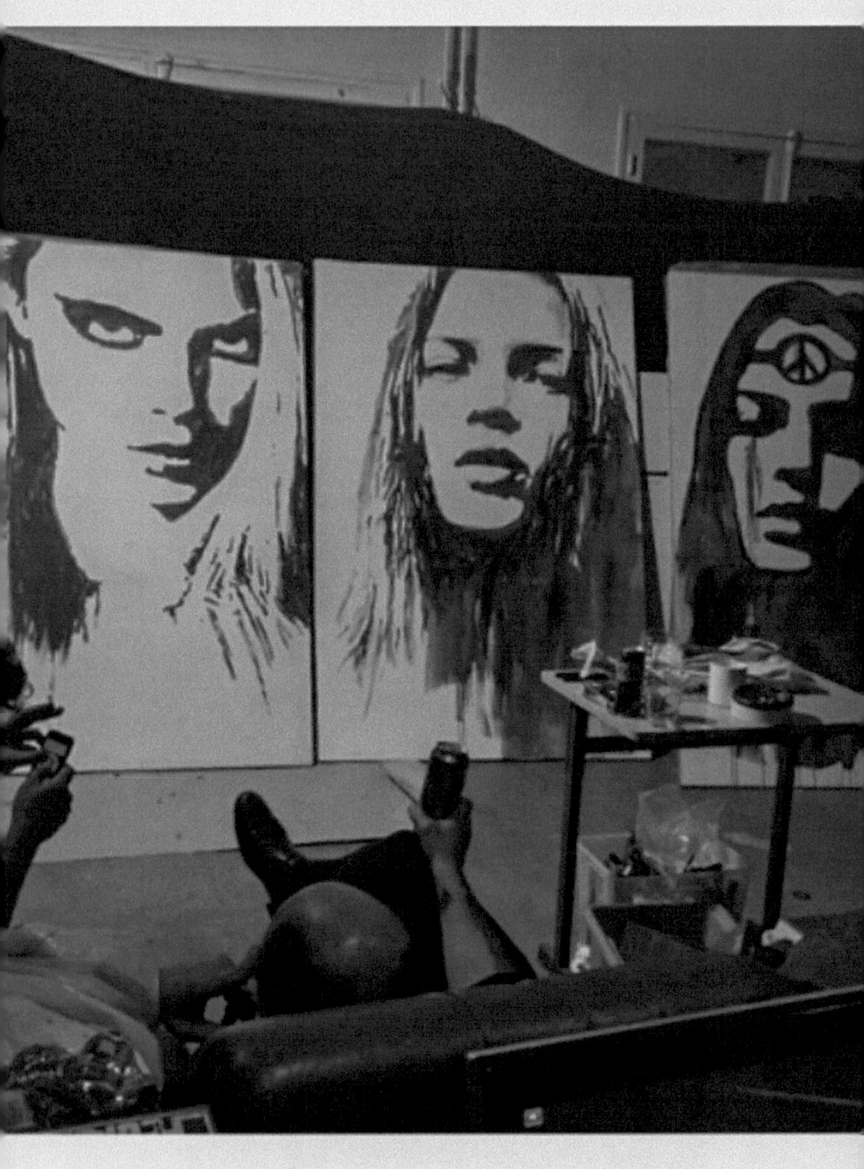

Atelier Paris Belleville

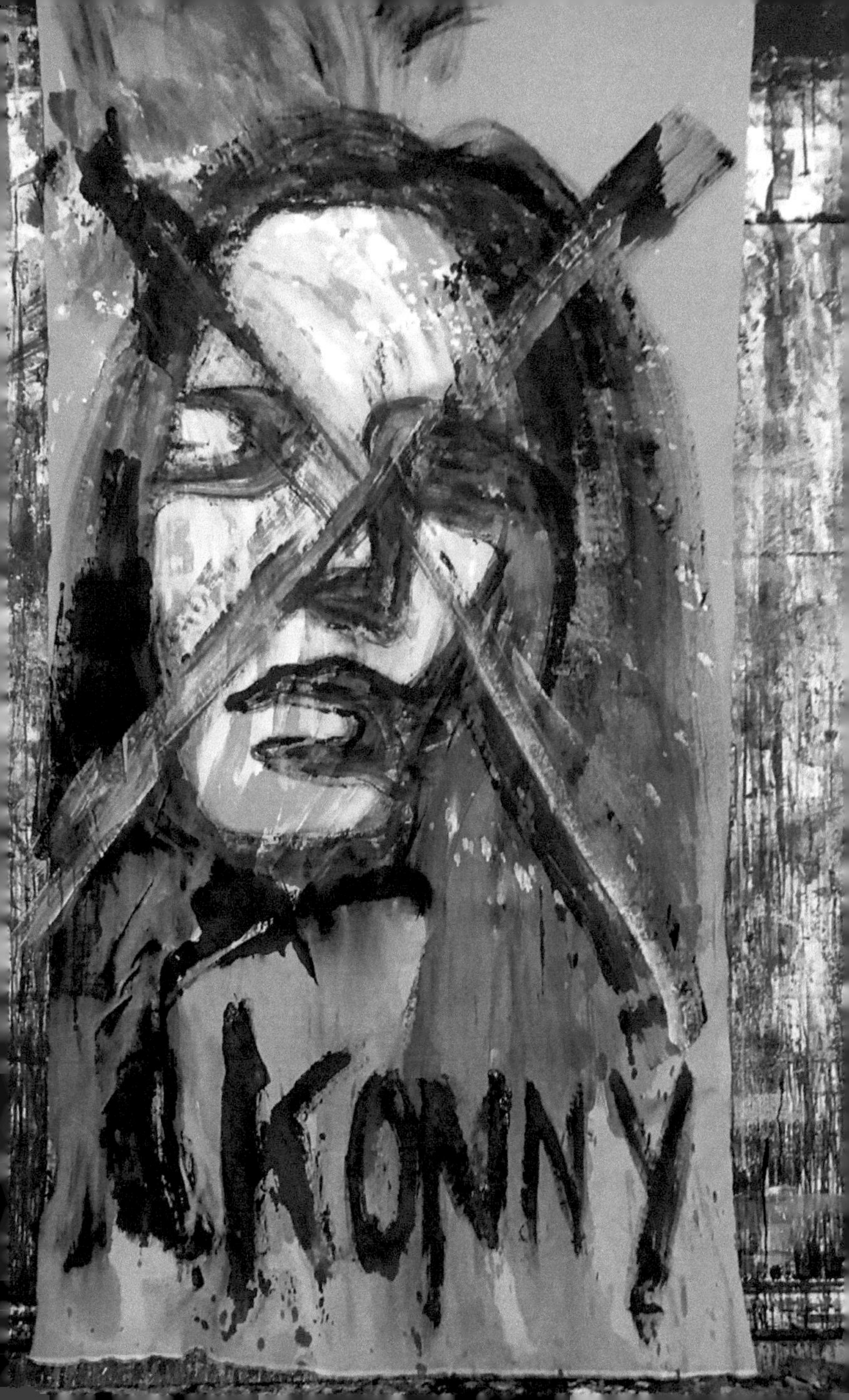
KONNY

Metro

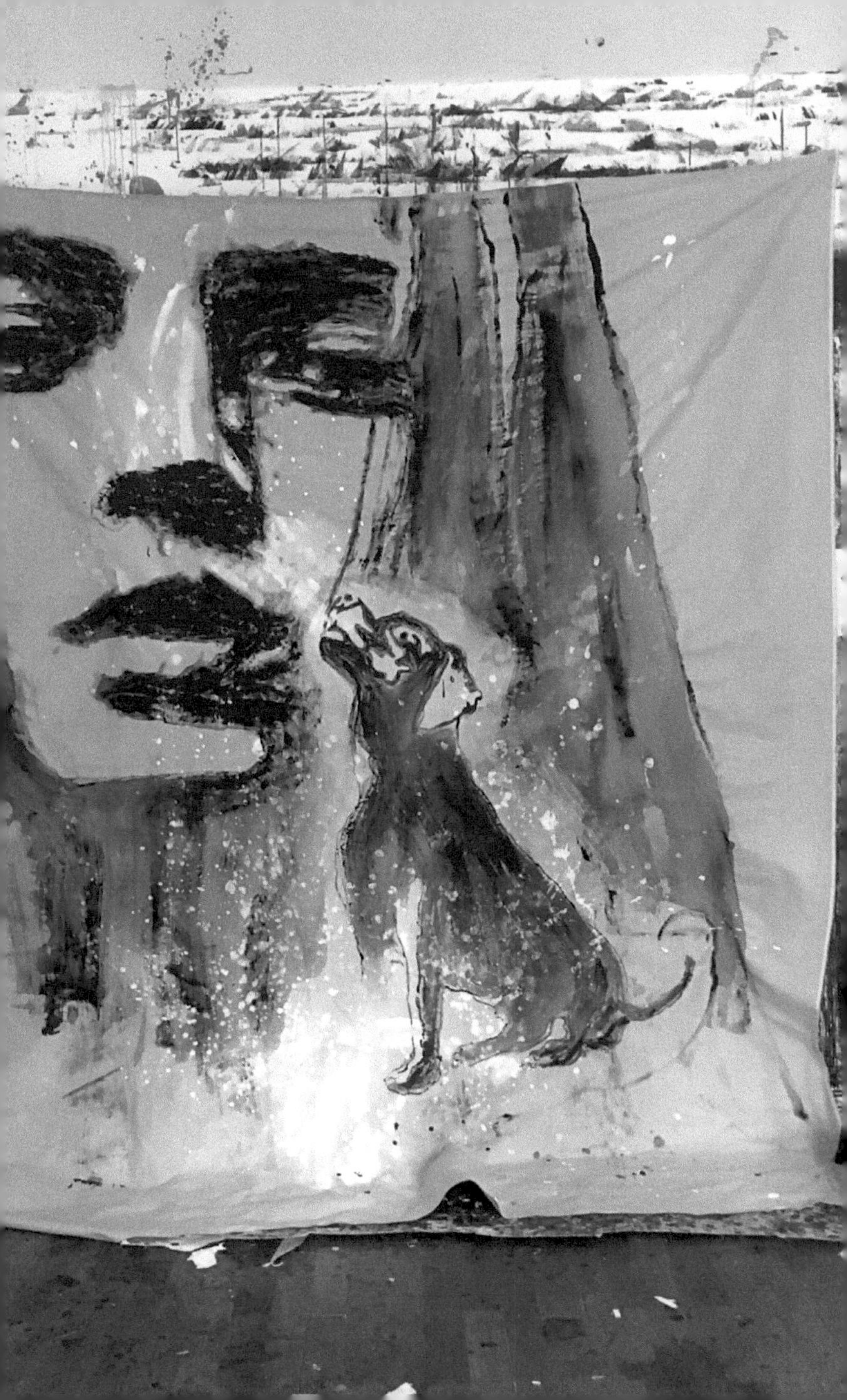

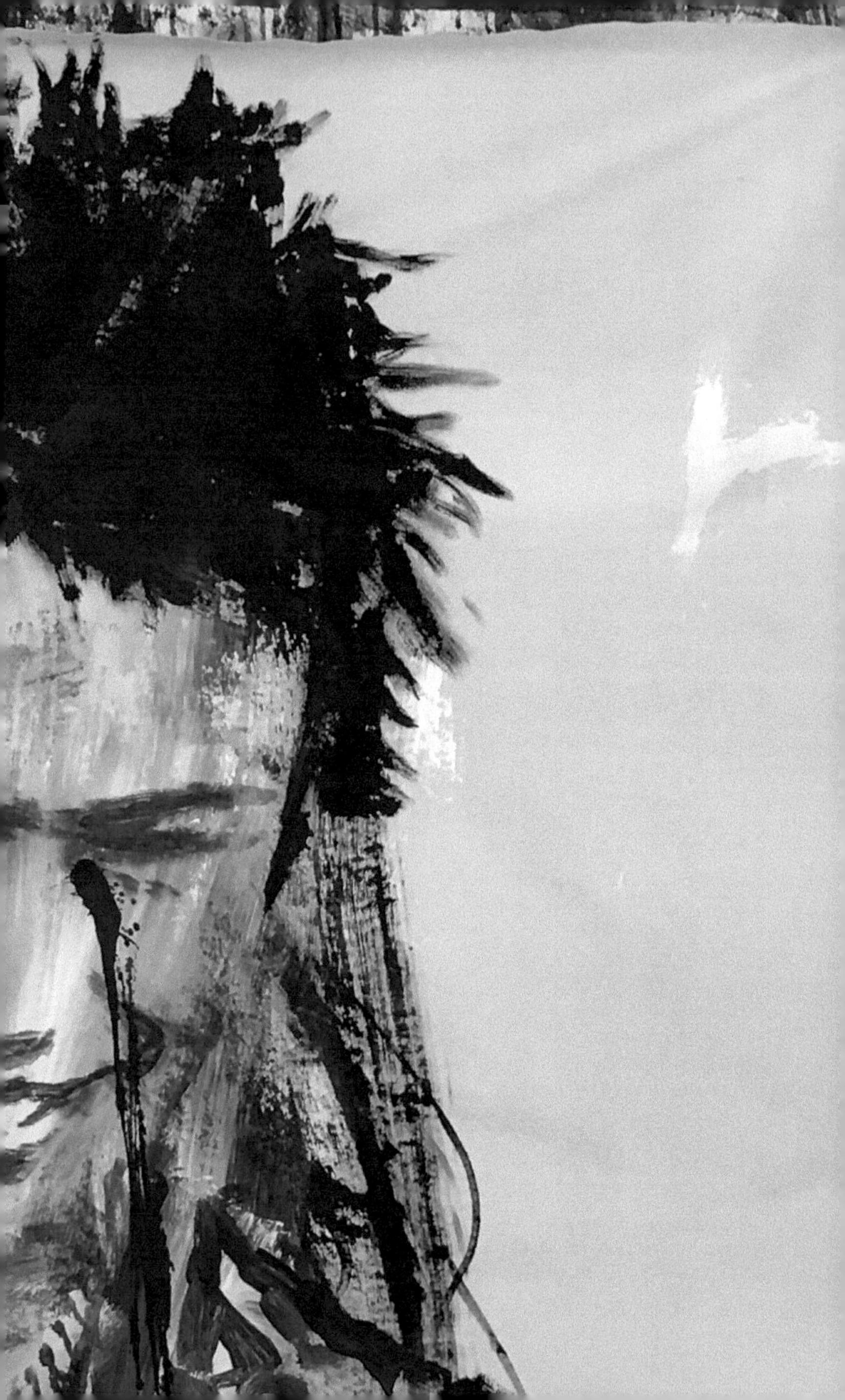

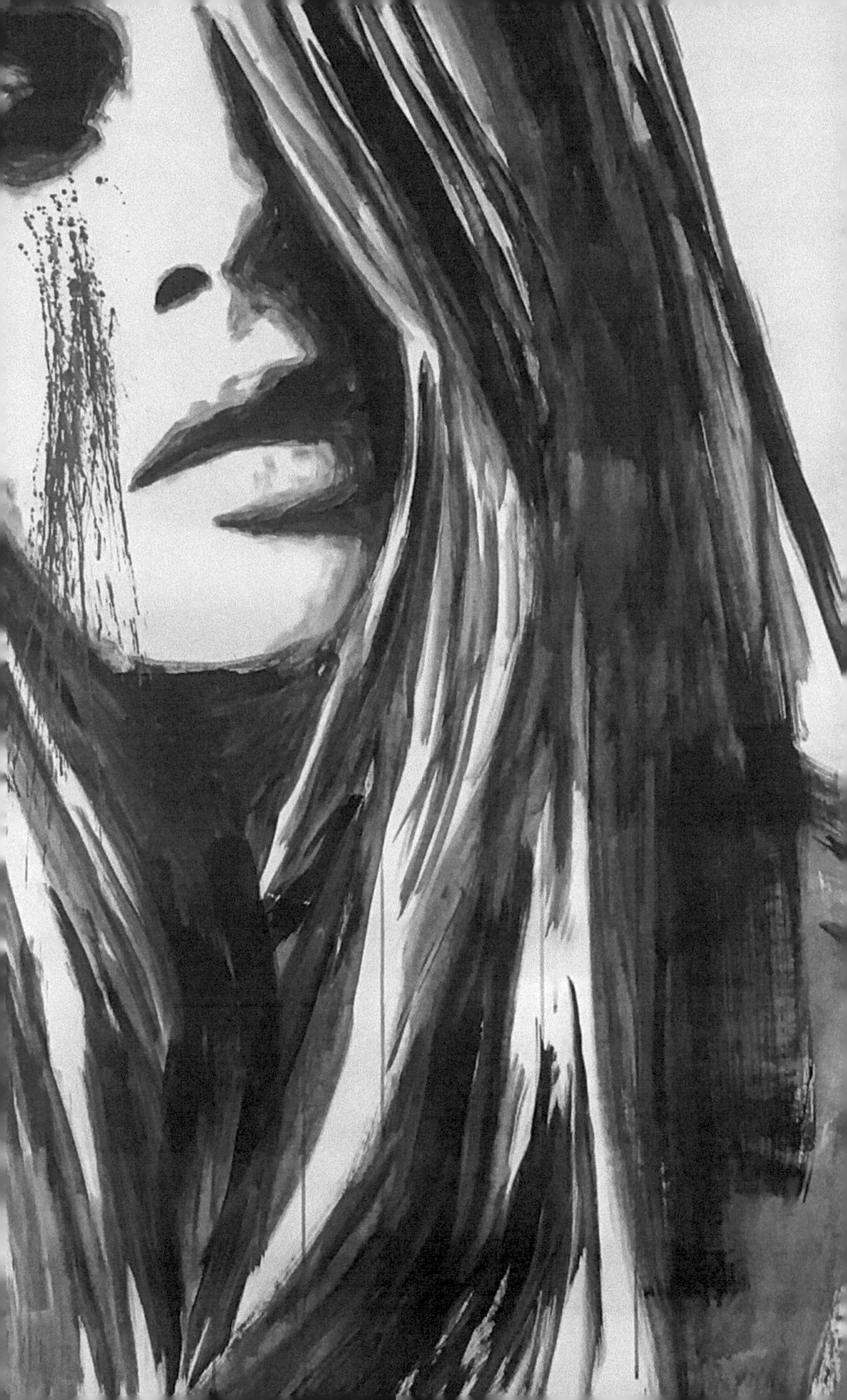

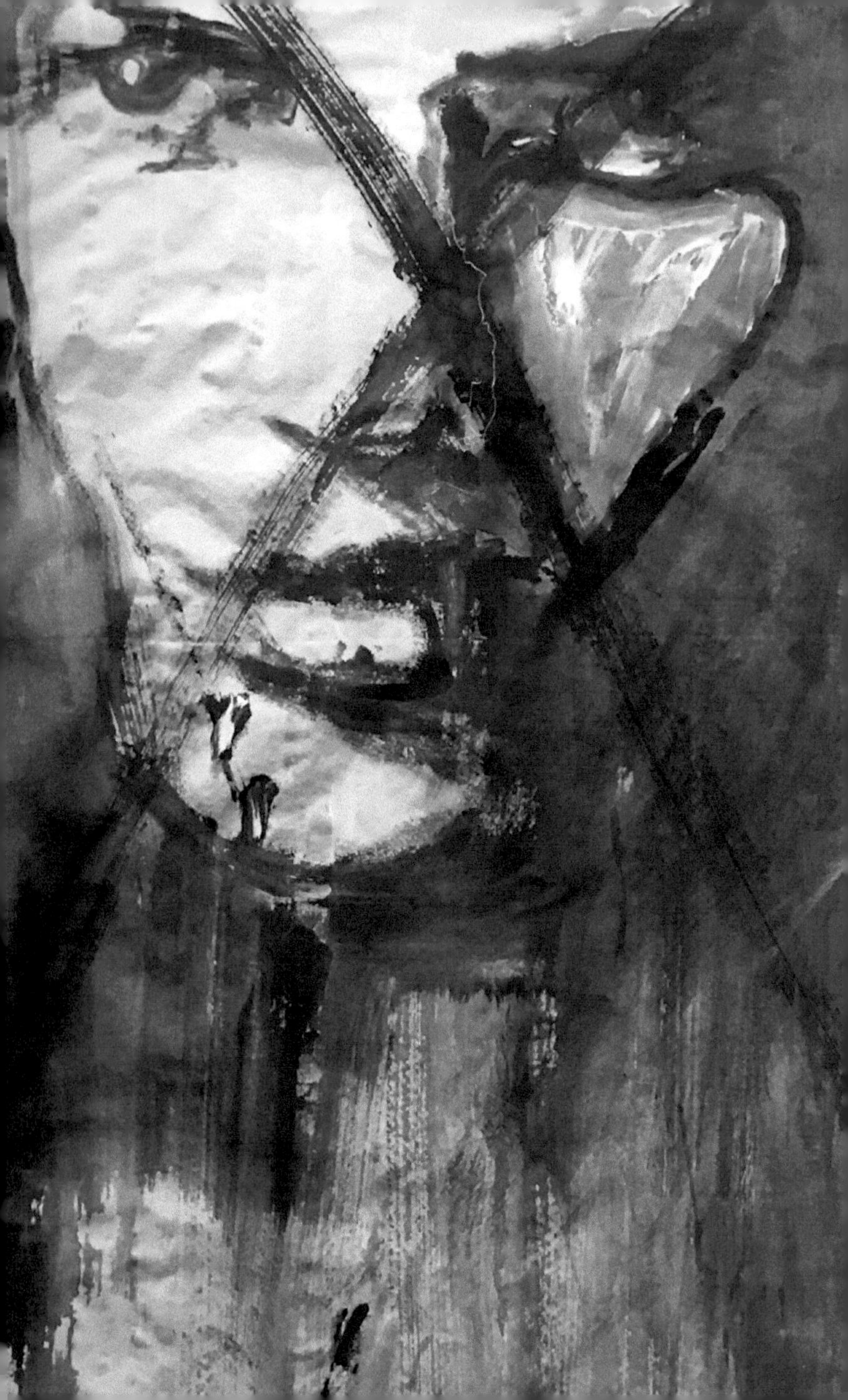

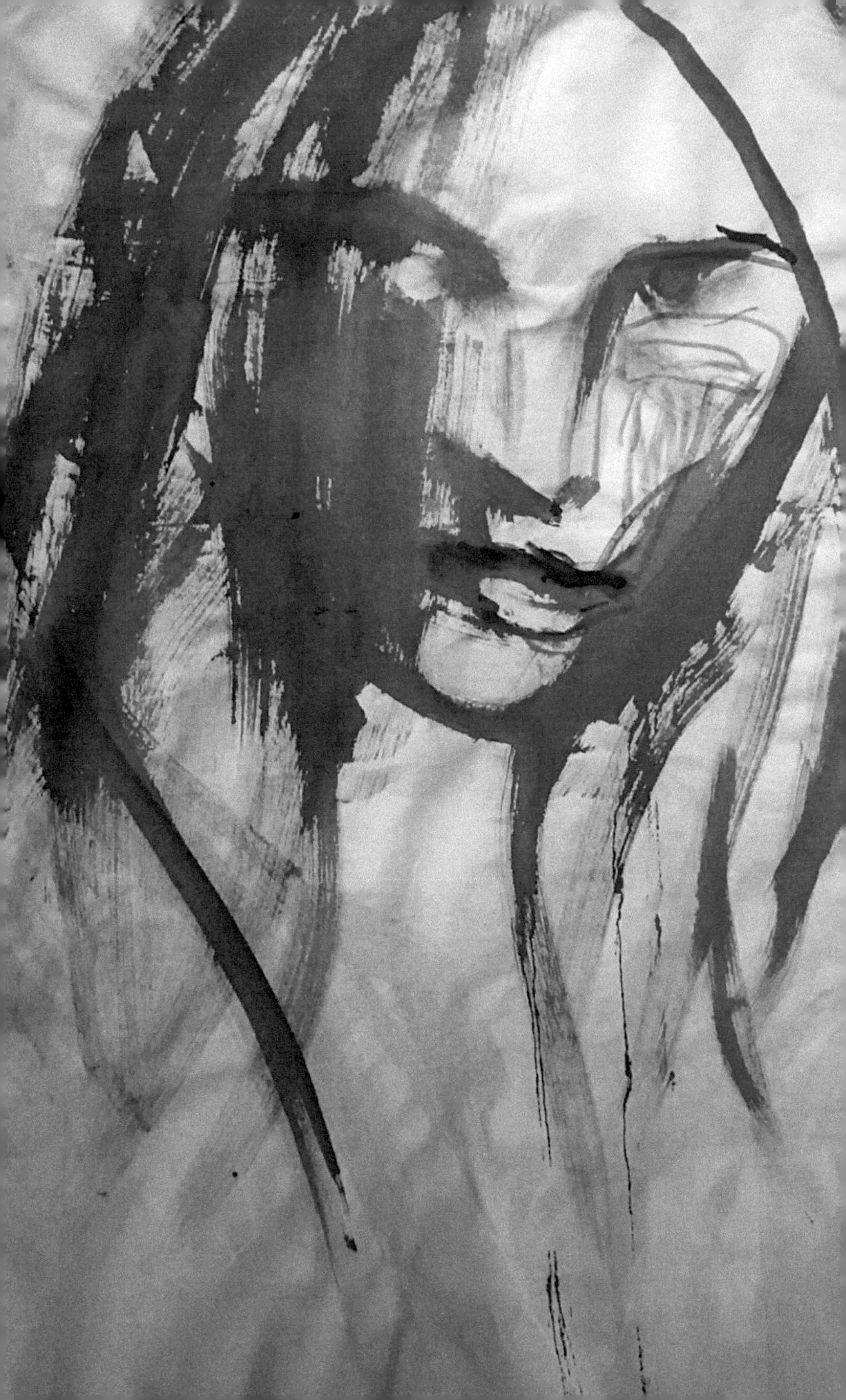

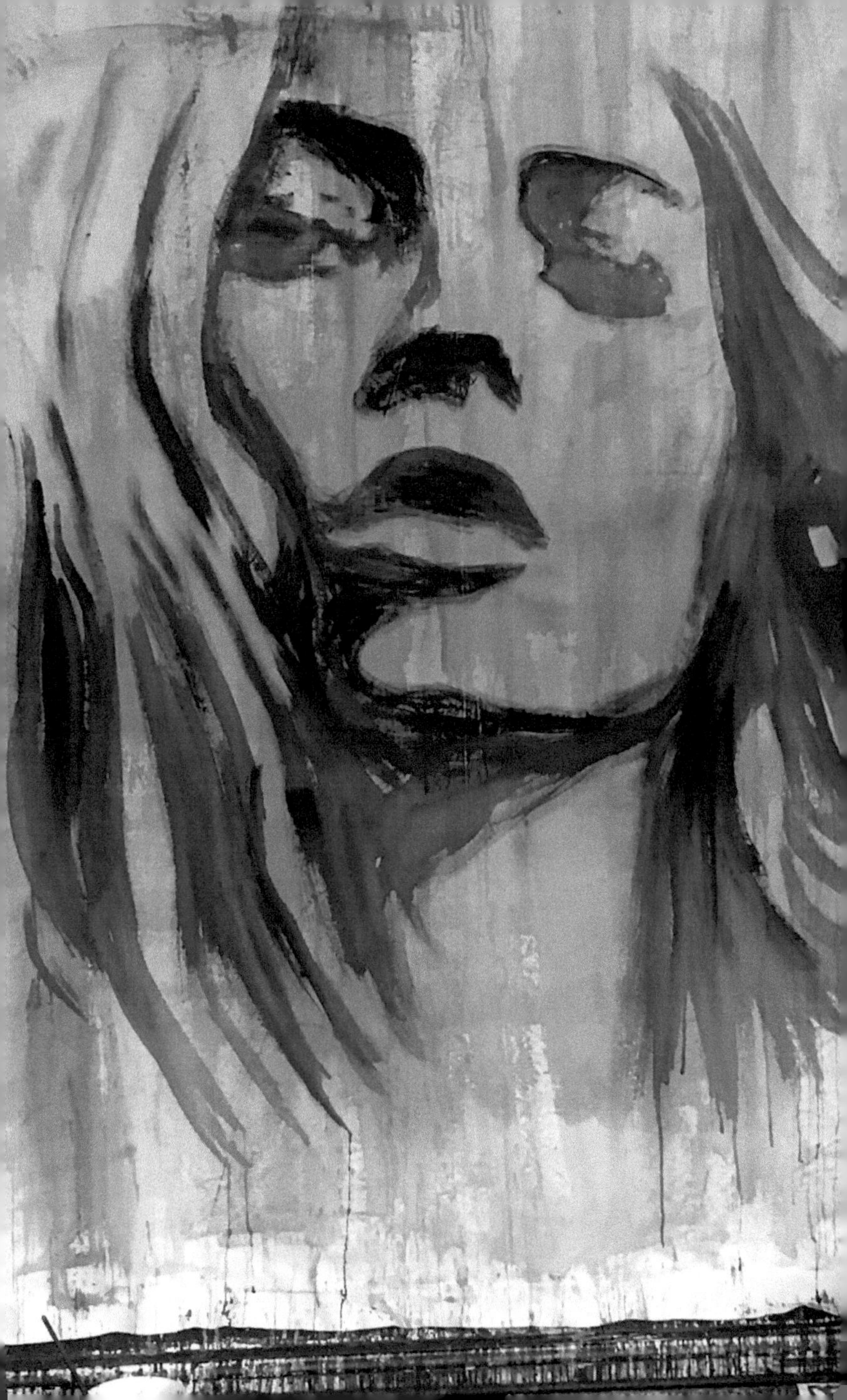

2020, 2021

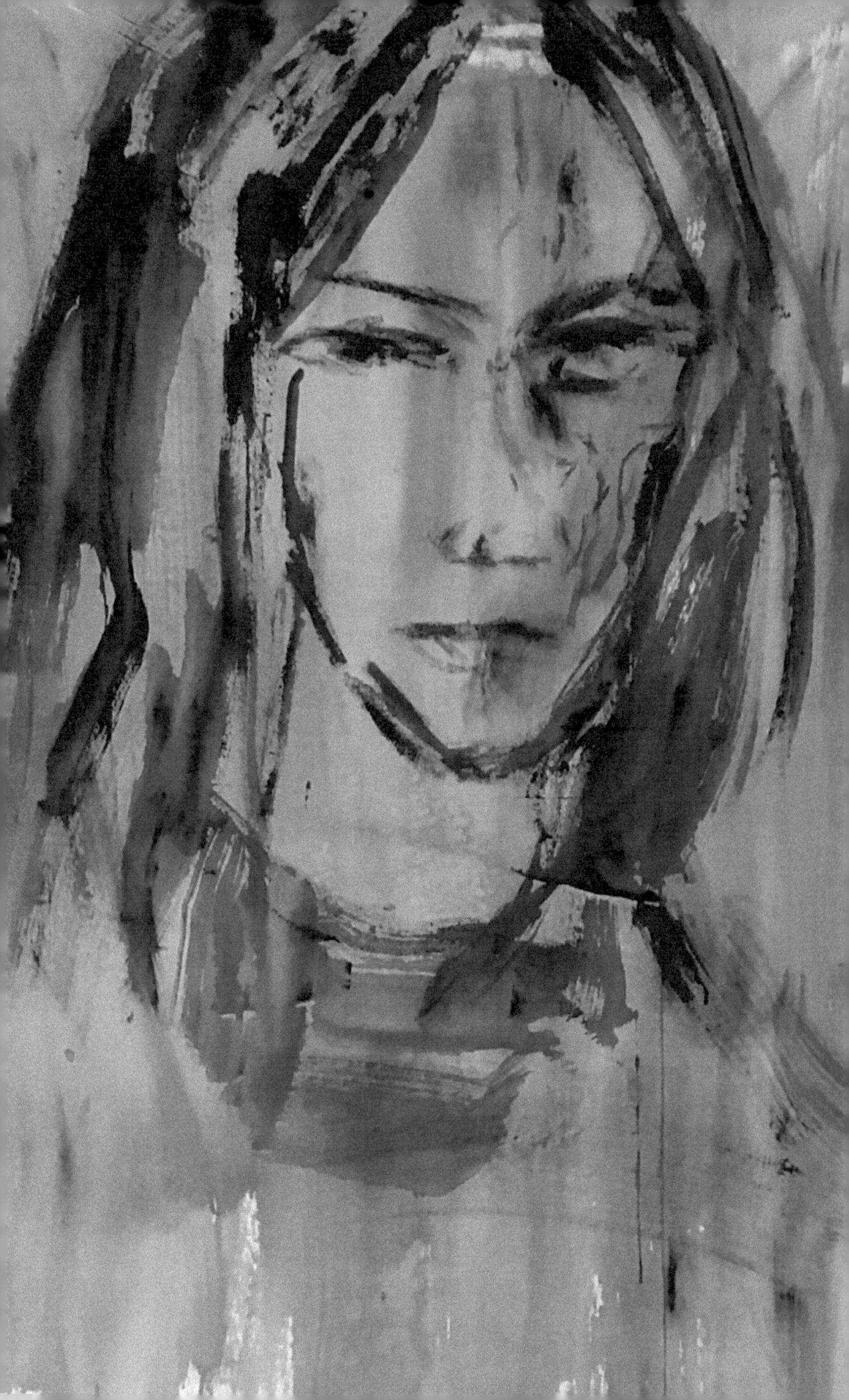

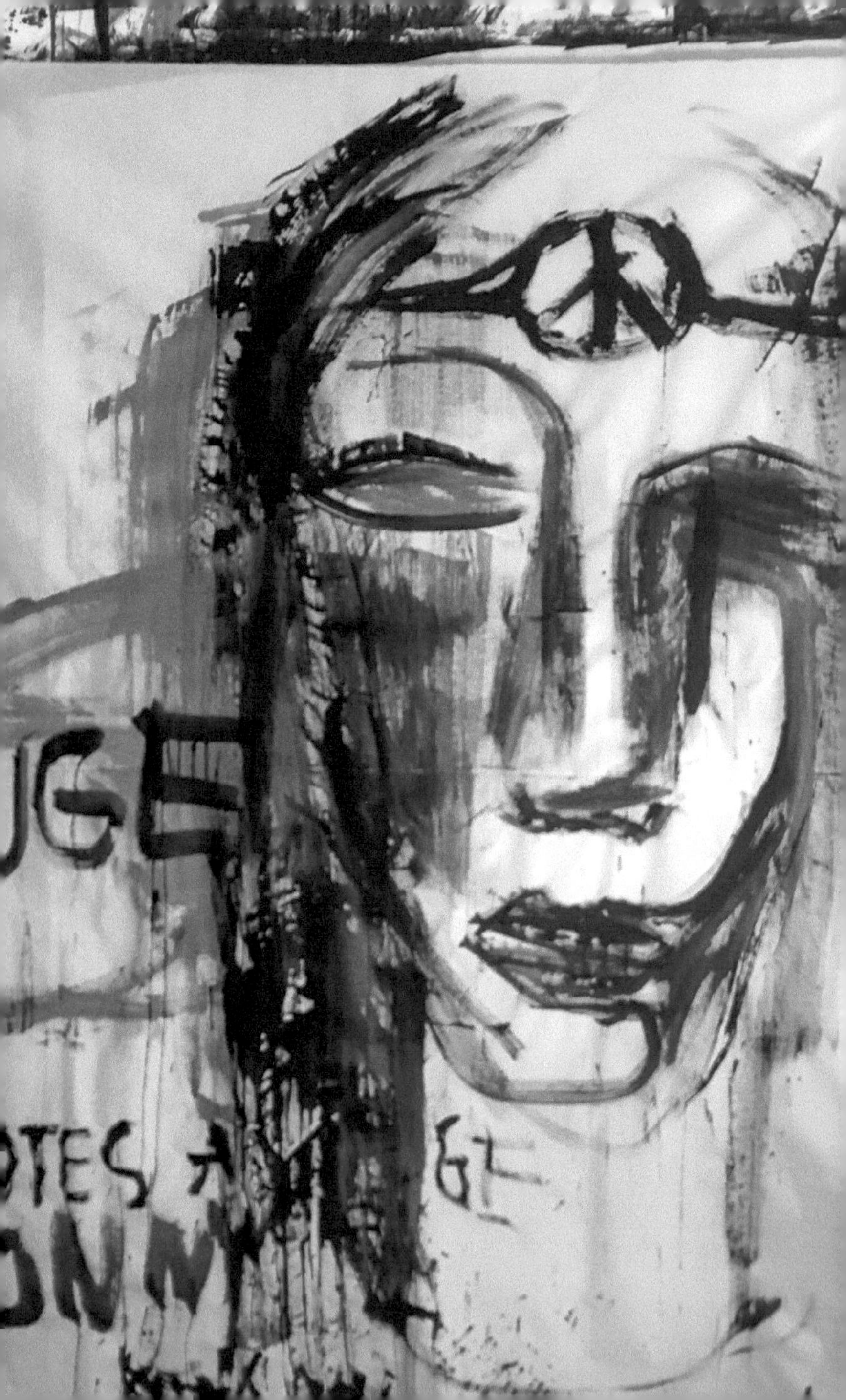
JGF
PTES A GF

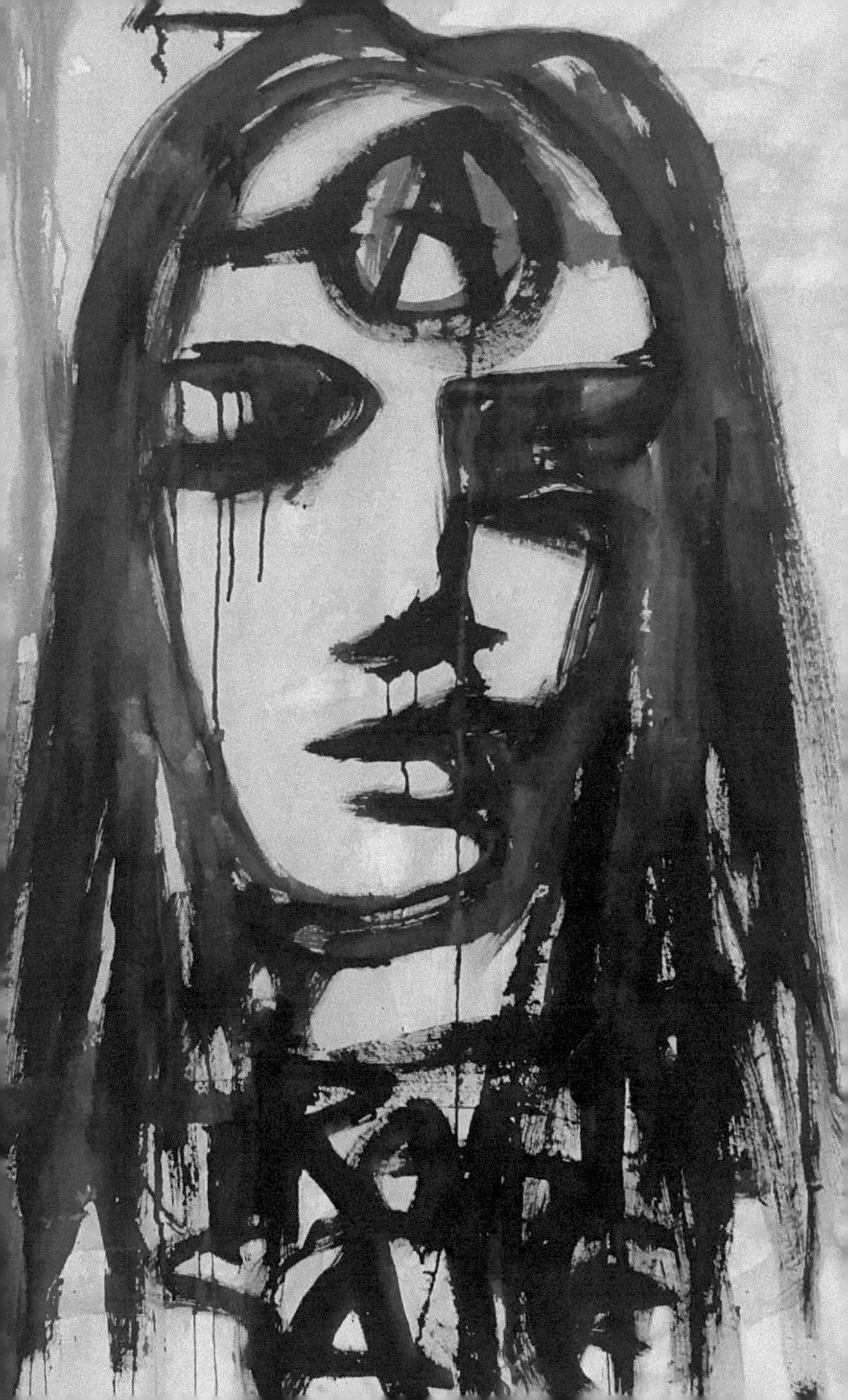

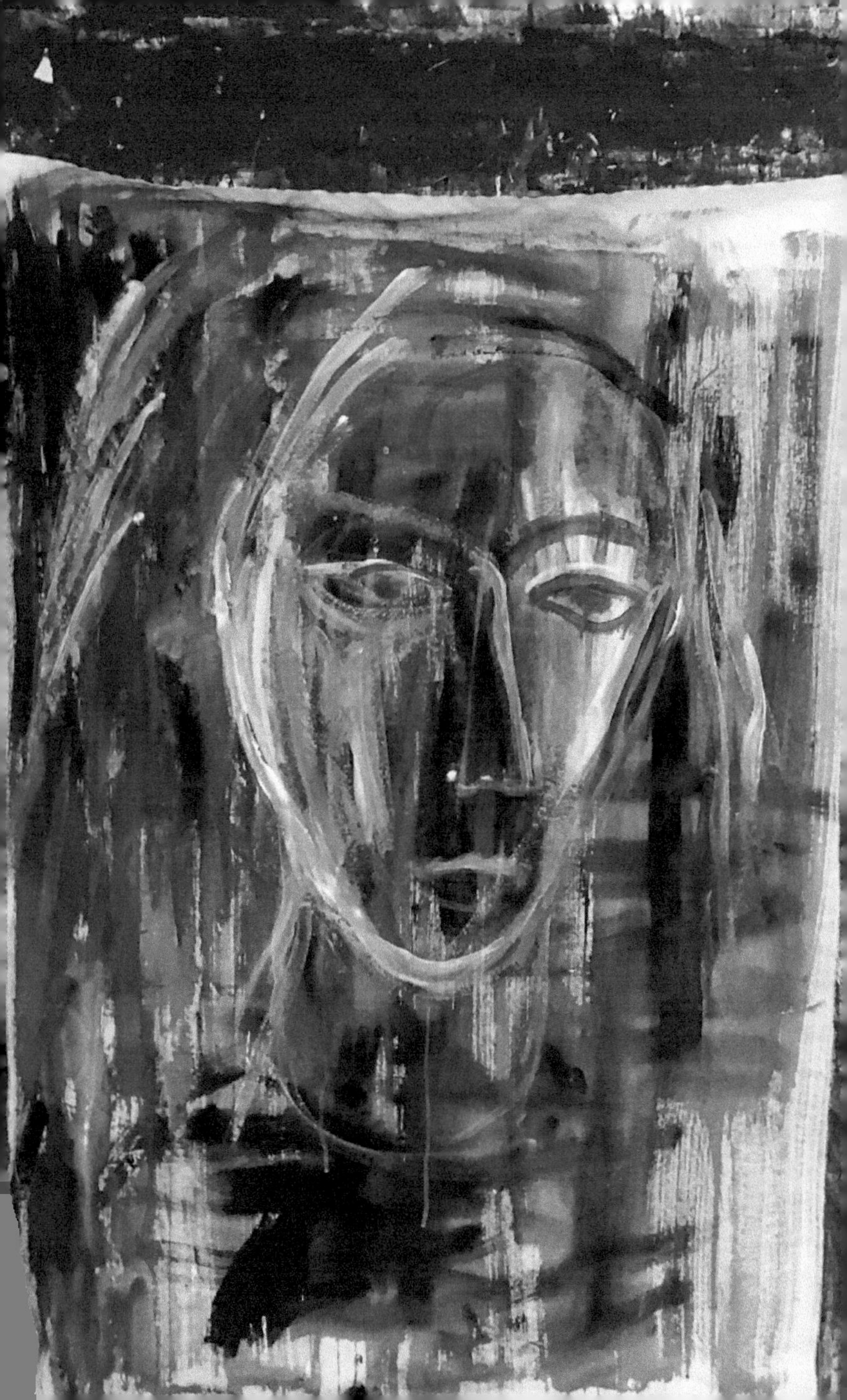

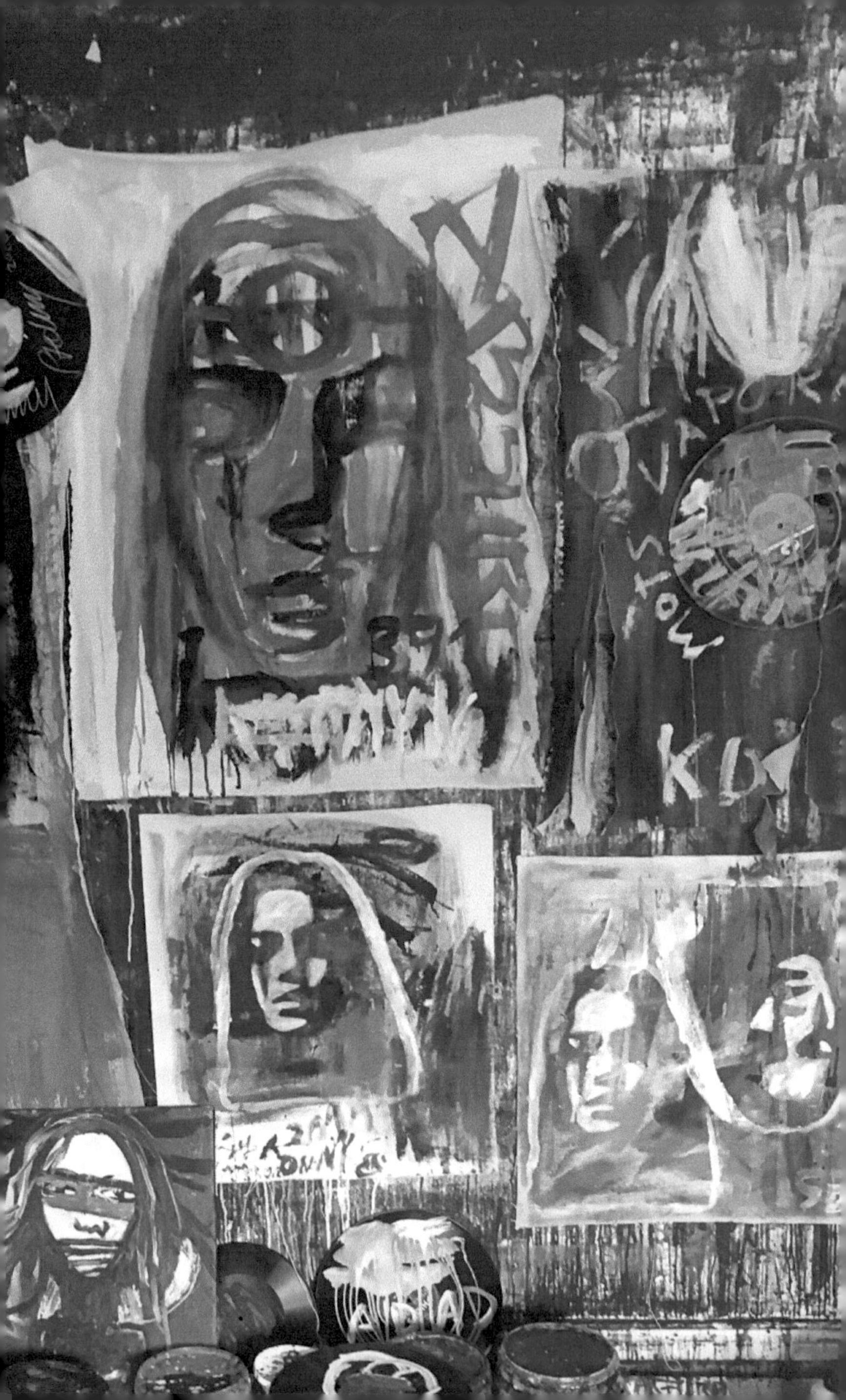

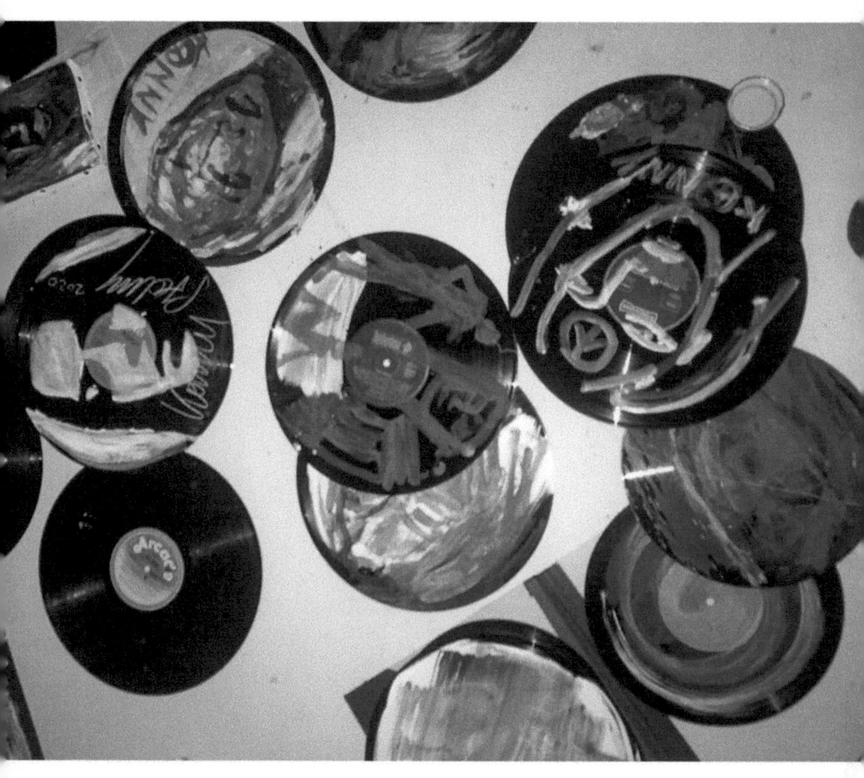

Atelier 2020

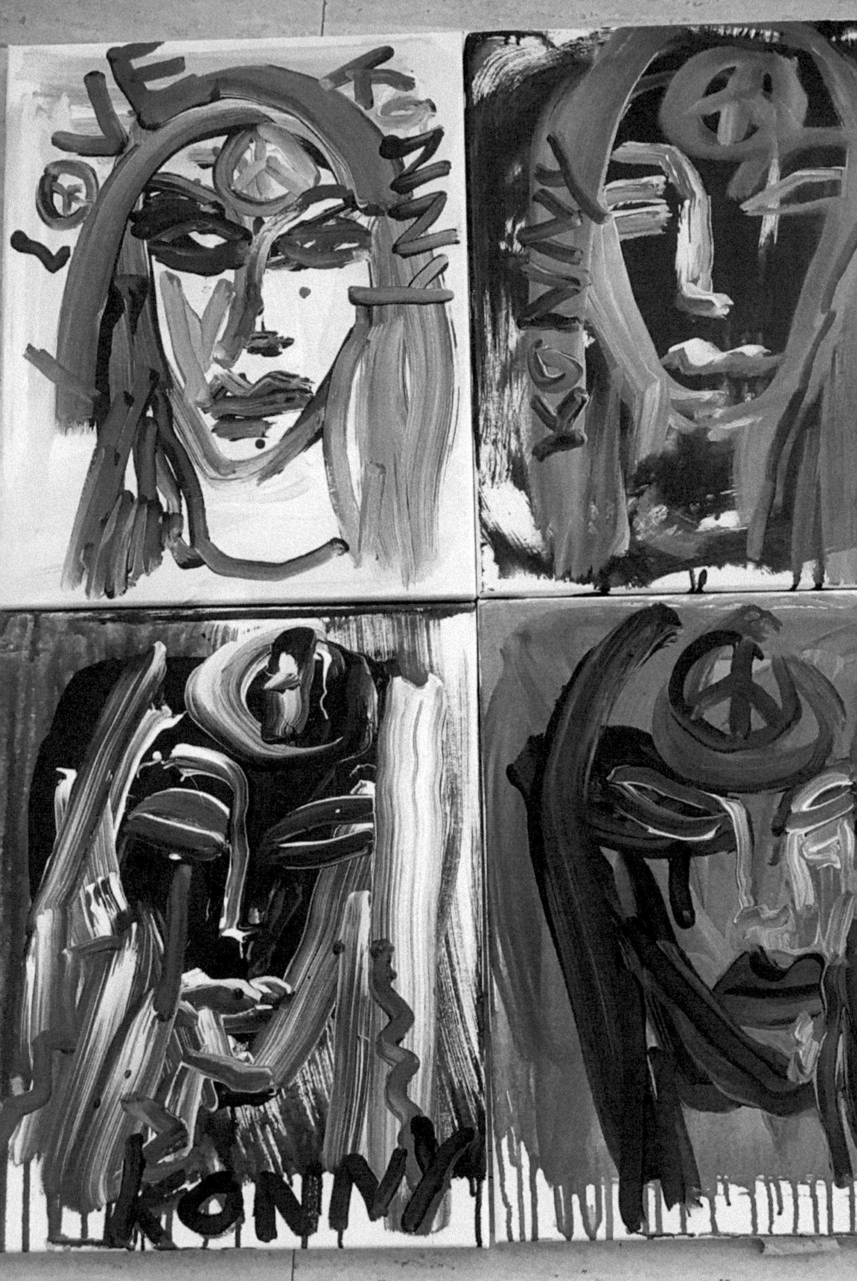

LOVE
KENNY
KENNY
KENNY
KONNY

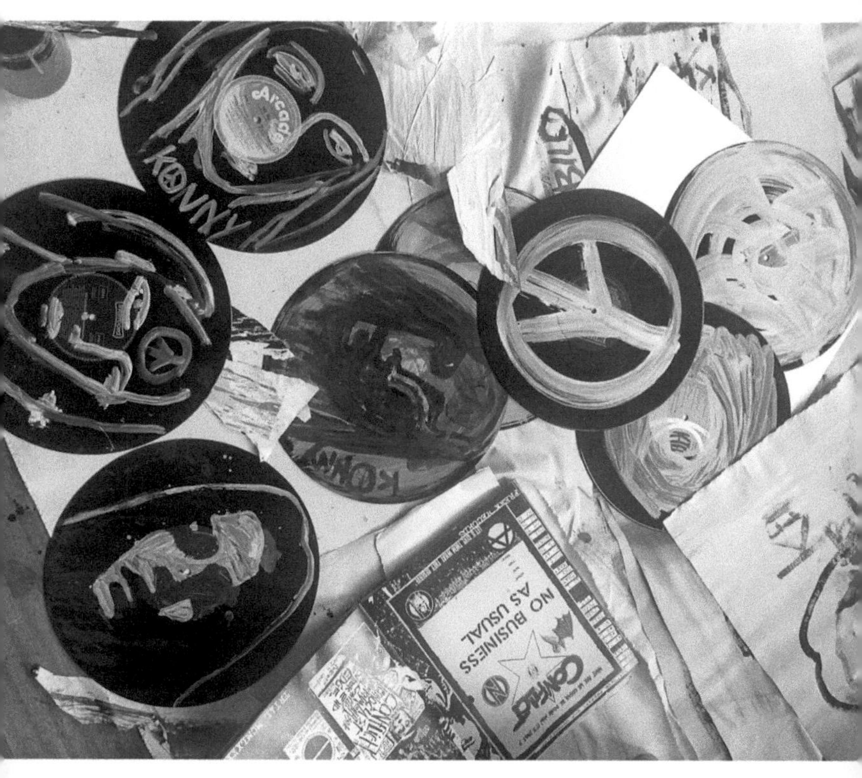

Galerie de la Clé Paris

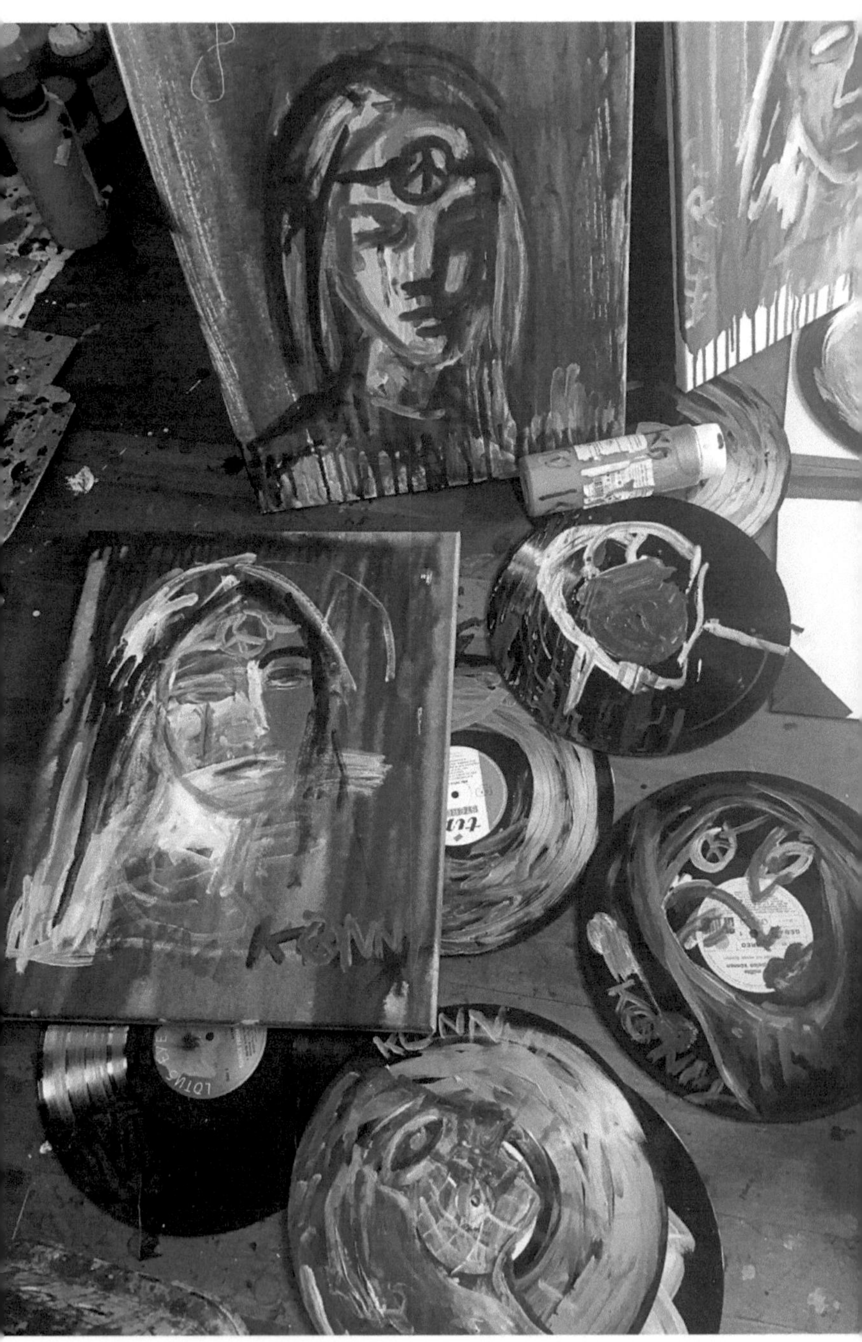

direct Serie 2020

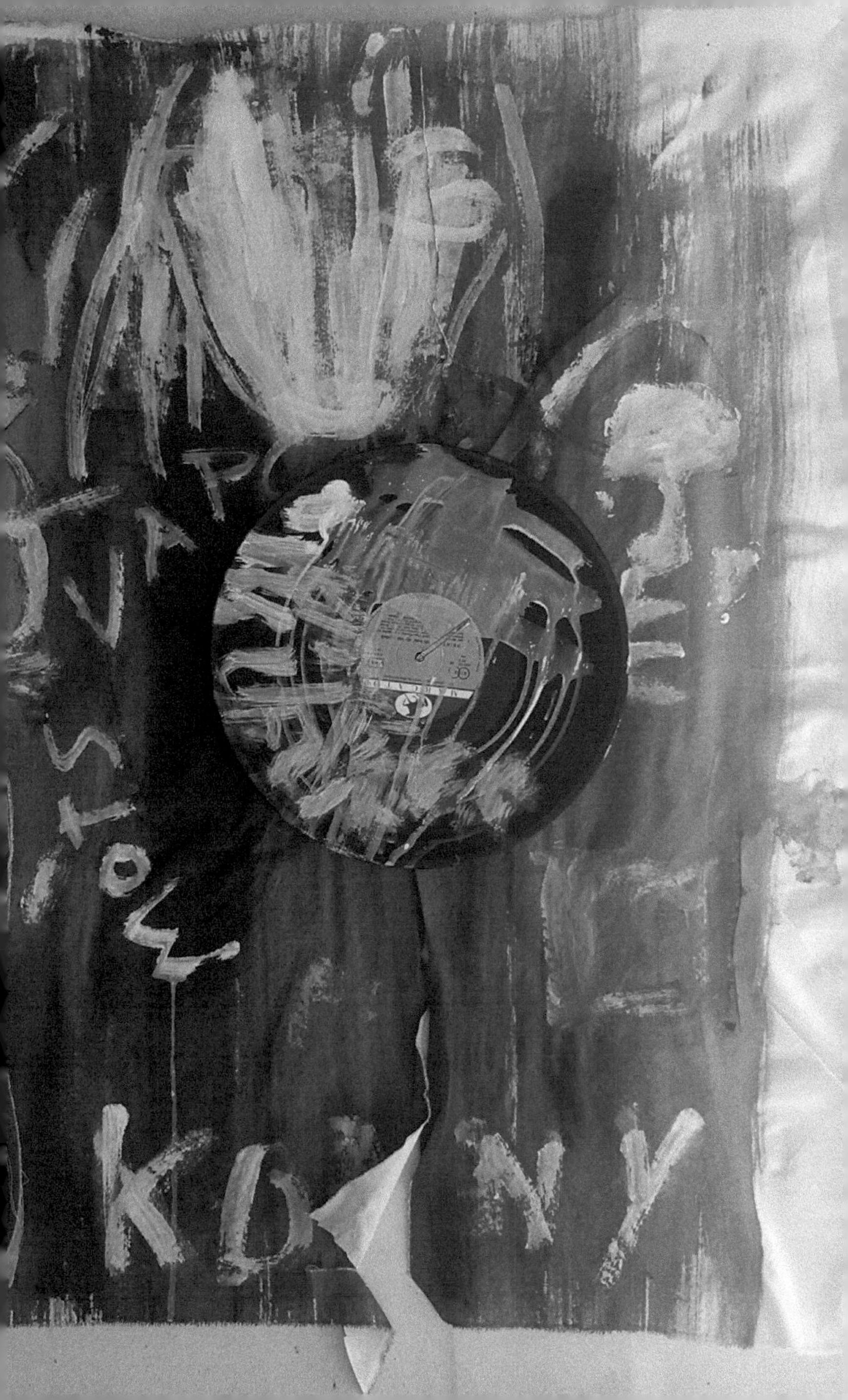

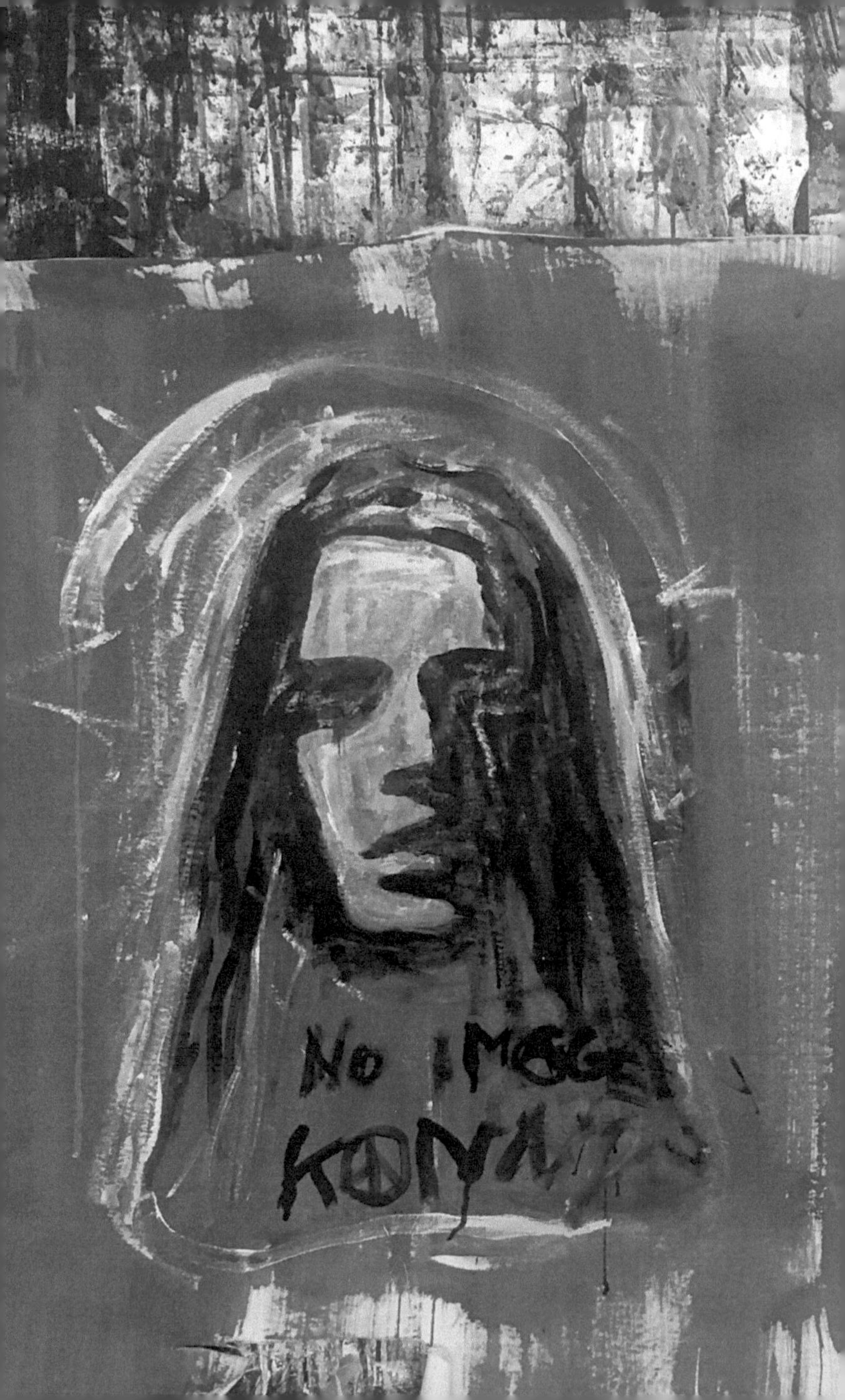
No Image
KONAI

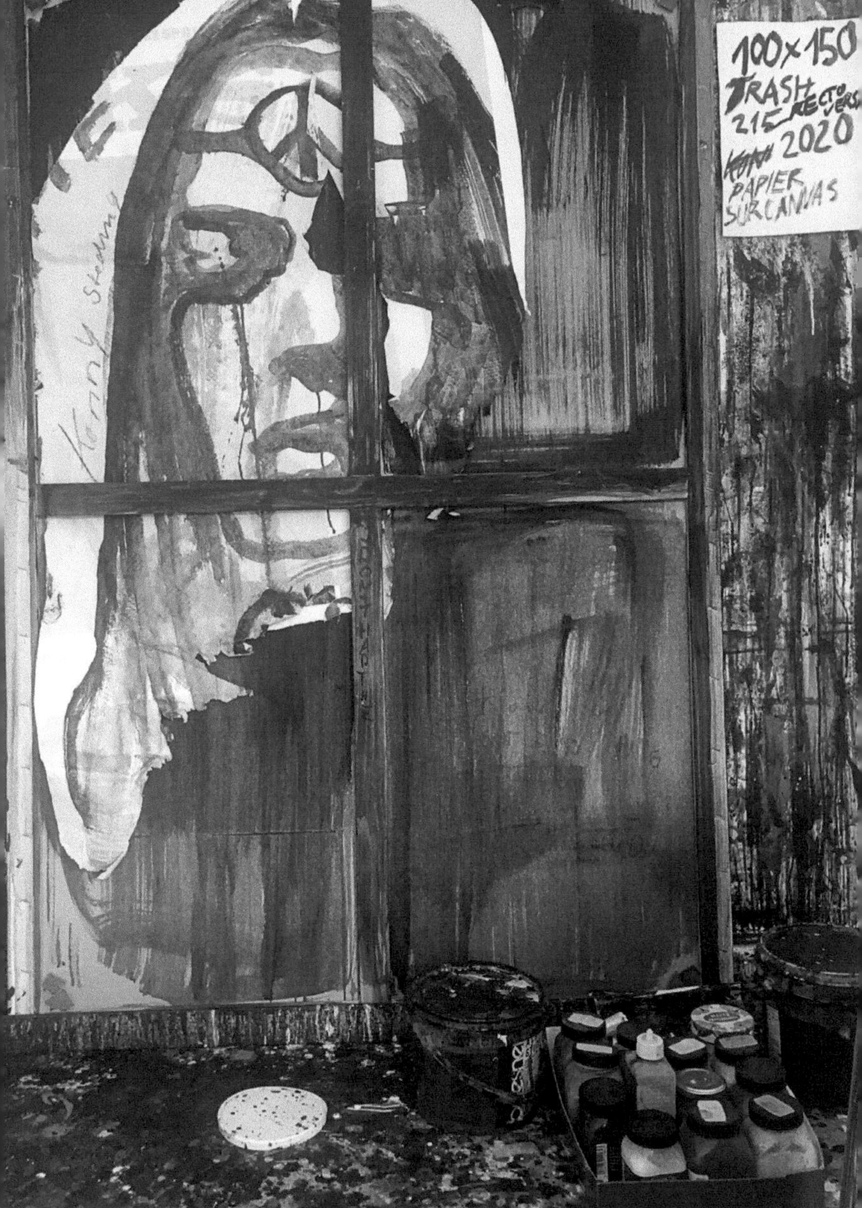
100x150
TRASH
215 RECTO VERS.
KOH 2020
PAPIER
SURCANVAS
Kenny Steeling

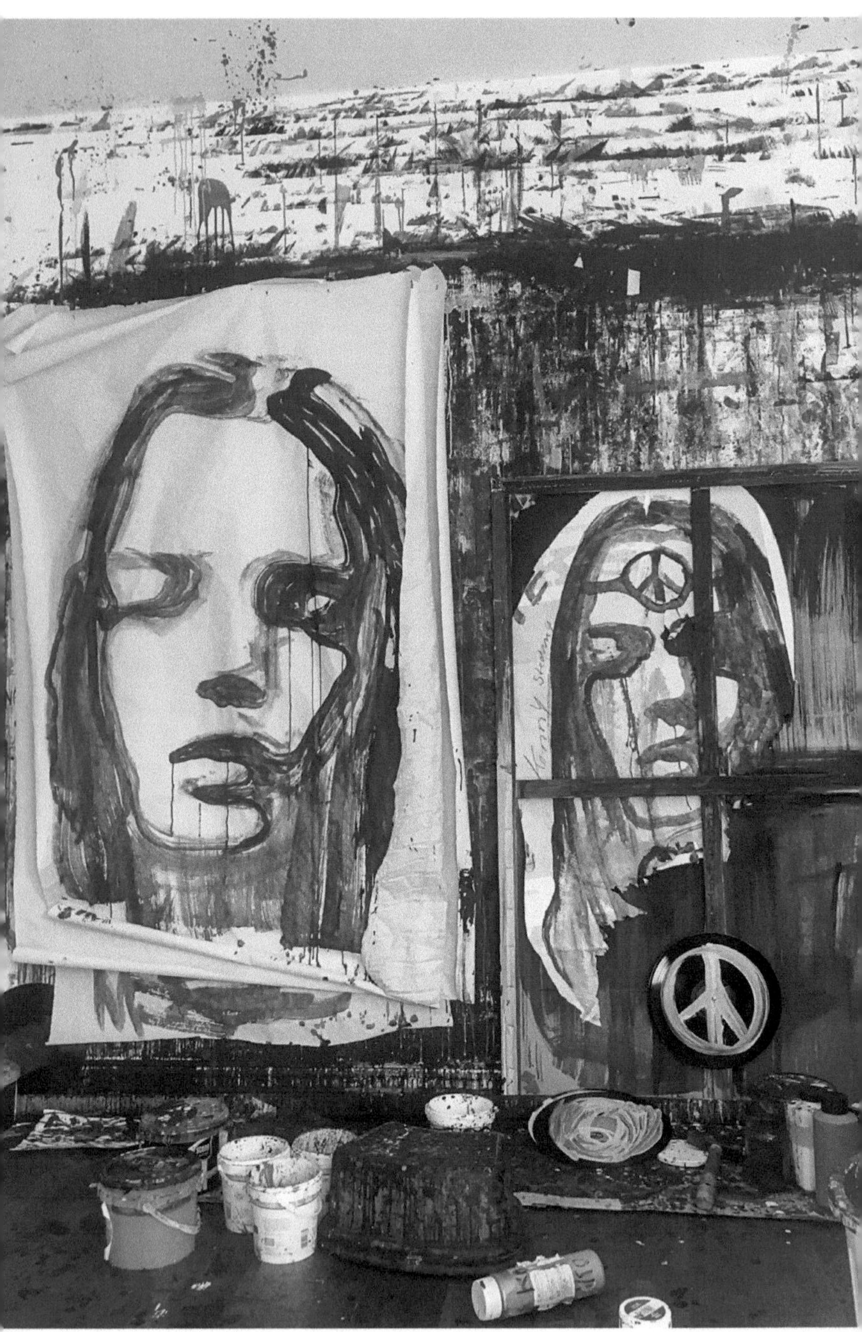

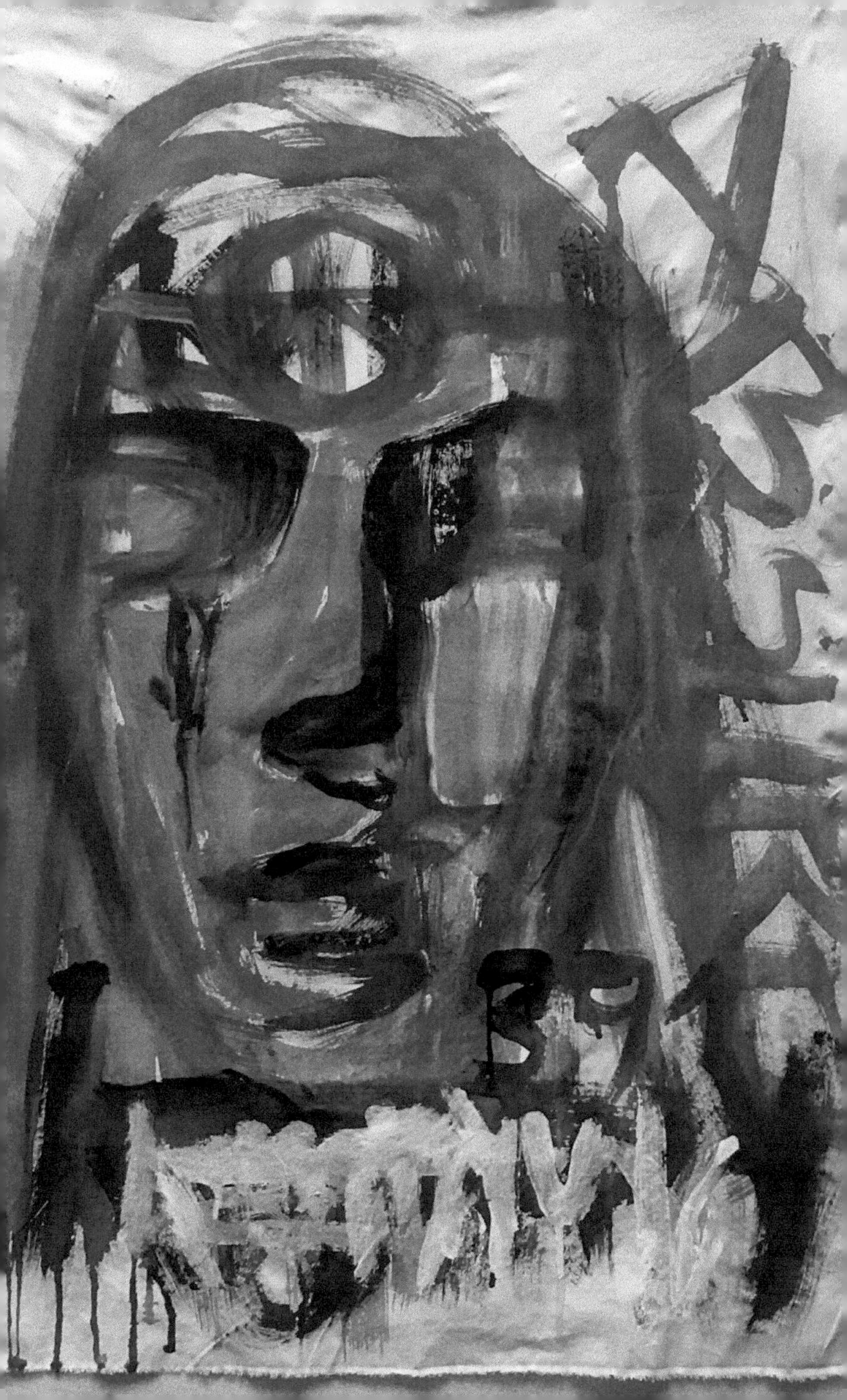

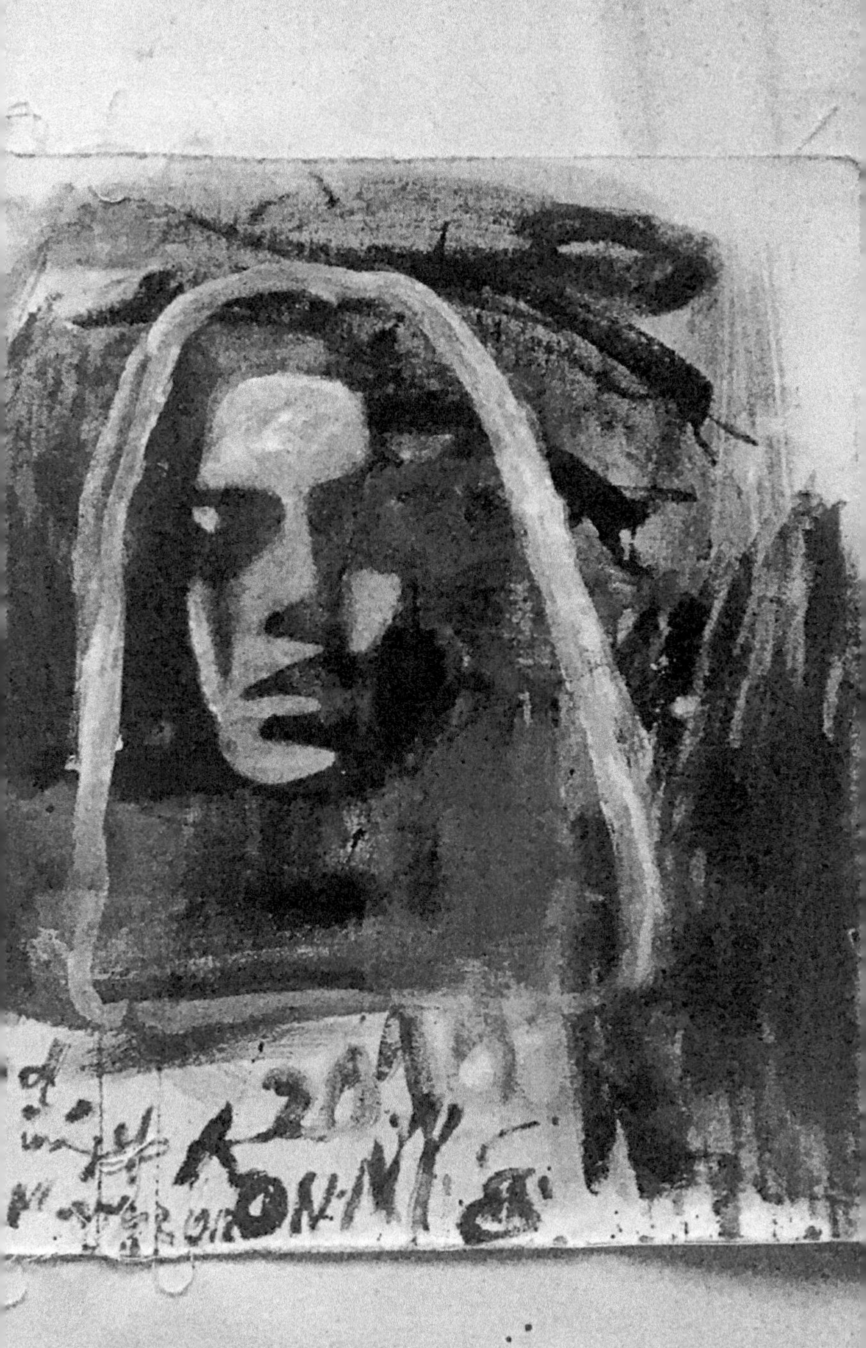

paintings from the trash 2020

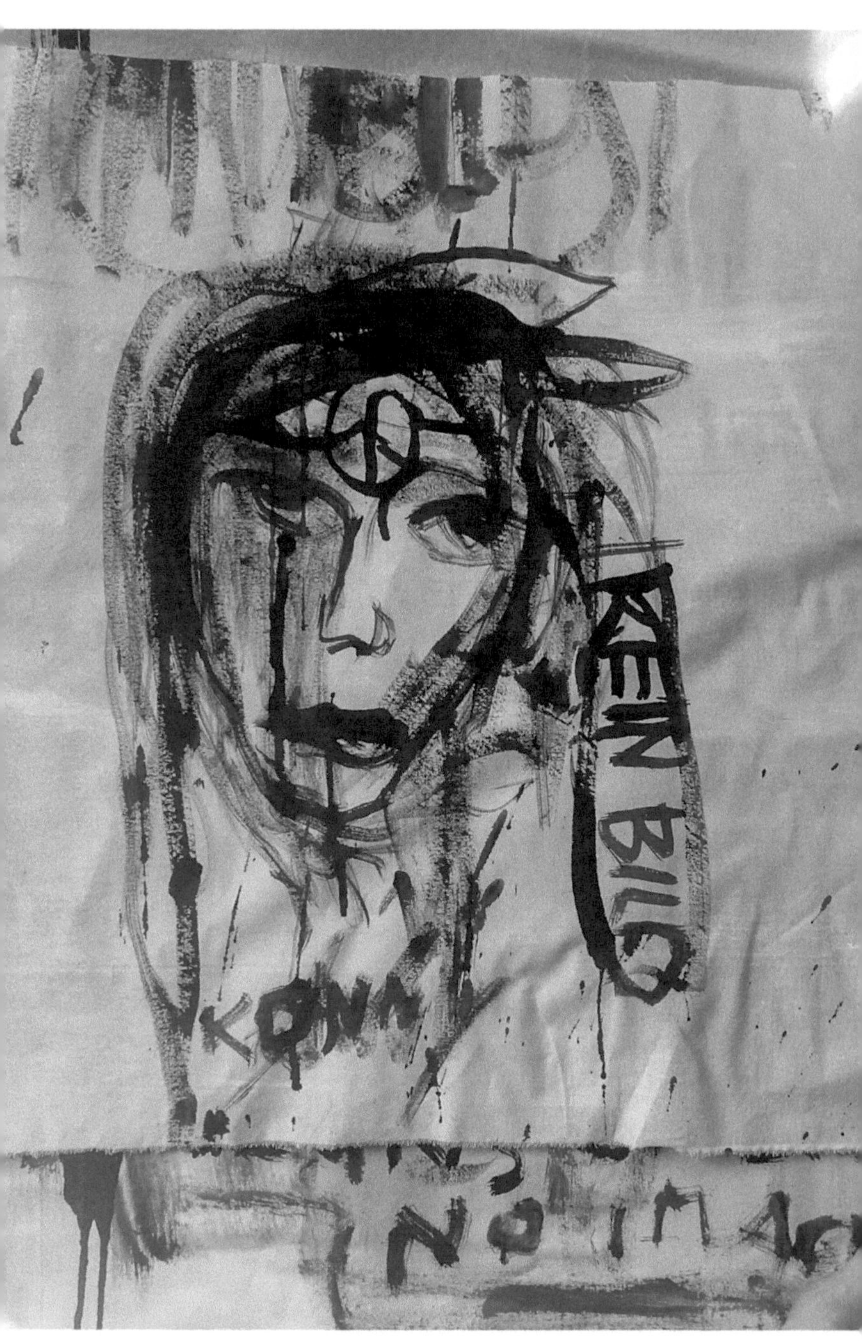

painting Kein Bild

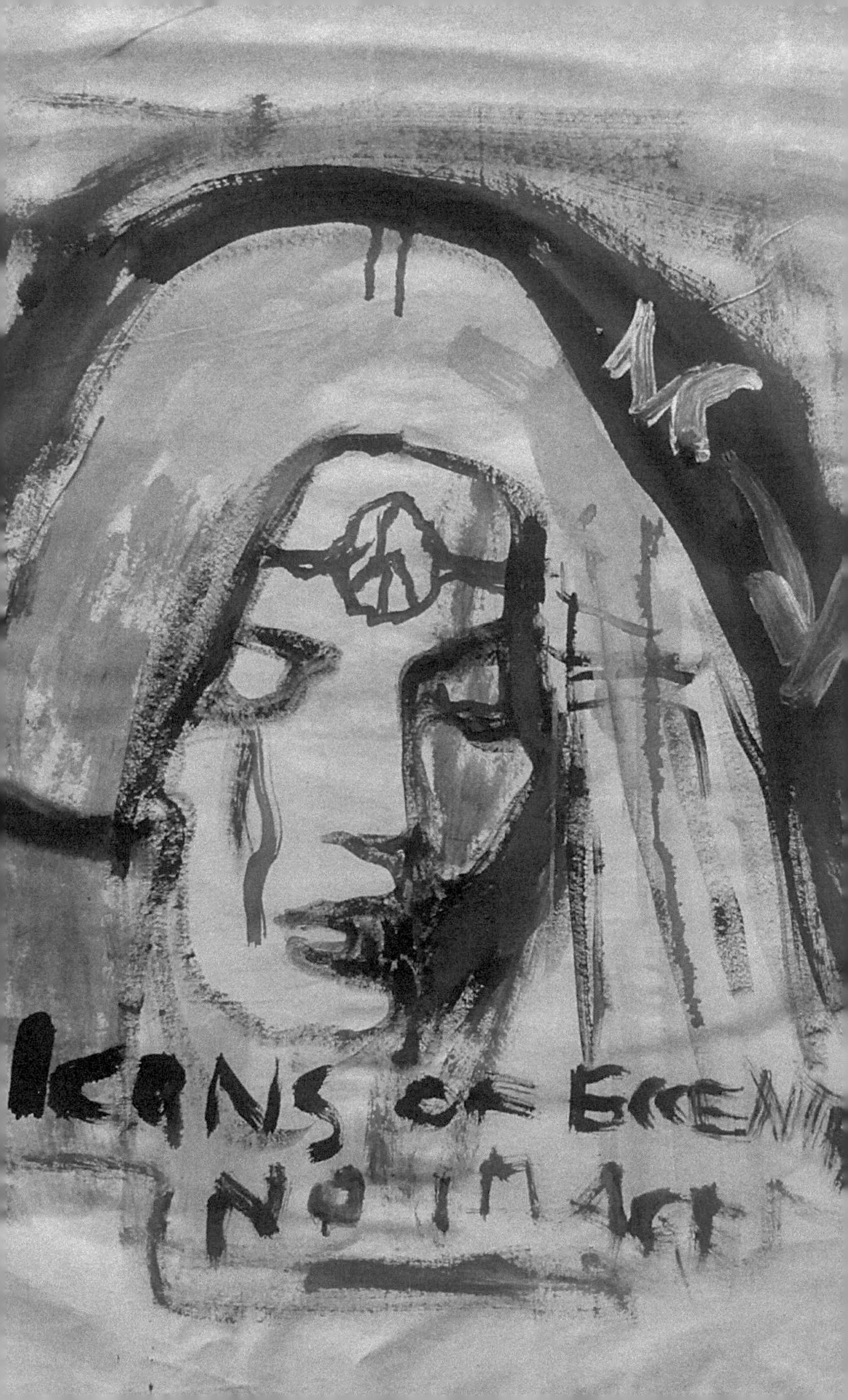

ICONS OF ECCENTRI
No in Art

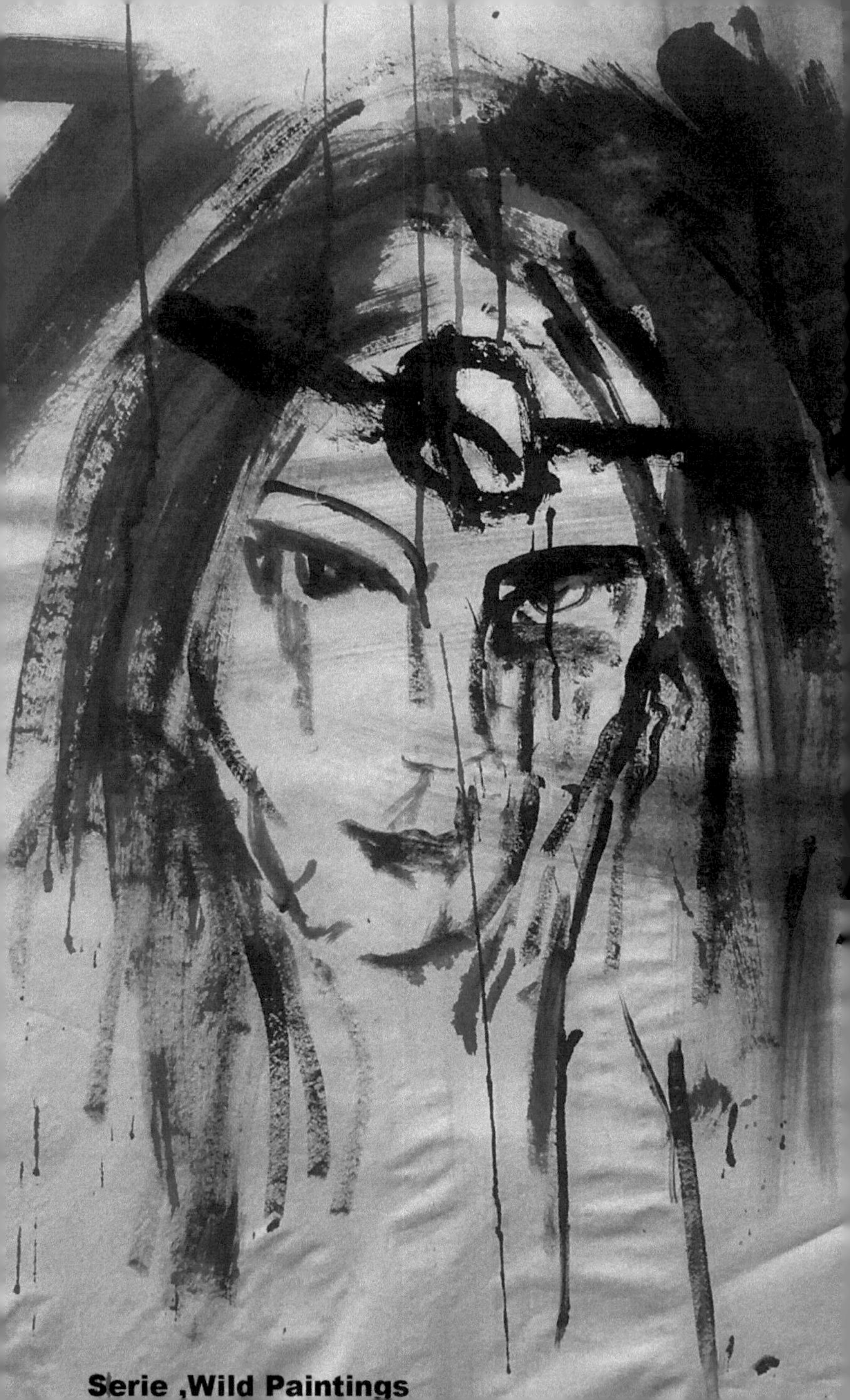

Serie ,Wild Paintings

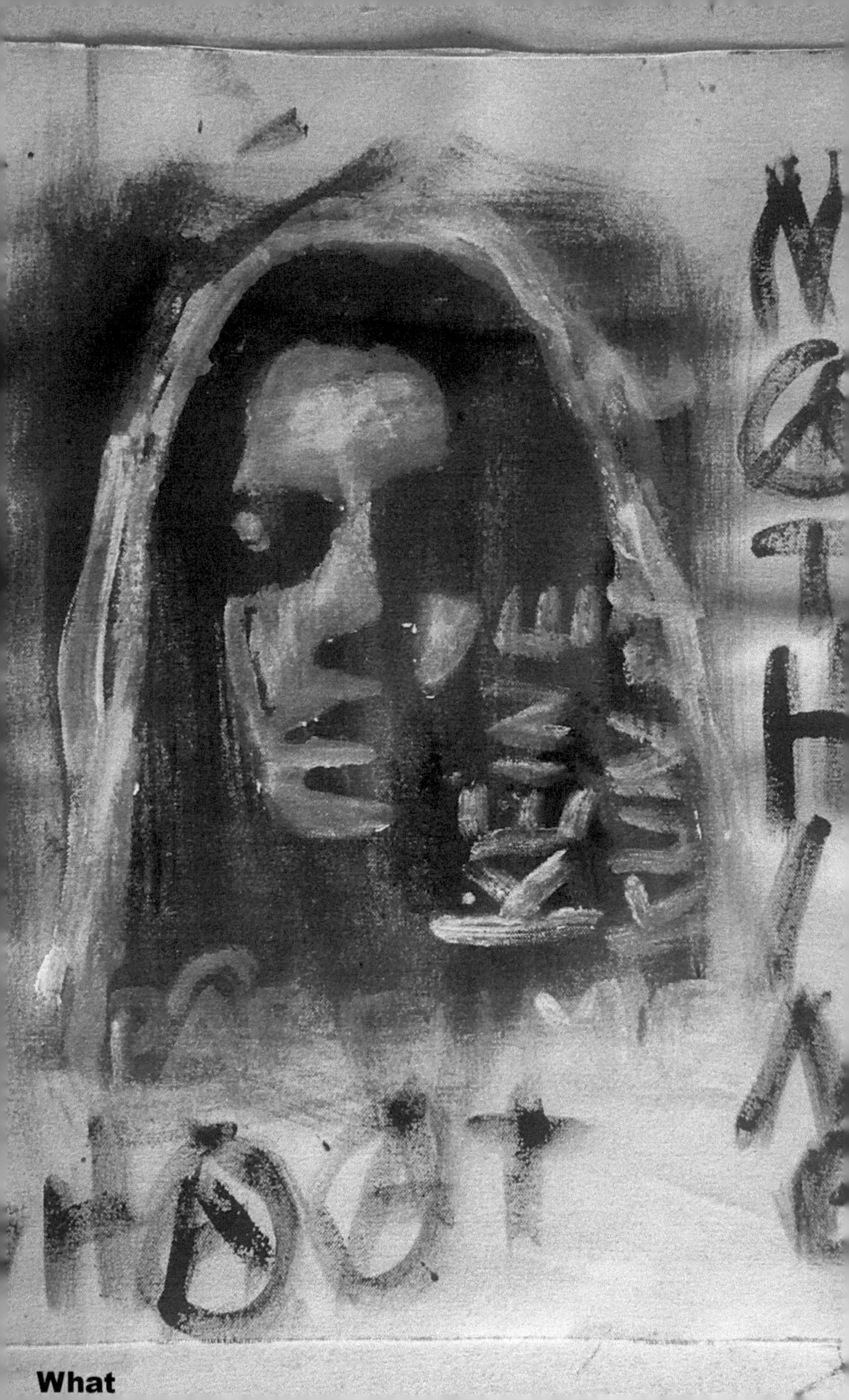
What

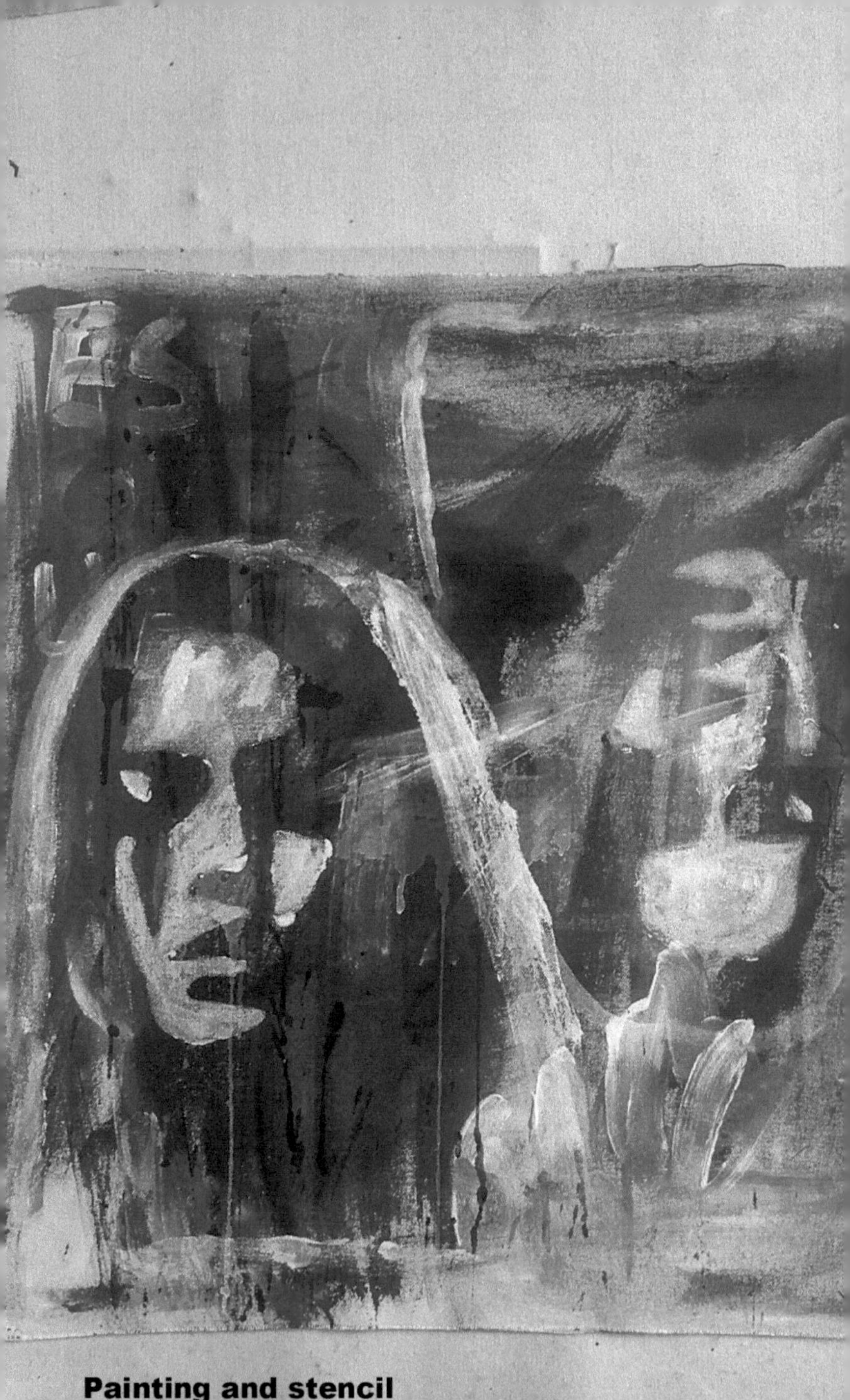

Painting and stencil

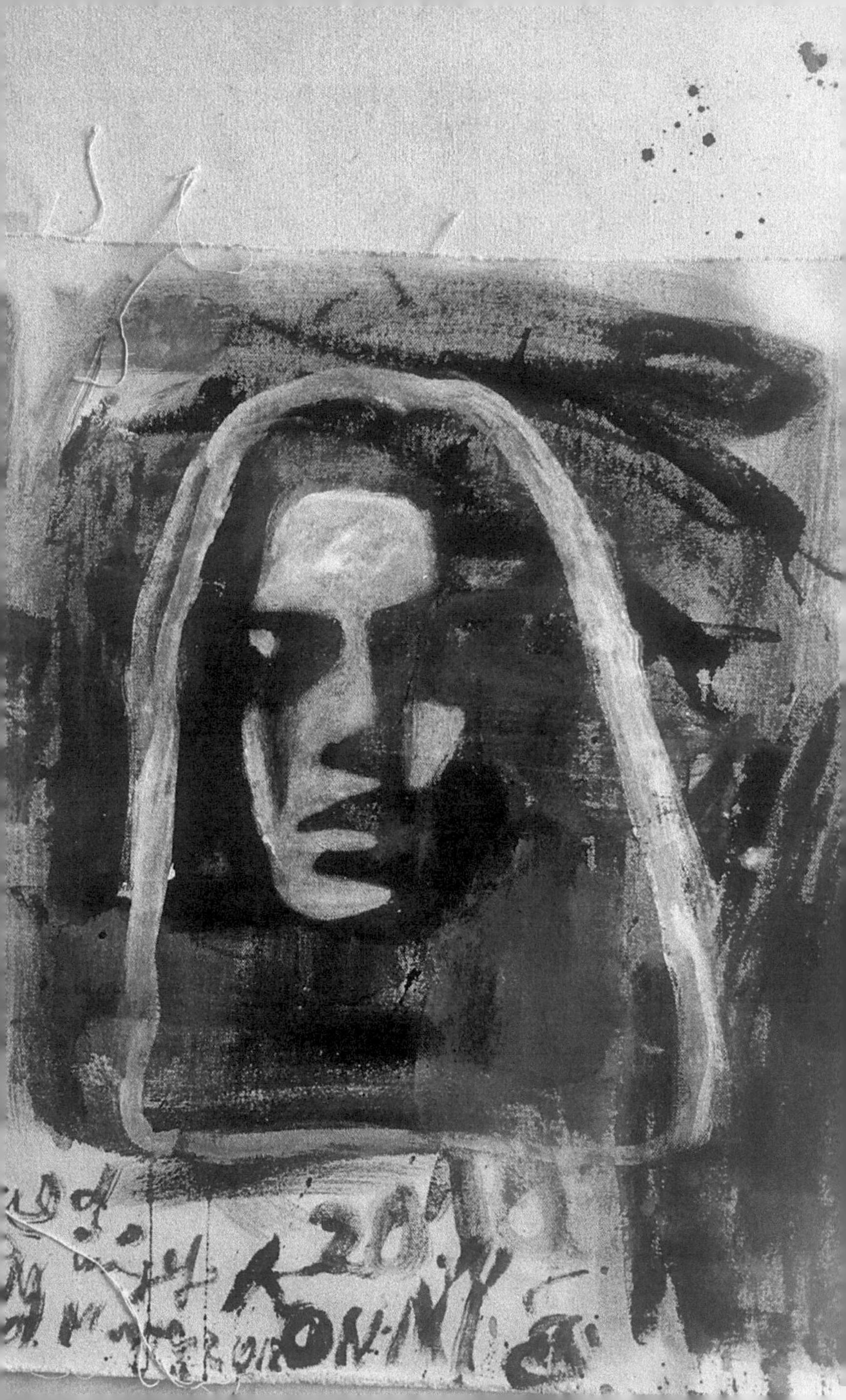

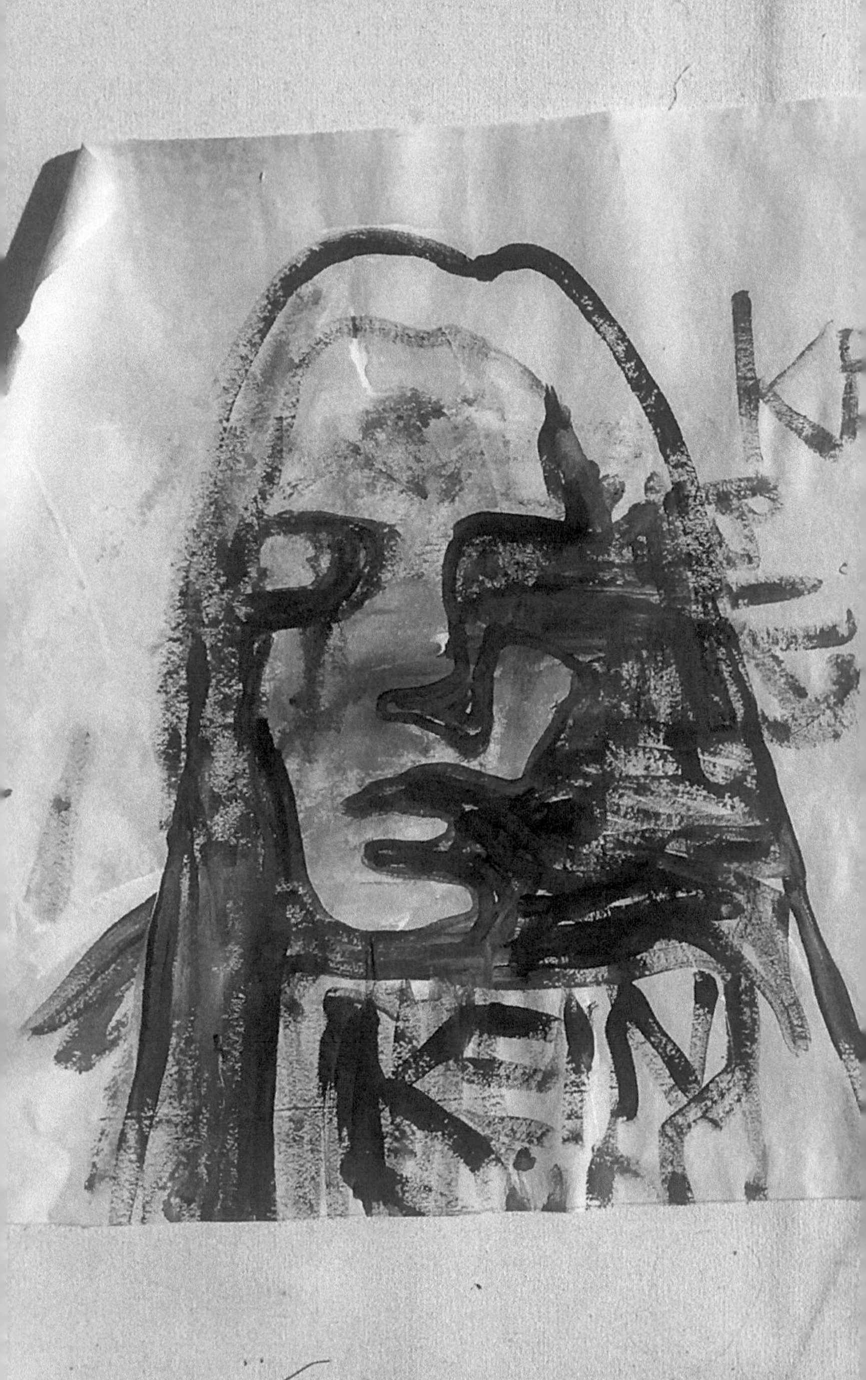

Mitternacht

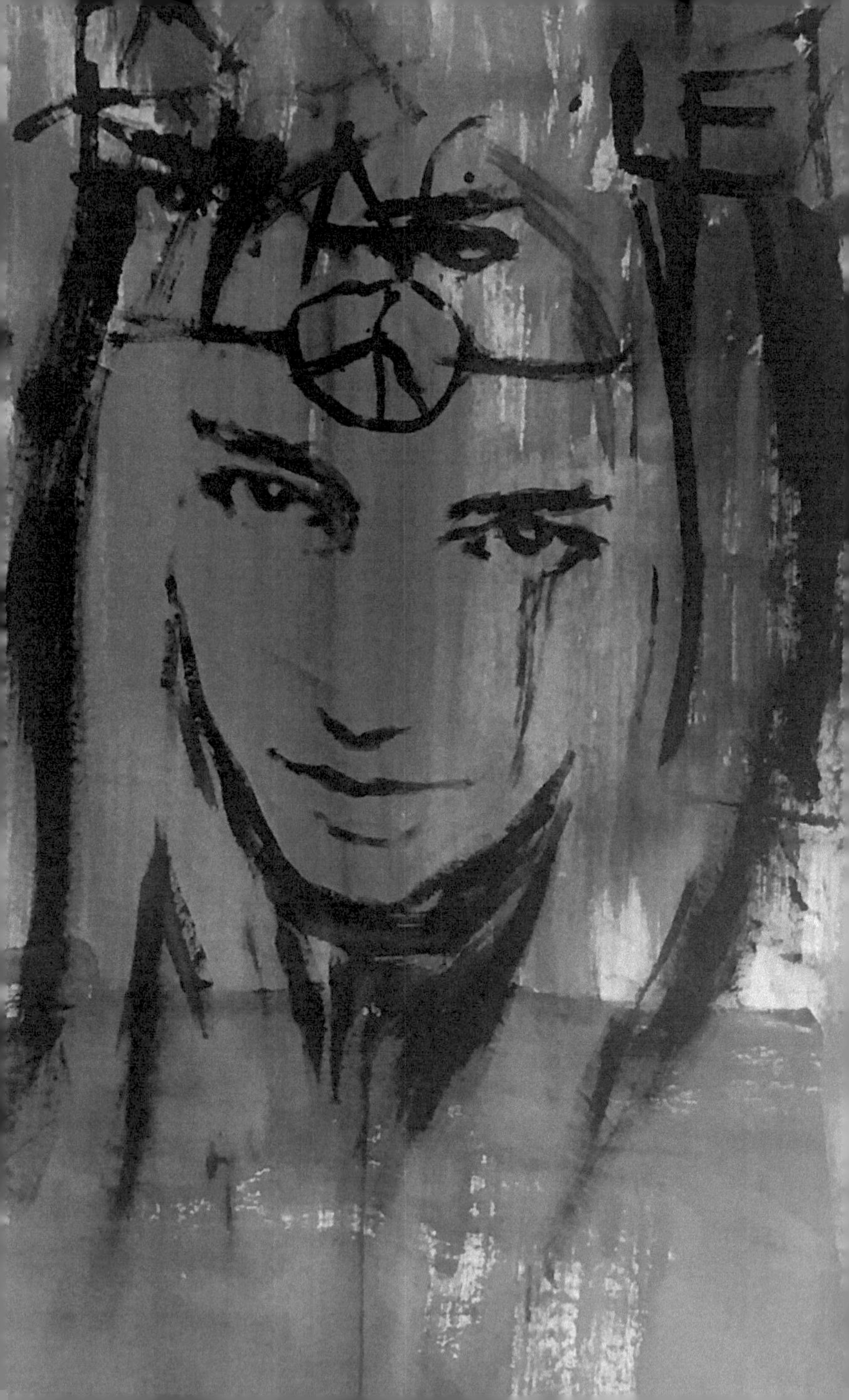

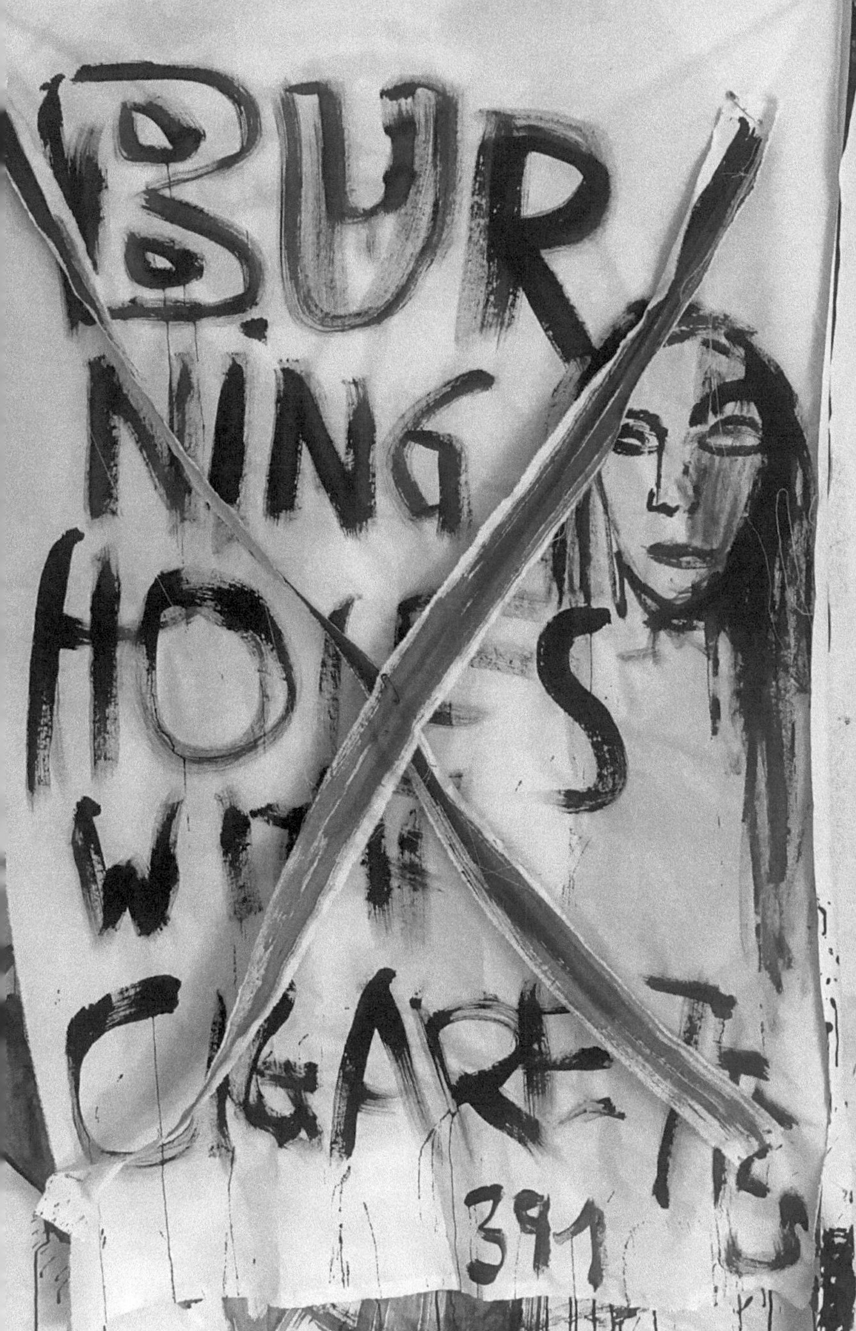

Serie Burning holes with cigarettes all night

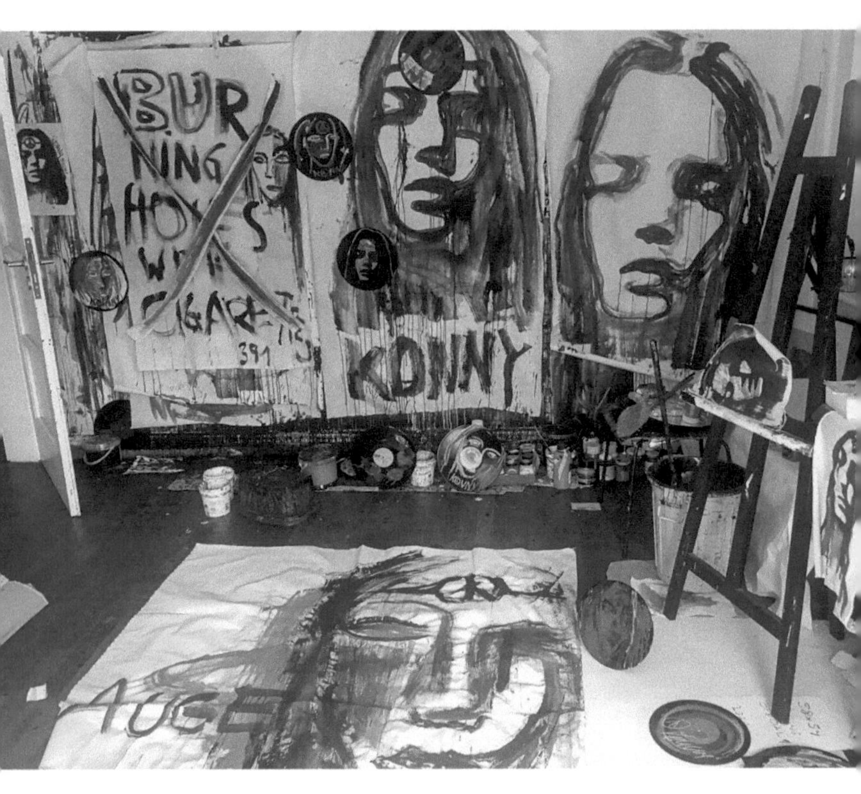

Serie 2020 Burning holes with cigarettes all night

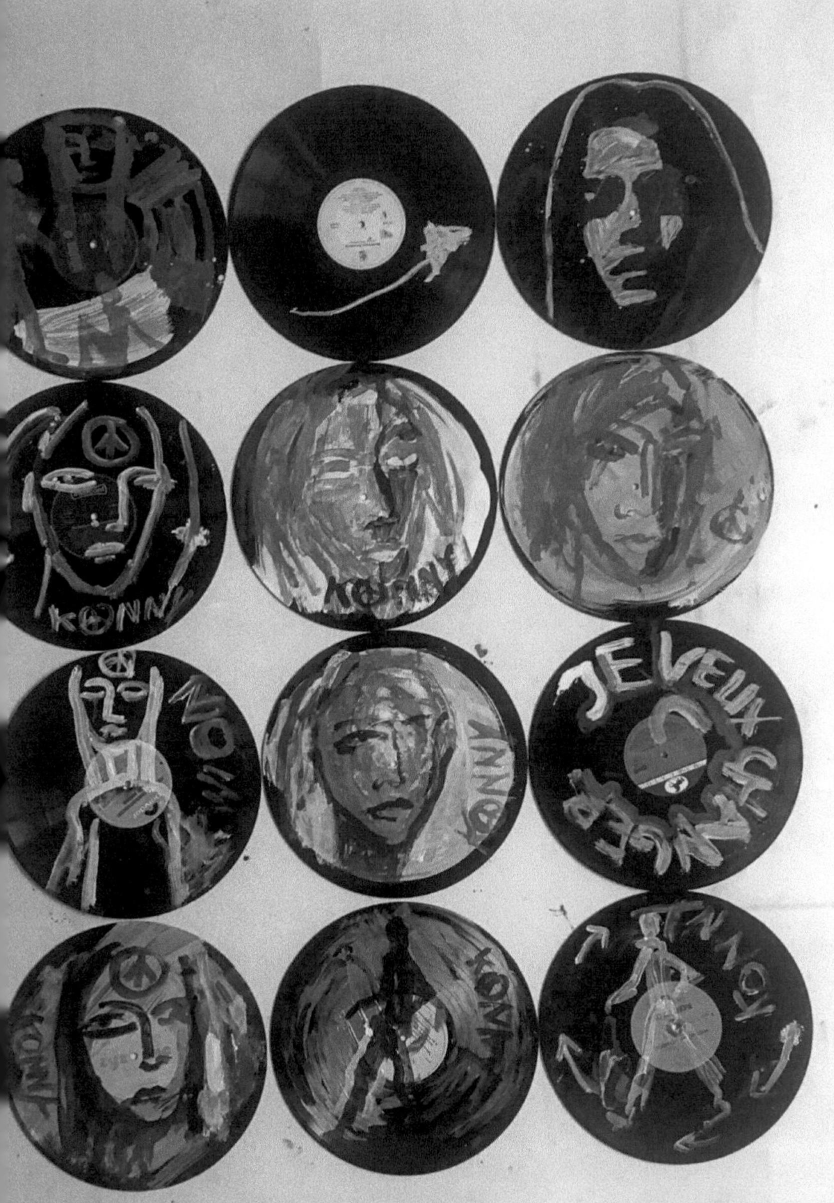

KONNY
JEVEUX CHANGER

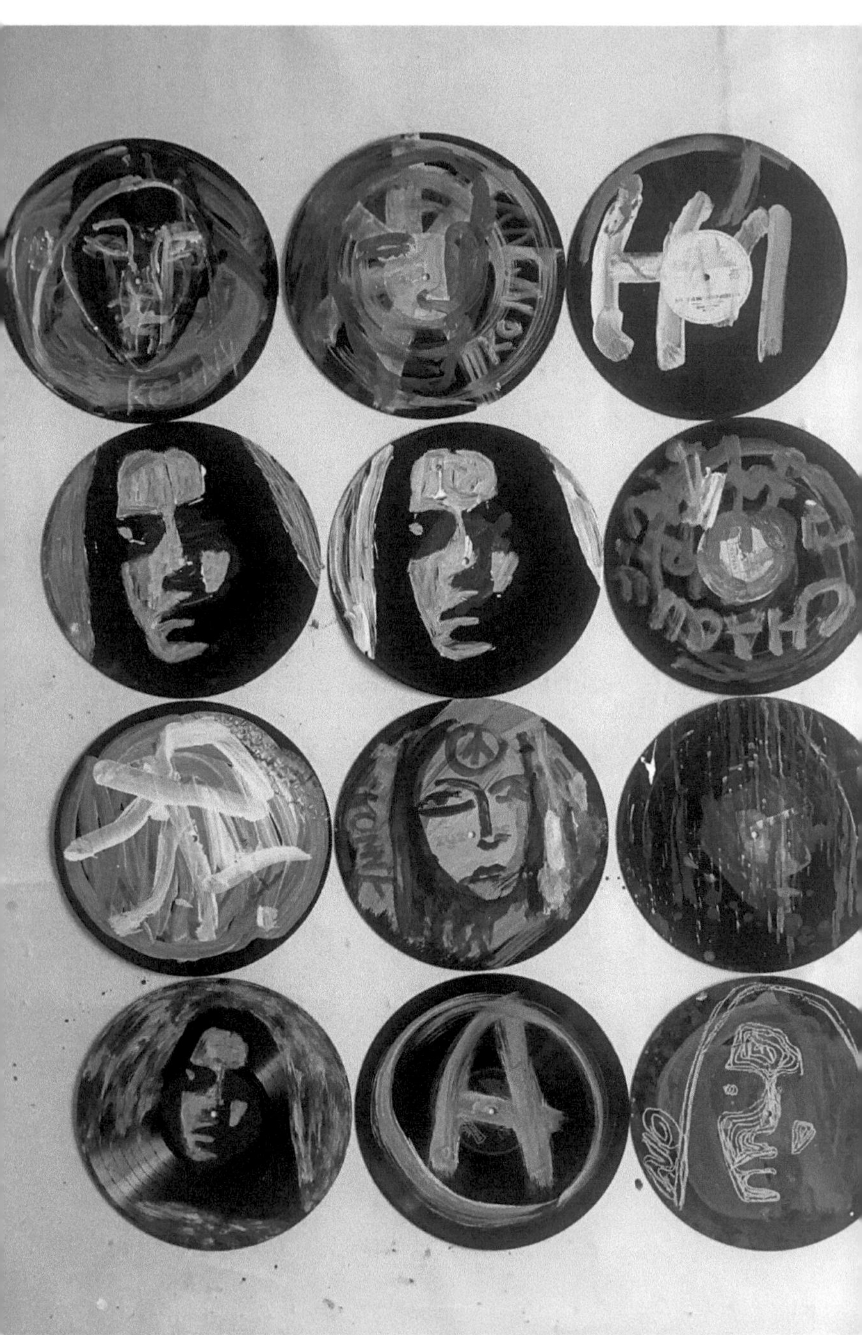

Serie AD AD

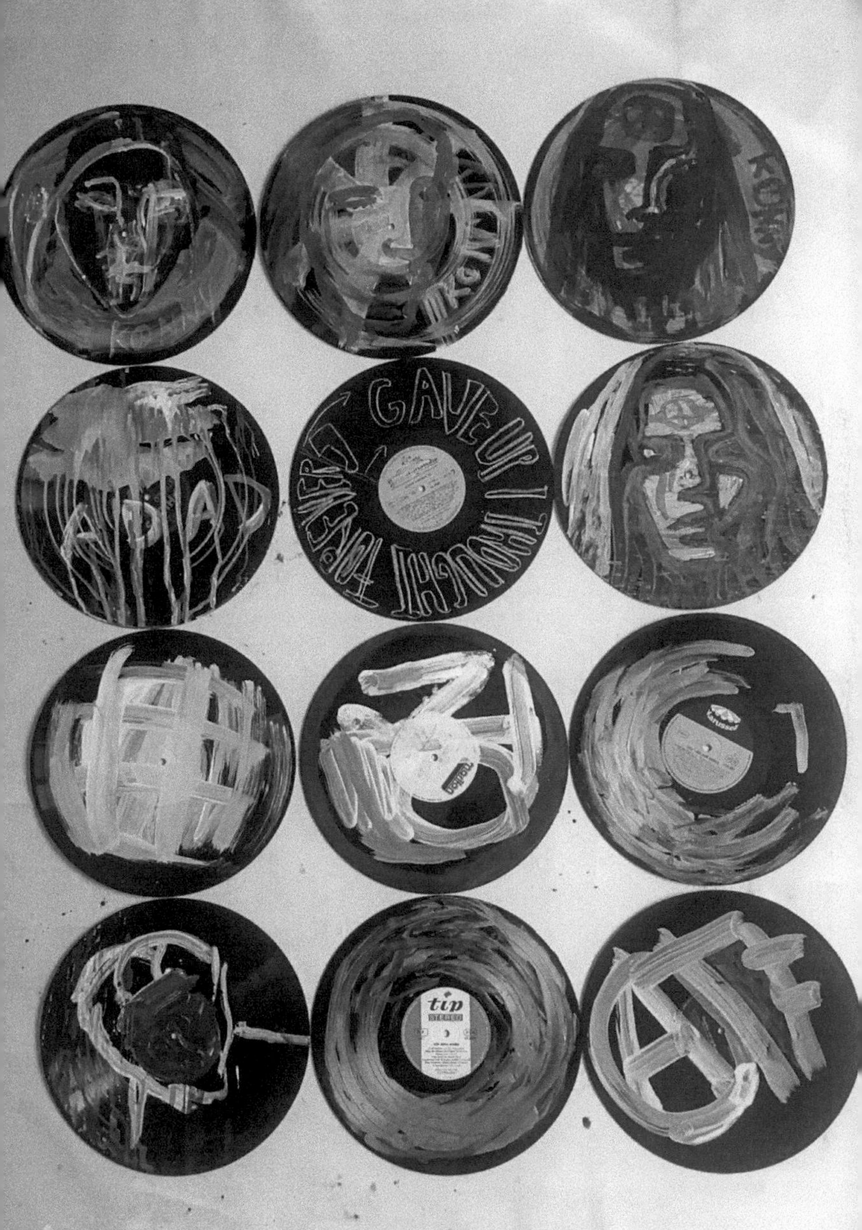
GAVE UP I THOUGHT FOREVER

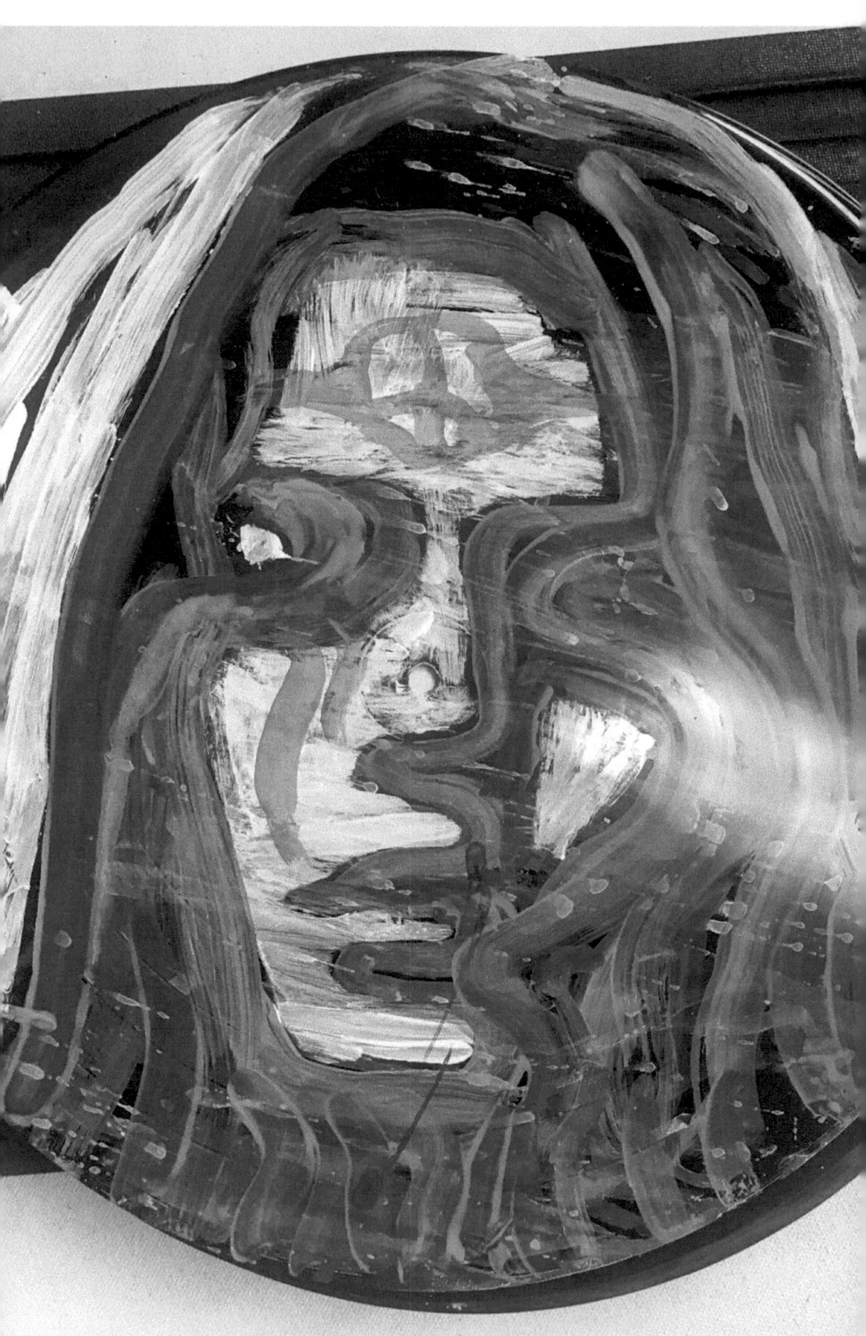

Serie AD DD Shoes from the trash

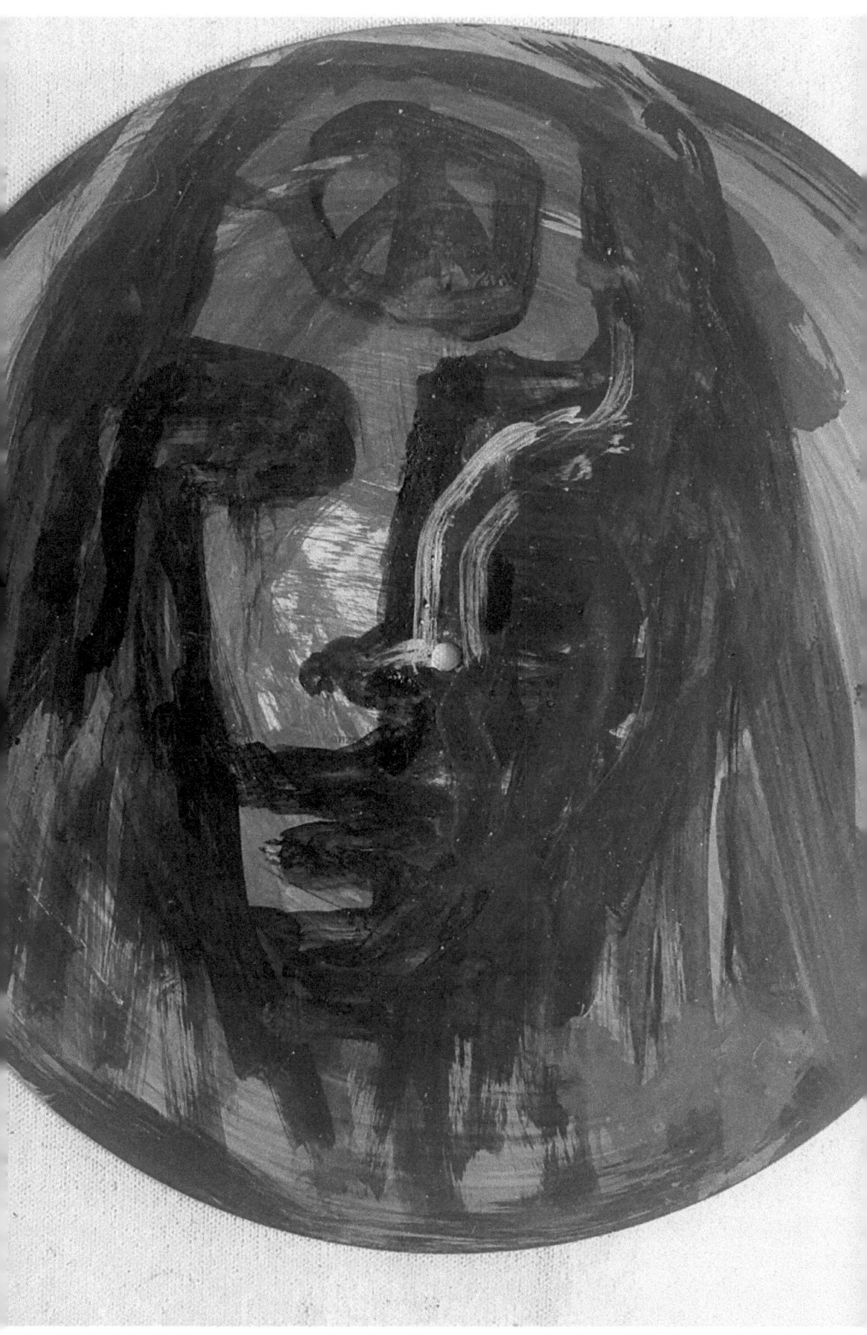

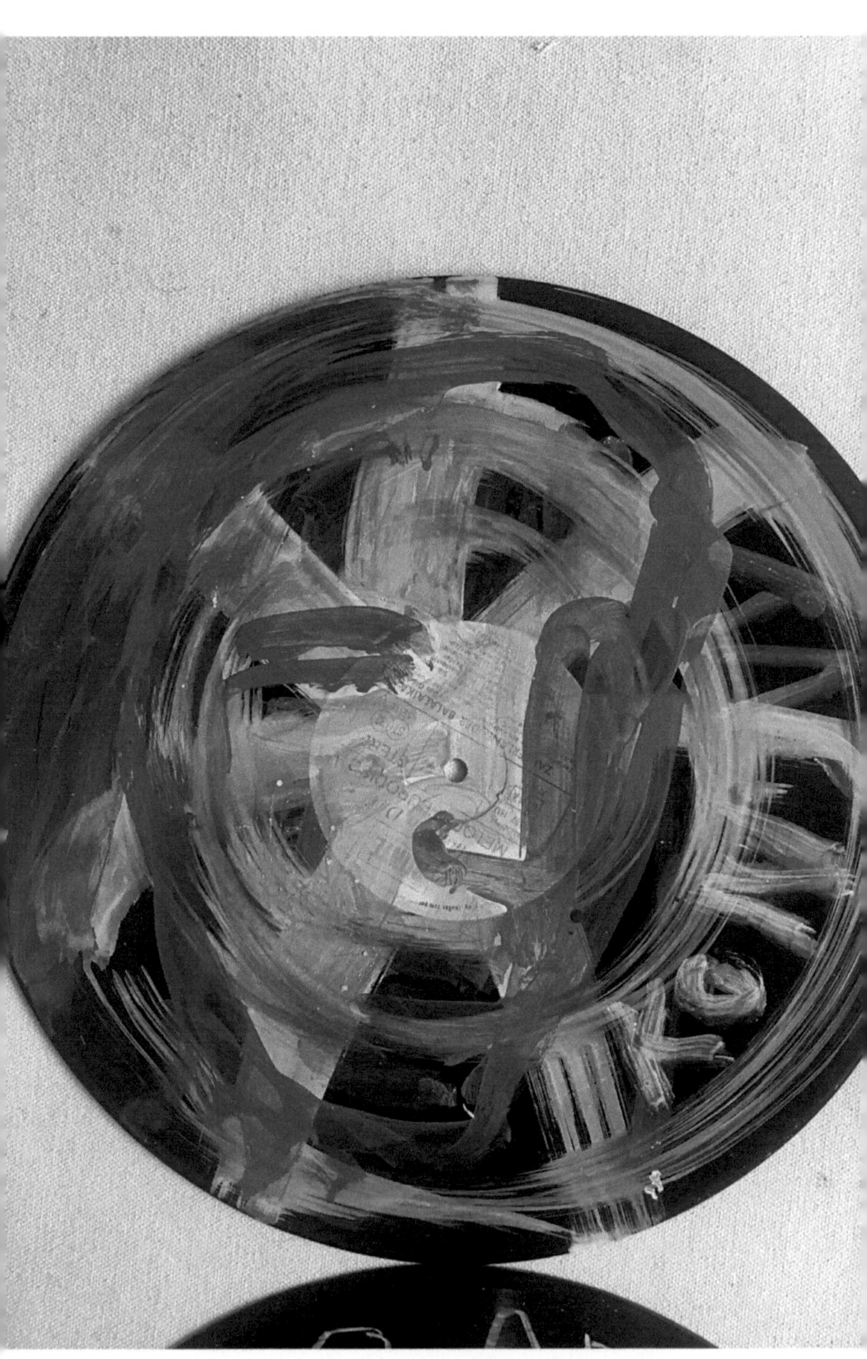

Serie AD AD Serie Sad painting 2020

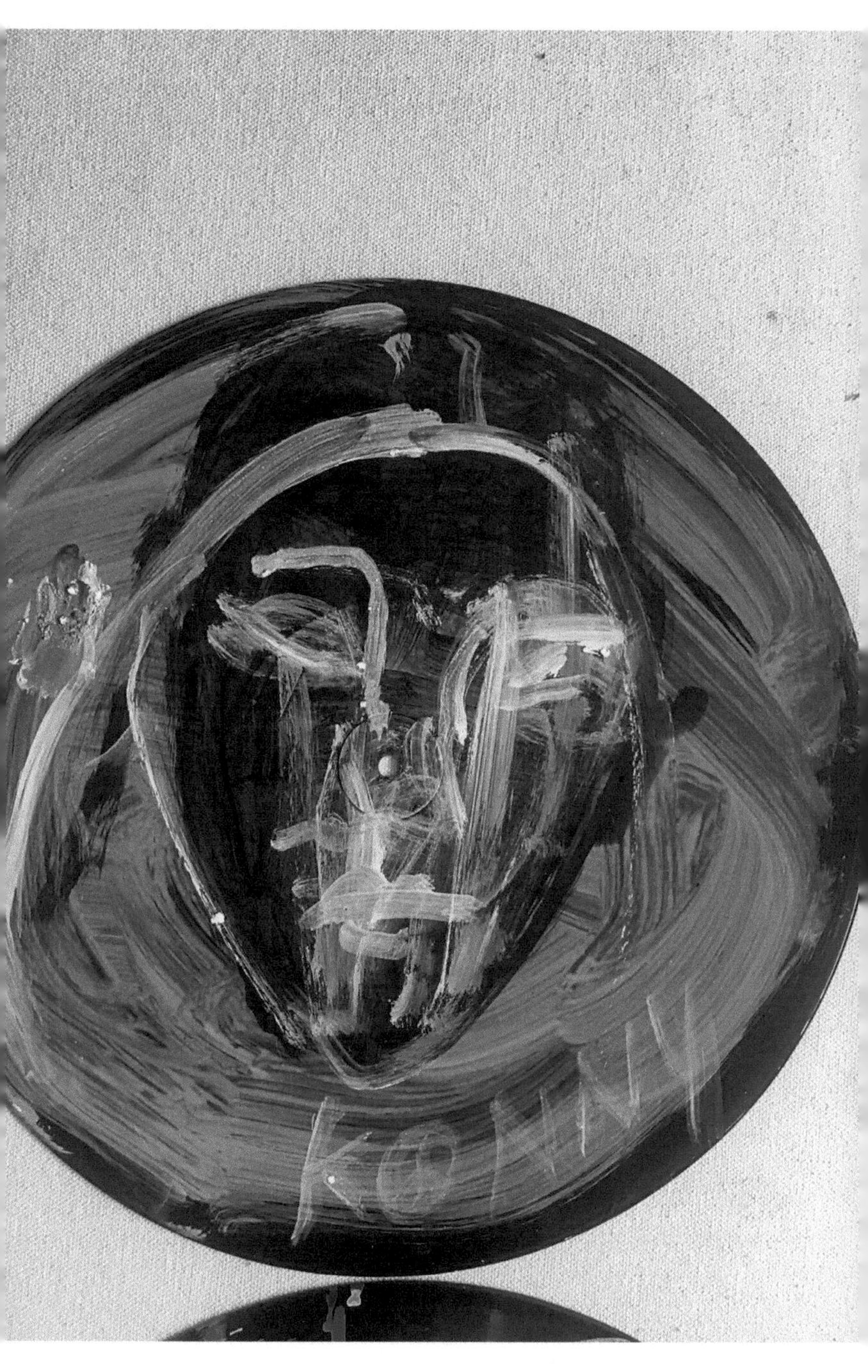
KONNY

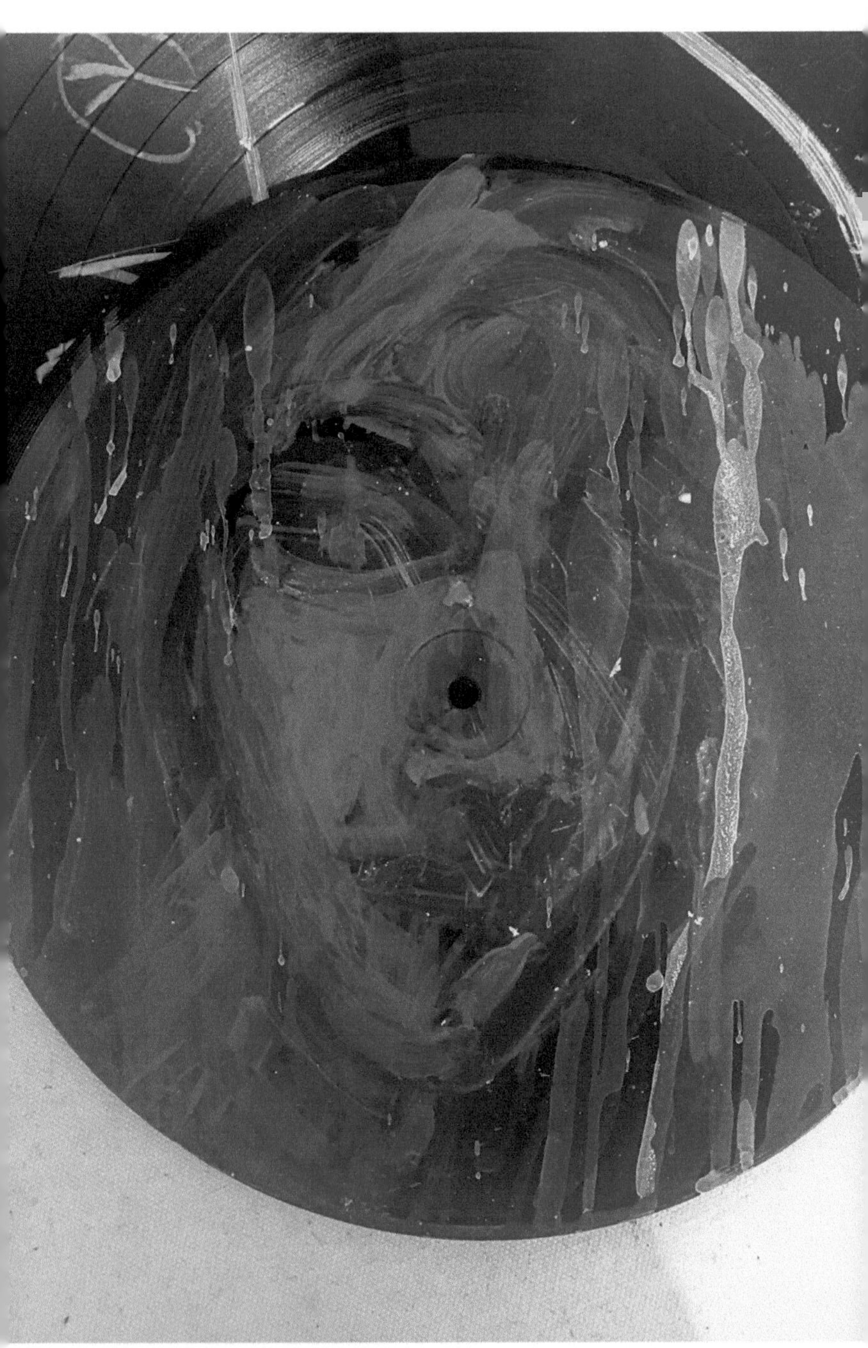

Black AD AD 2020

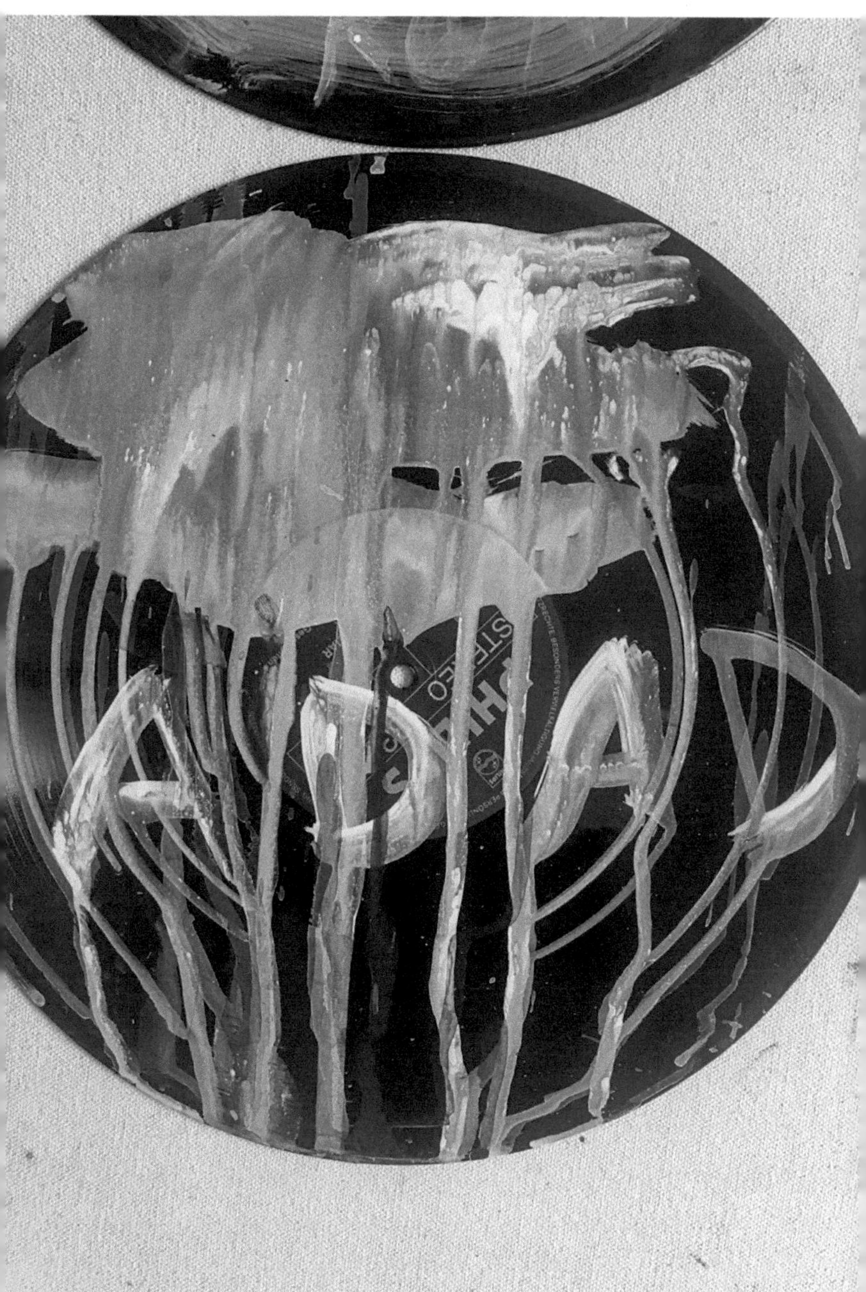

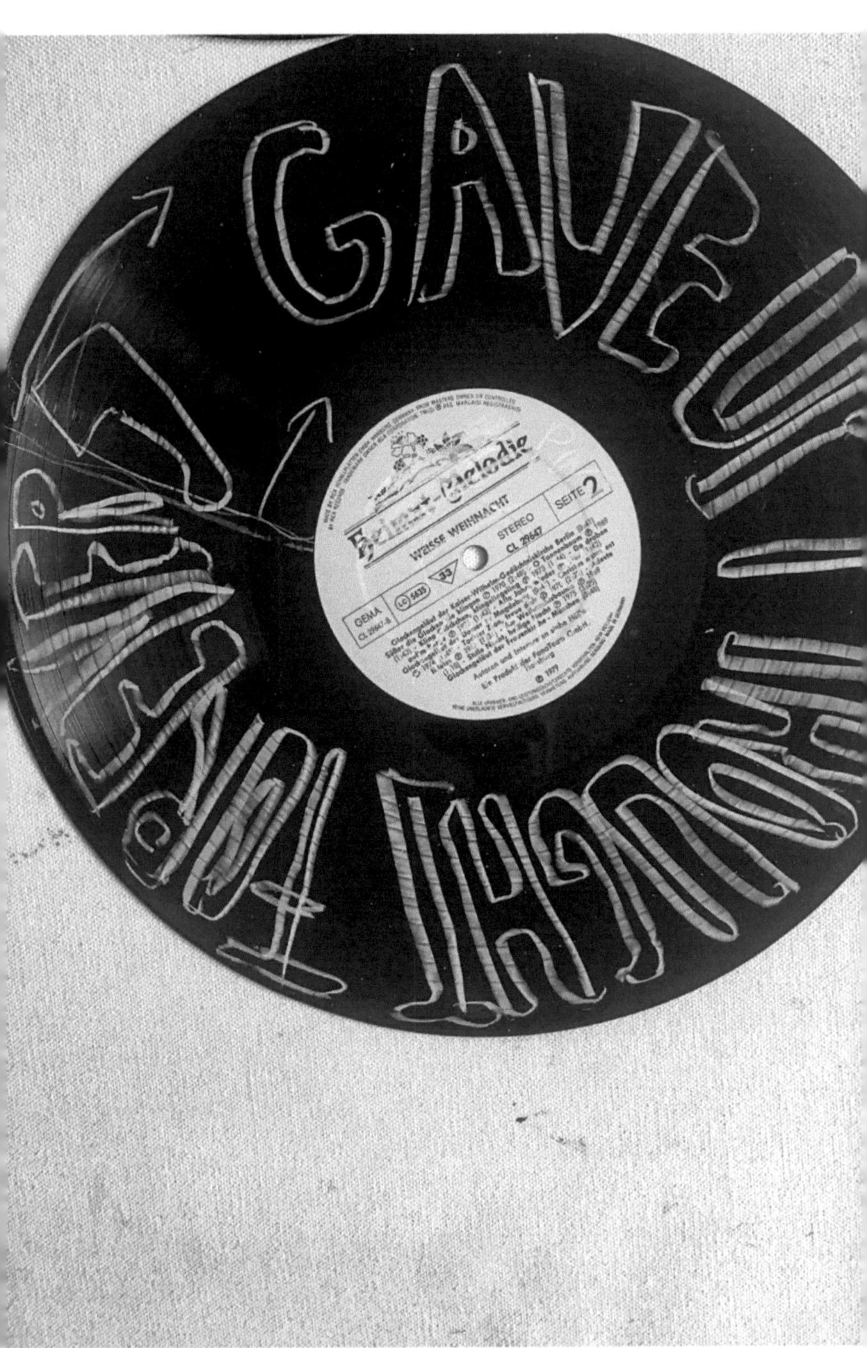

I Gave up serie 2020

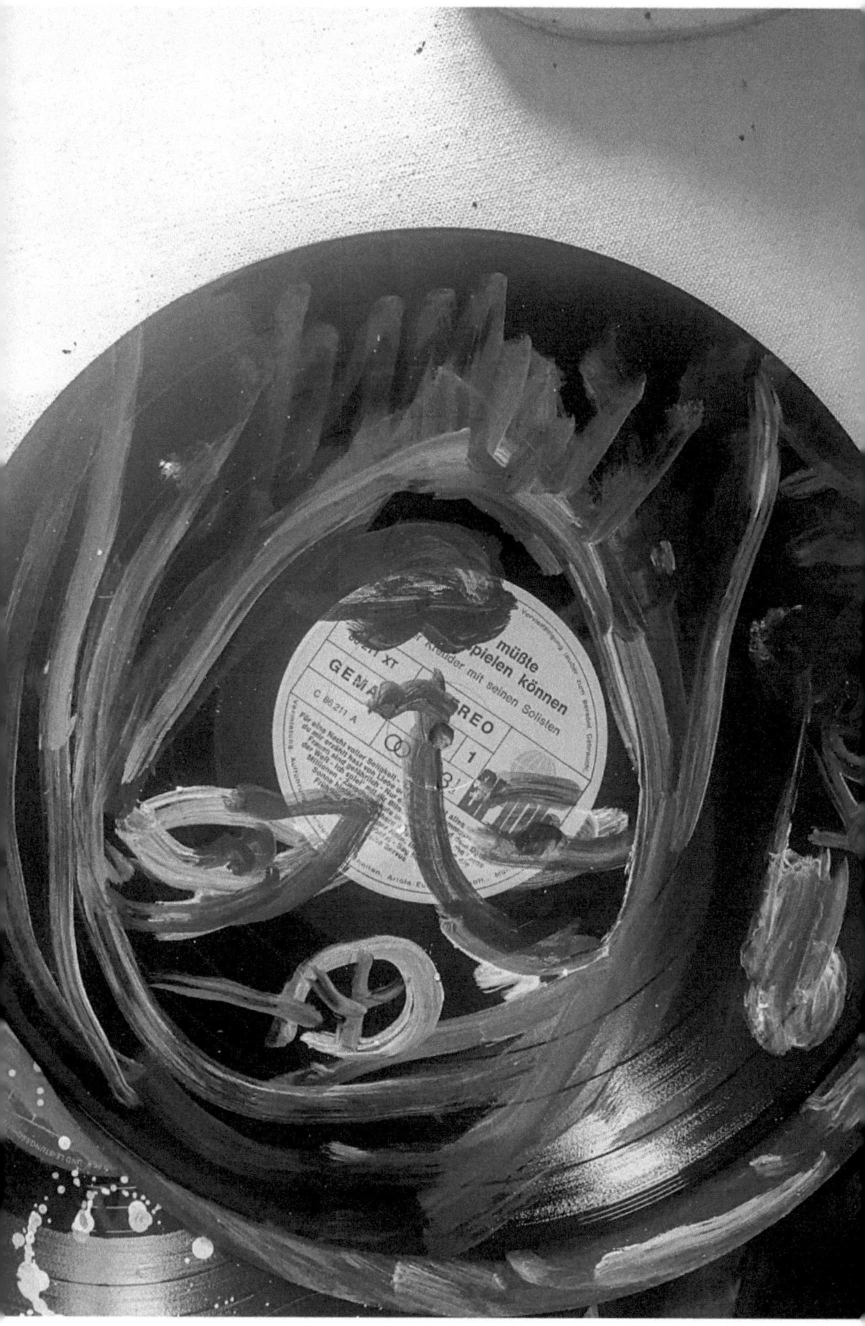
müßte
Kreuder mit seinen Solisten
spielen können
86211 XT
GEMA STEREO
C 86 211 A
1

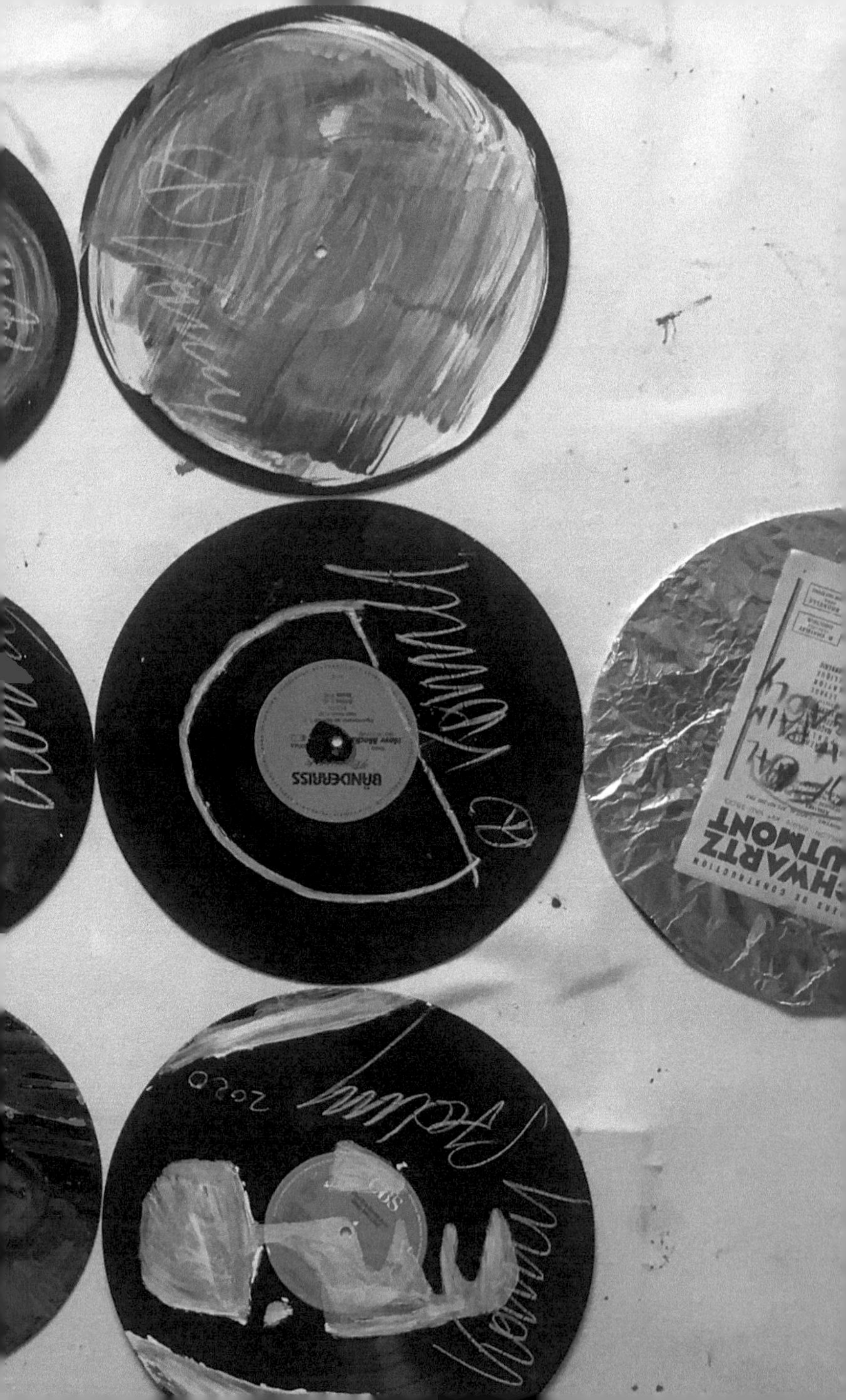

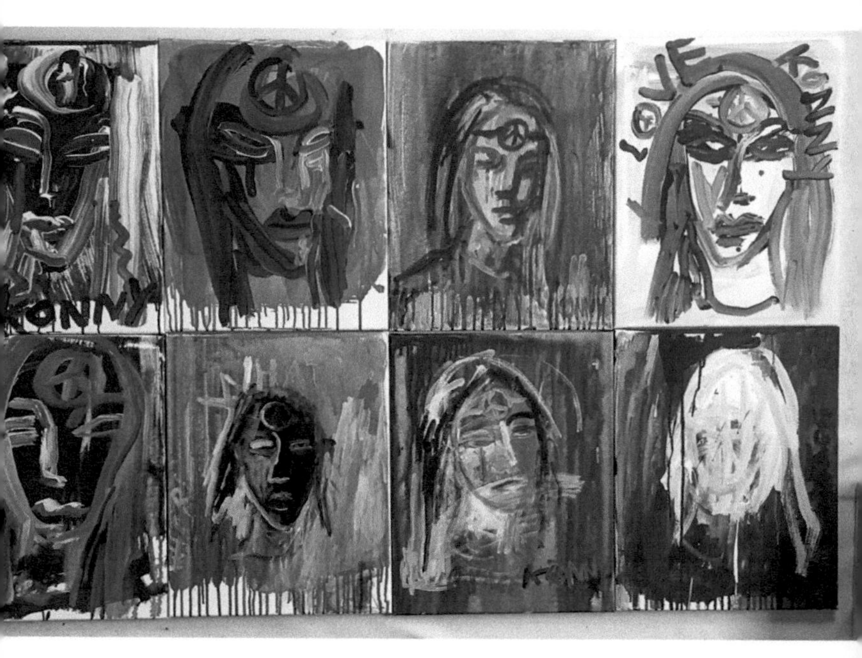

Trash Konny

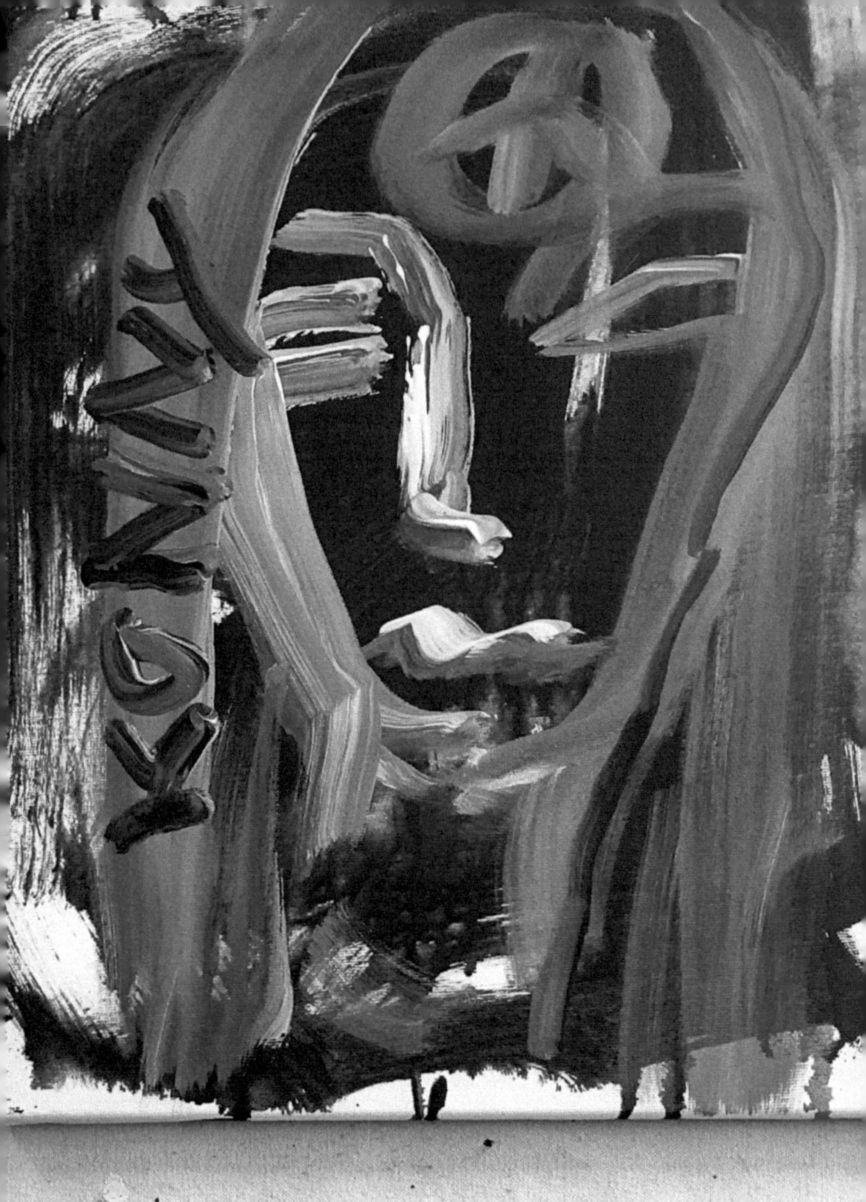

I gave up

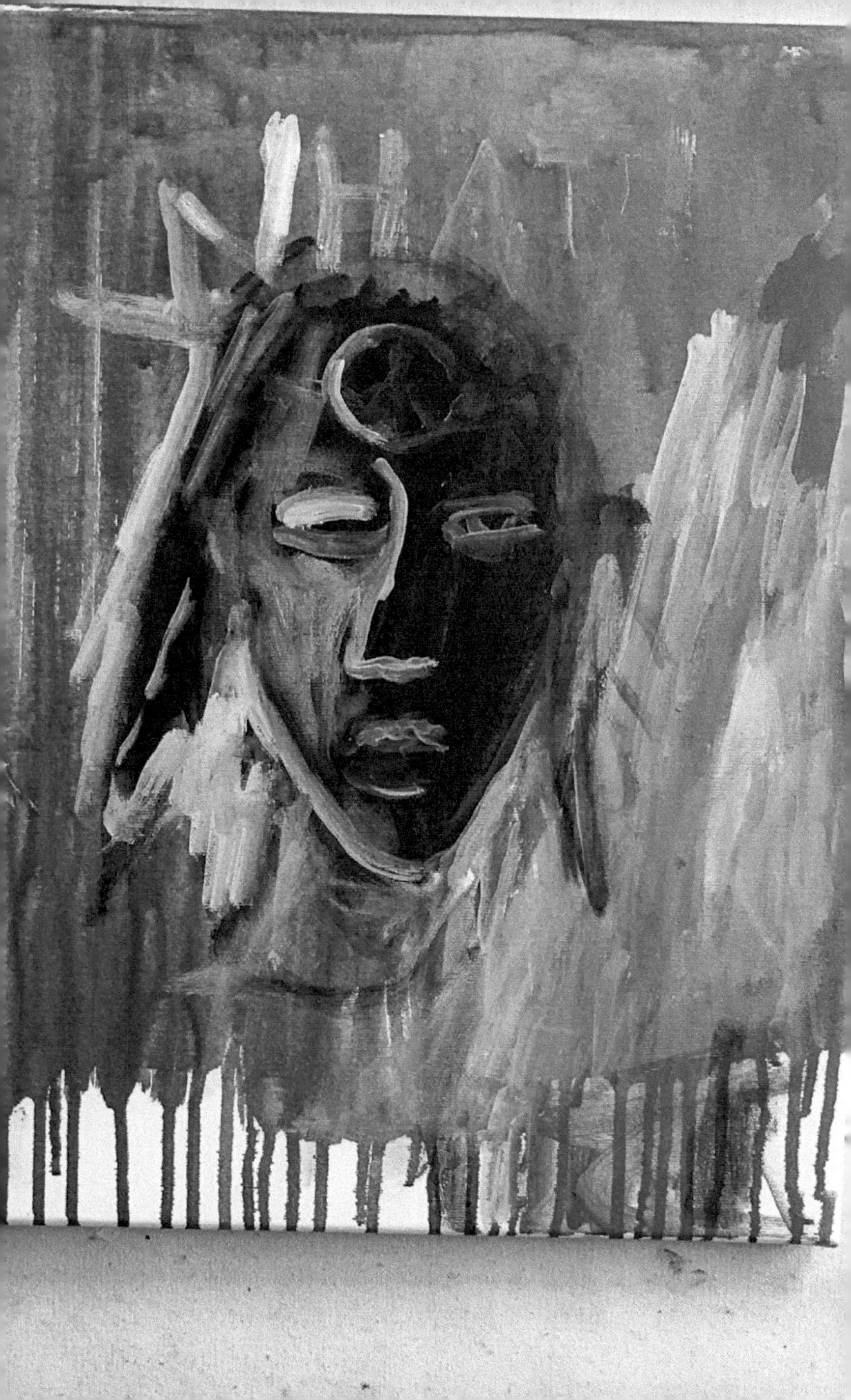

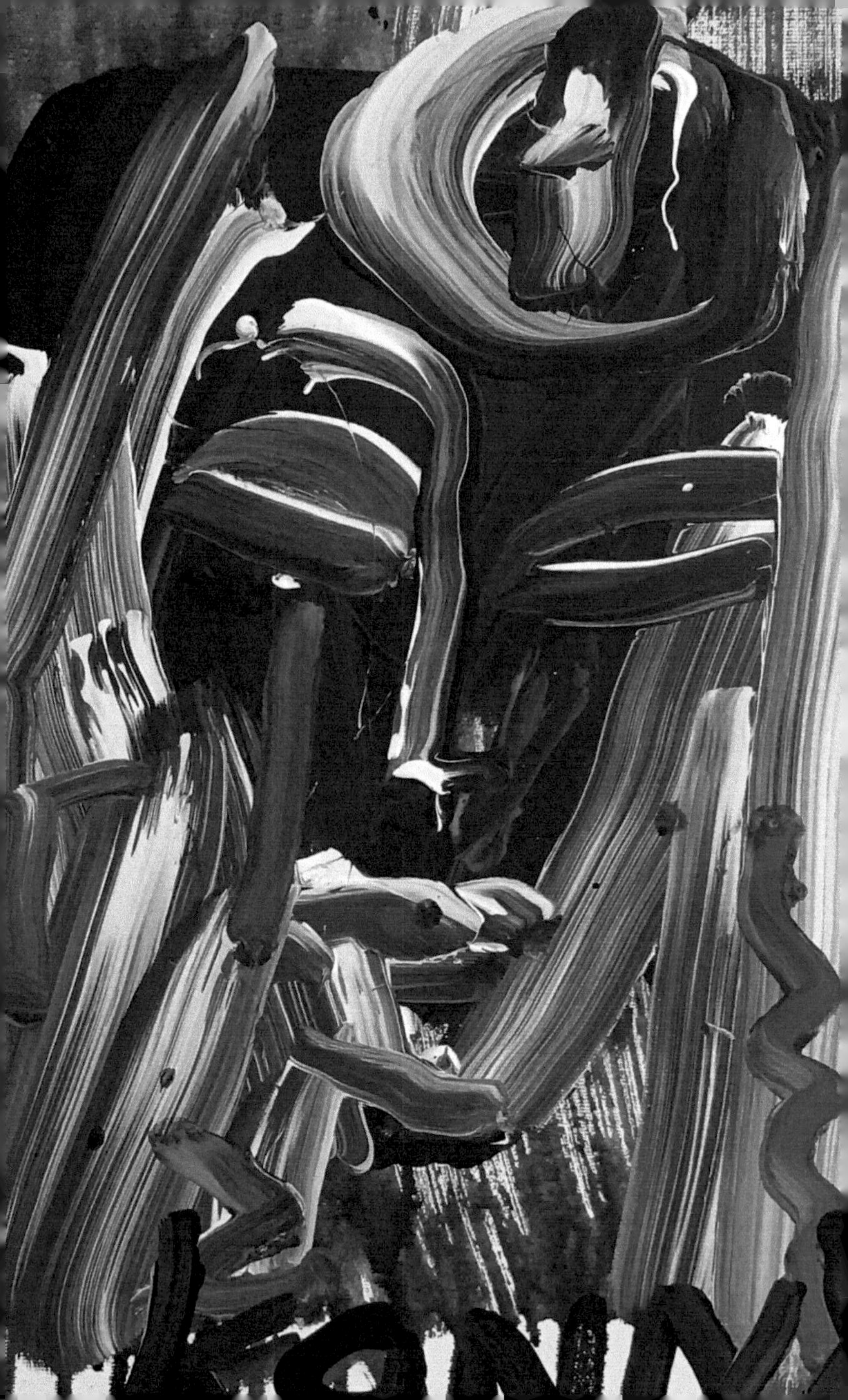

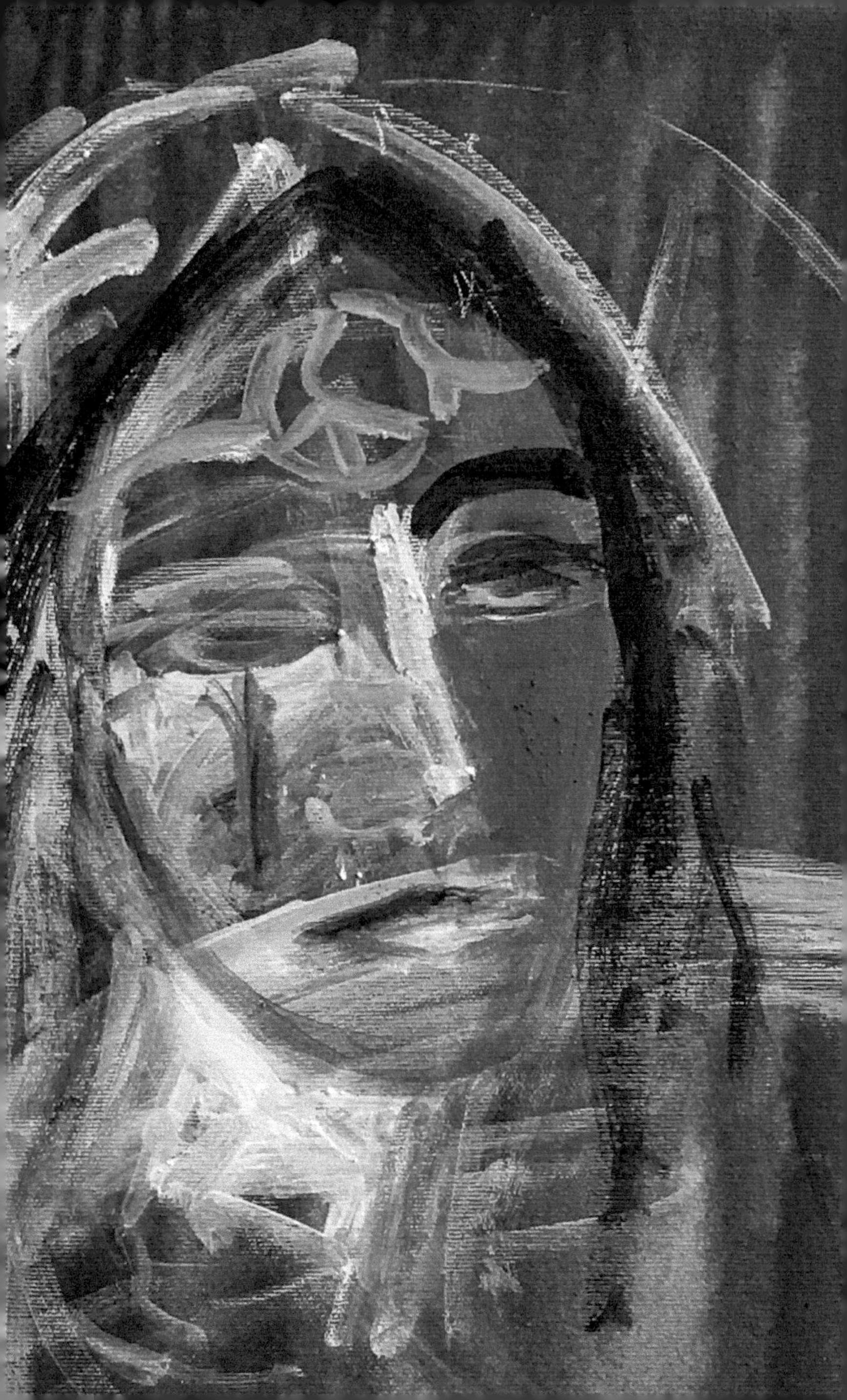

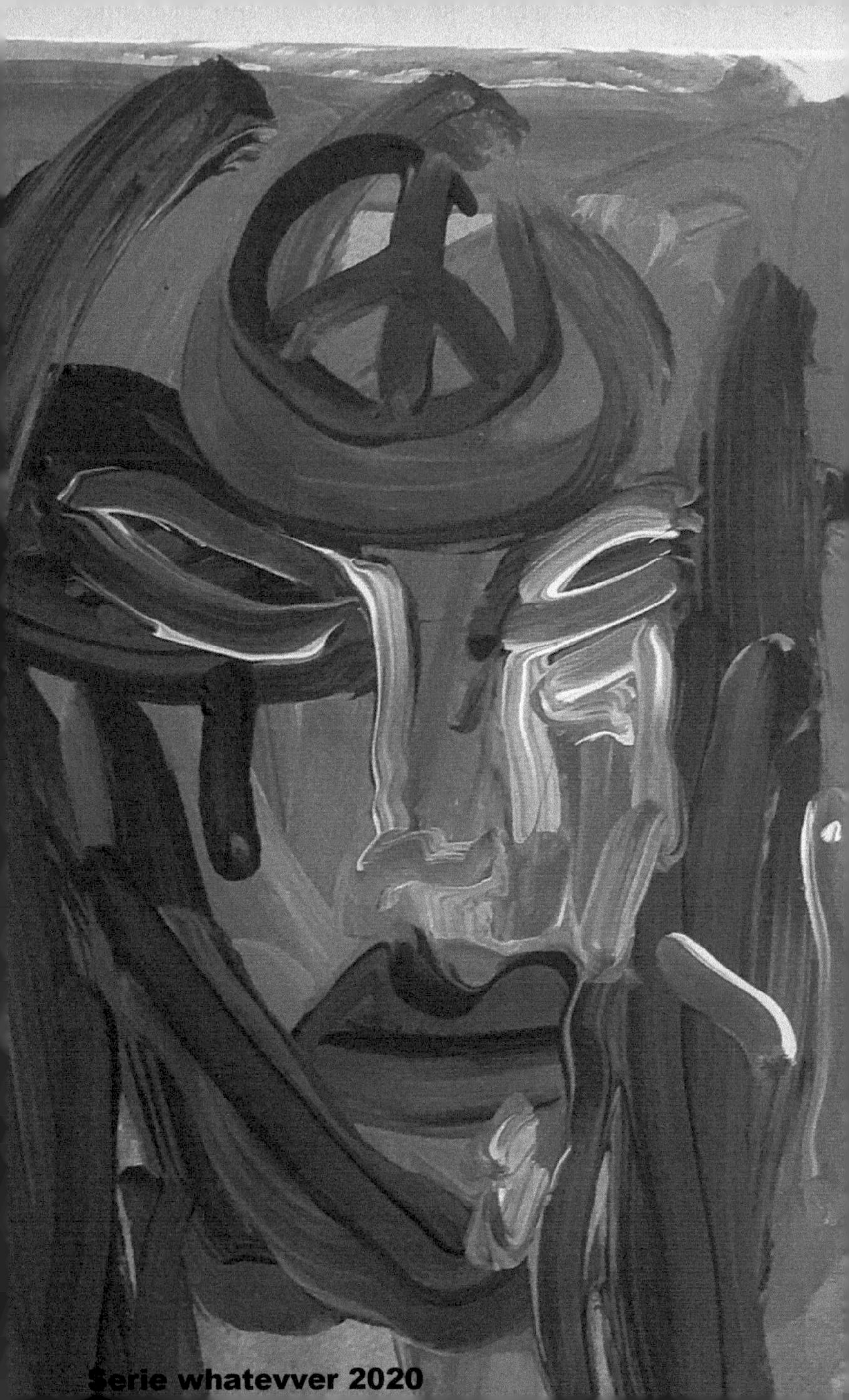
Serie whatevver 2020

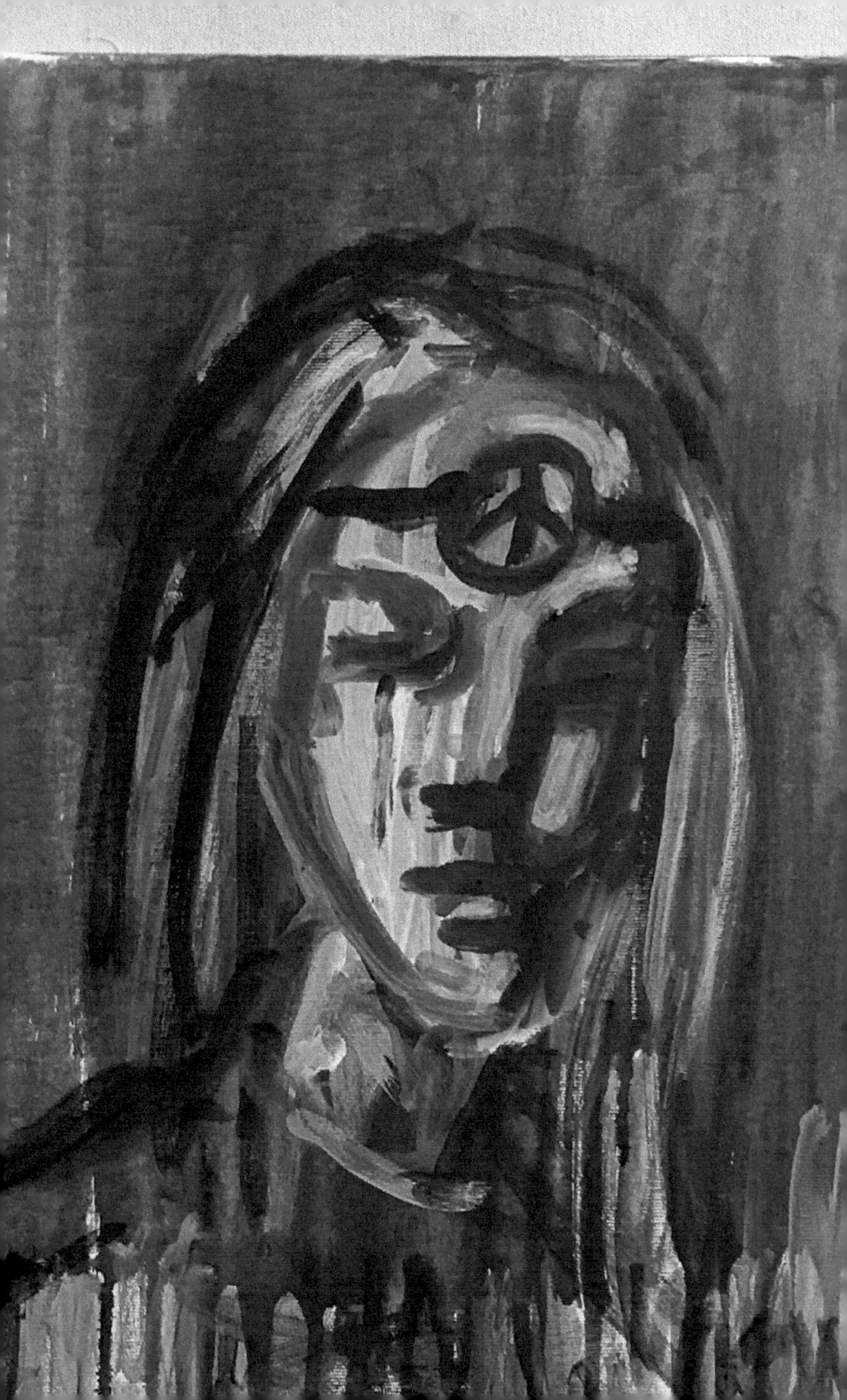

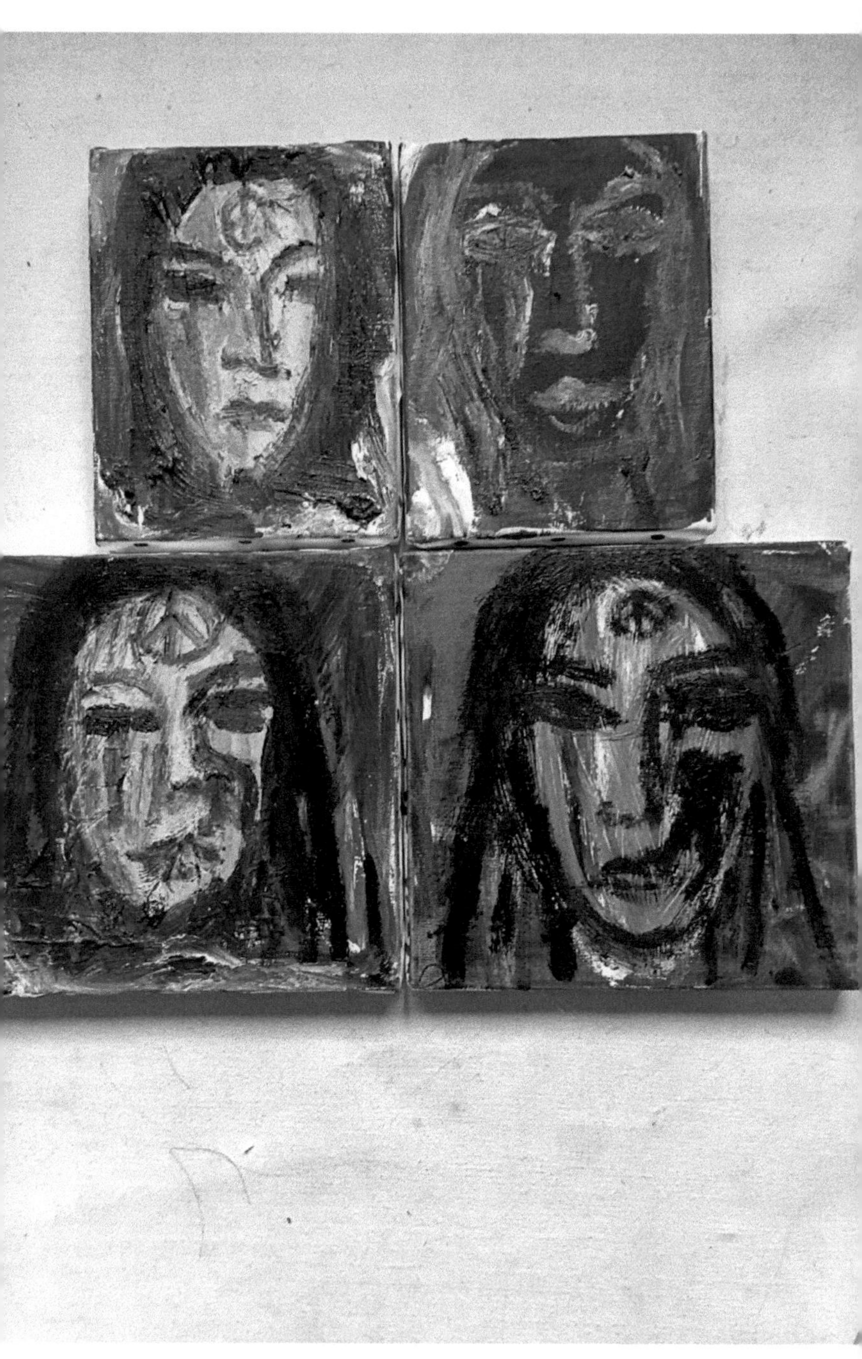

Serie 2020 nothing is real

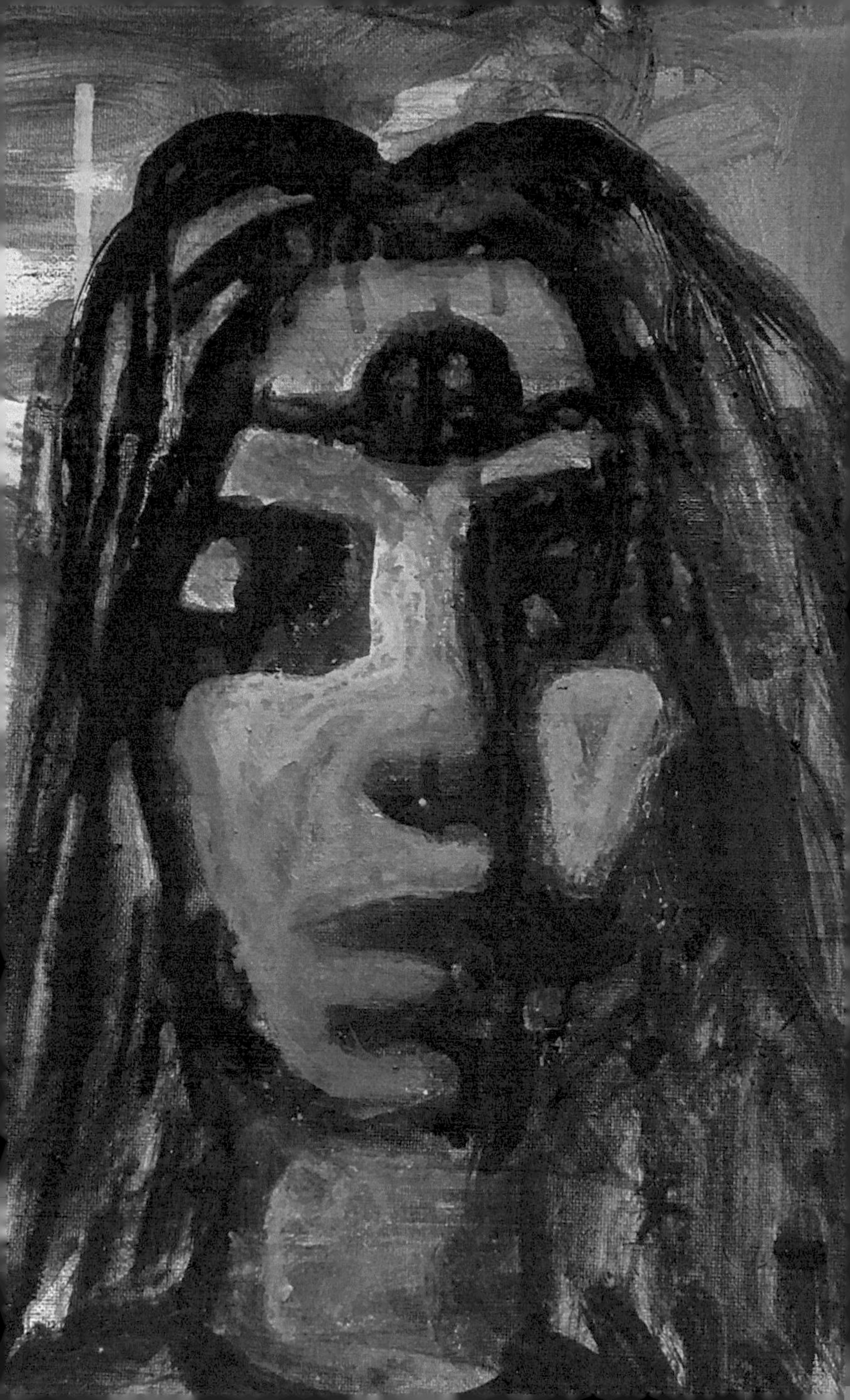

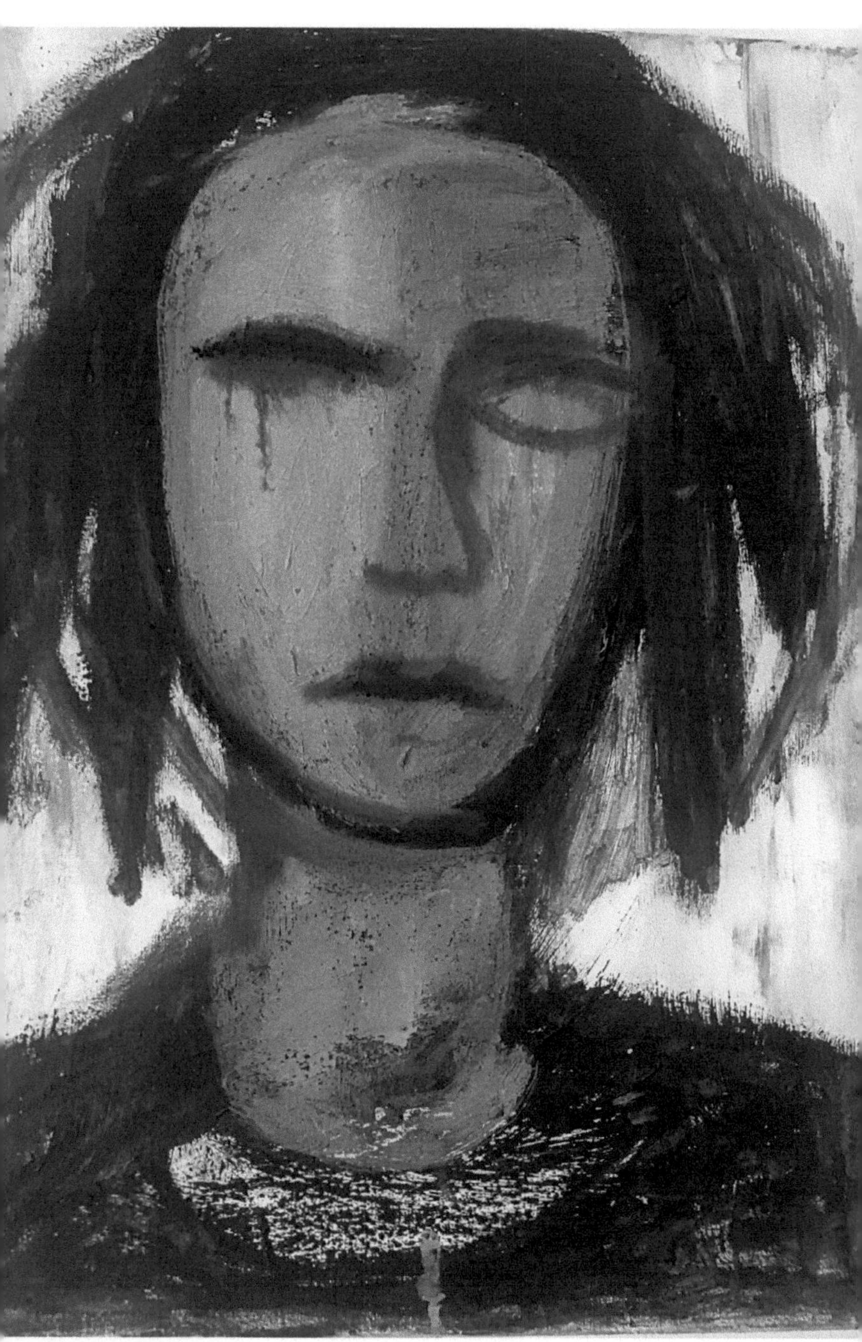

Serie 2004

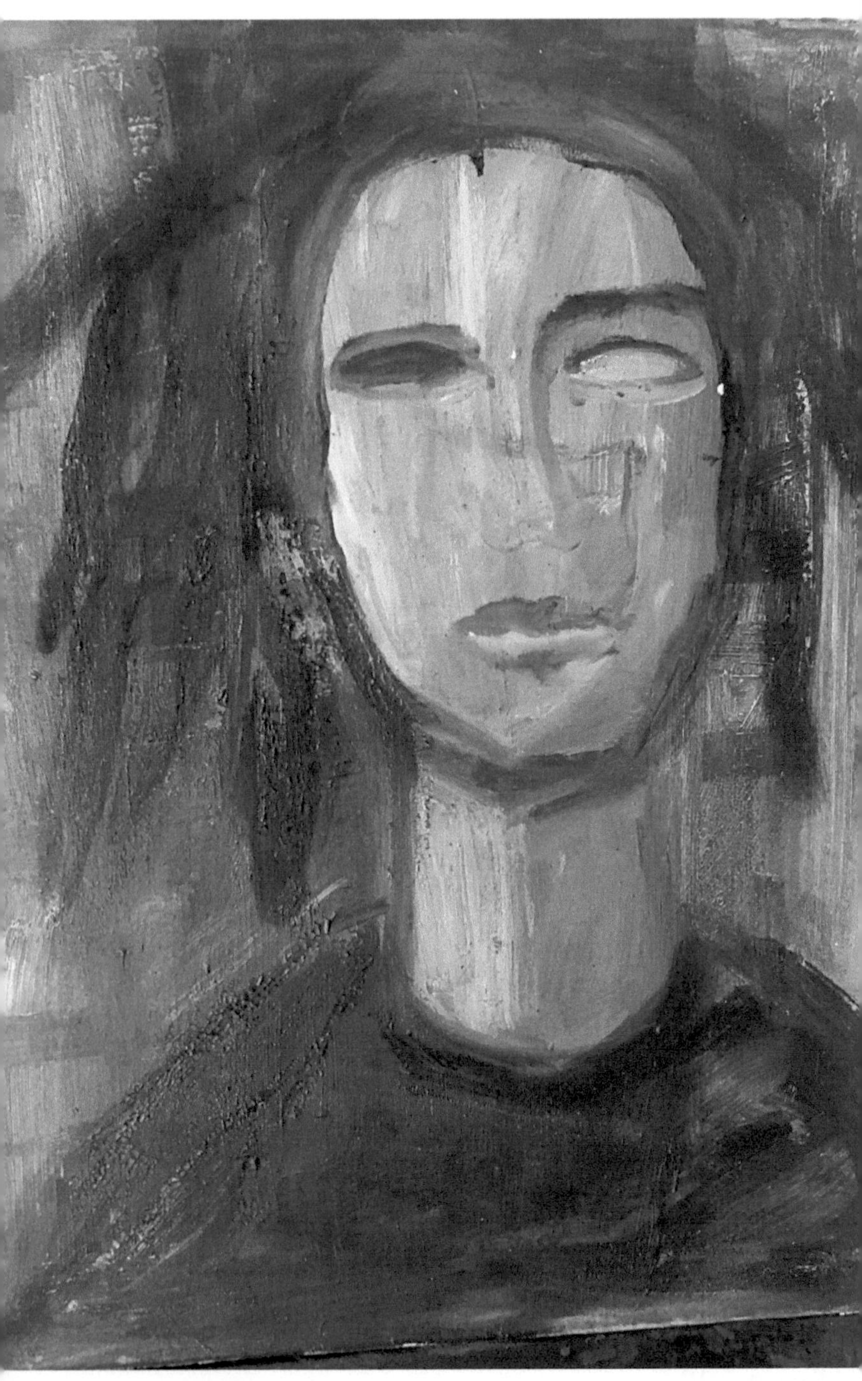

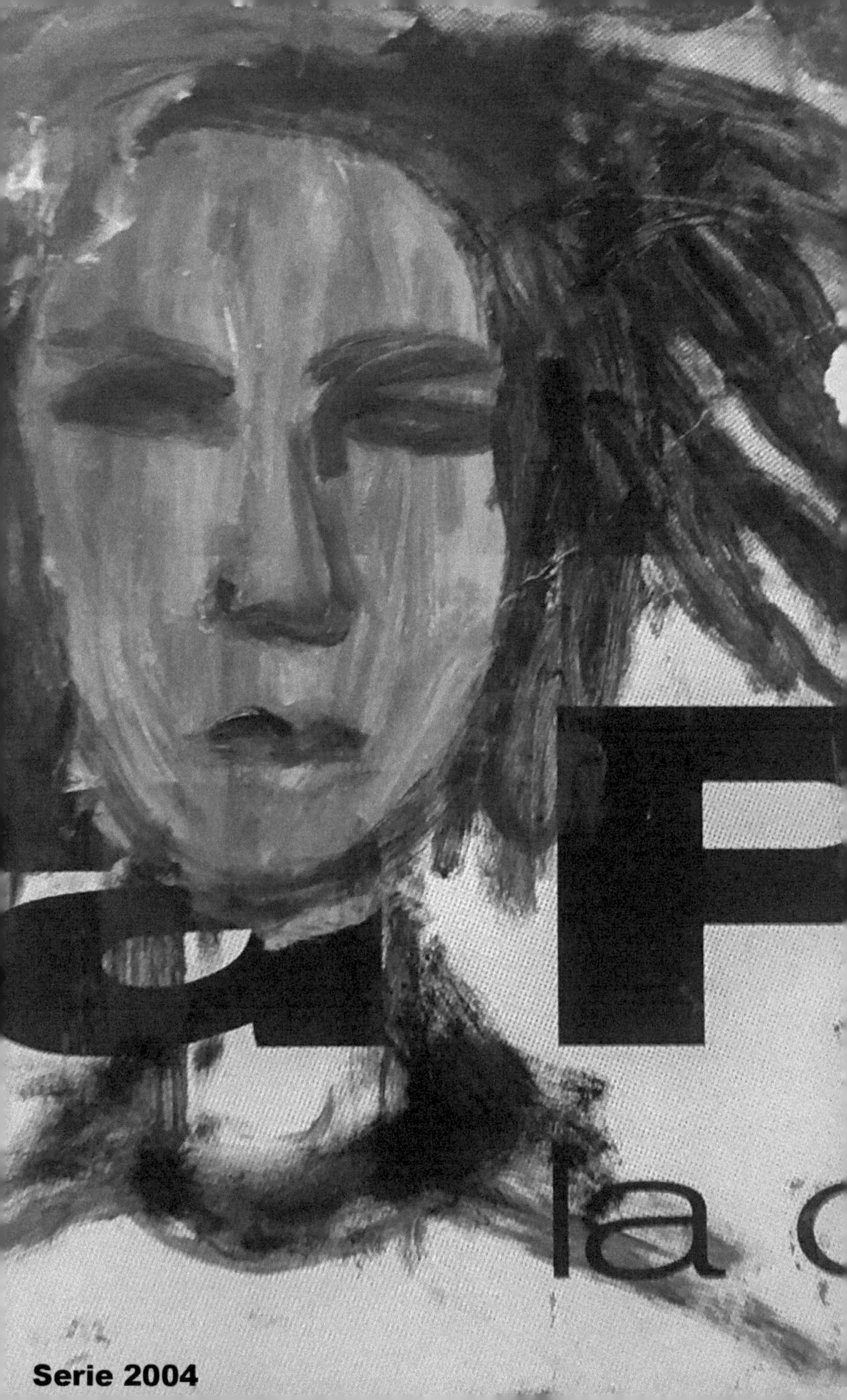
Serie 2004

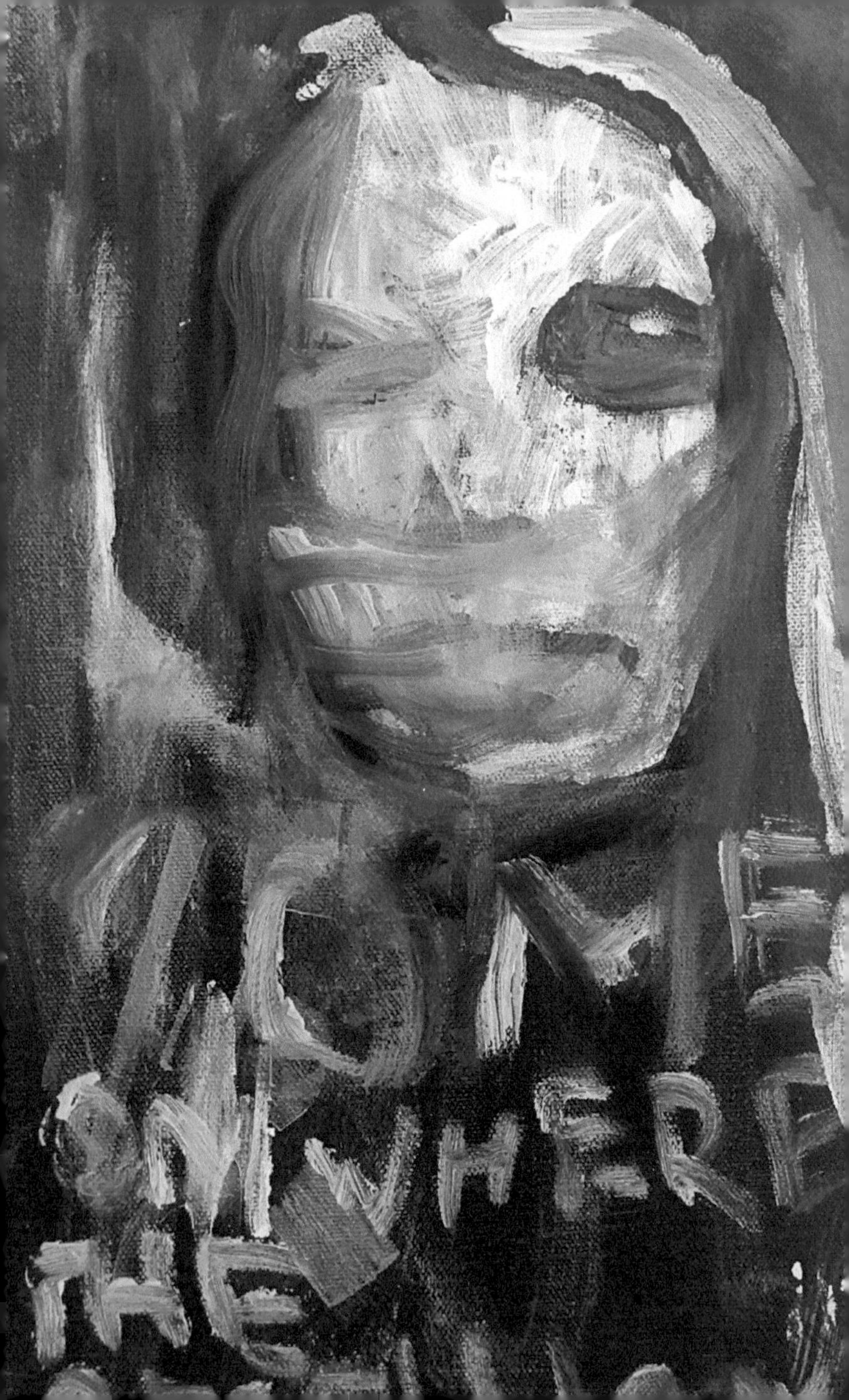

NO
WHERE
THE

Oil on canvvas 2008 Serie Hey Come on......

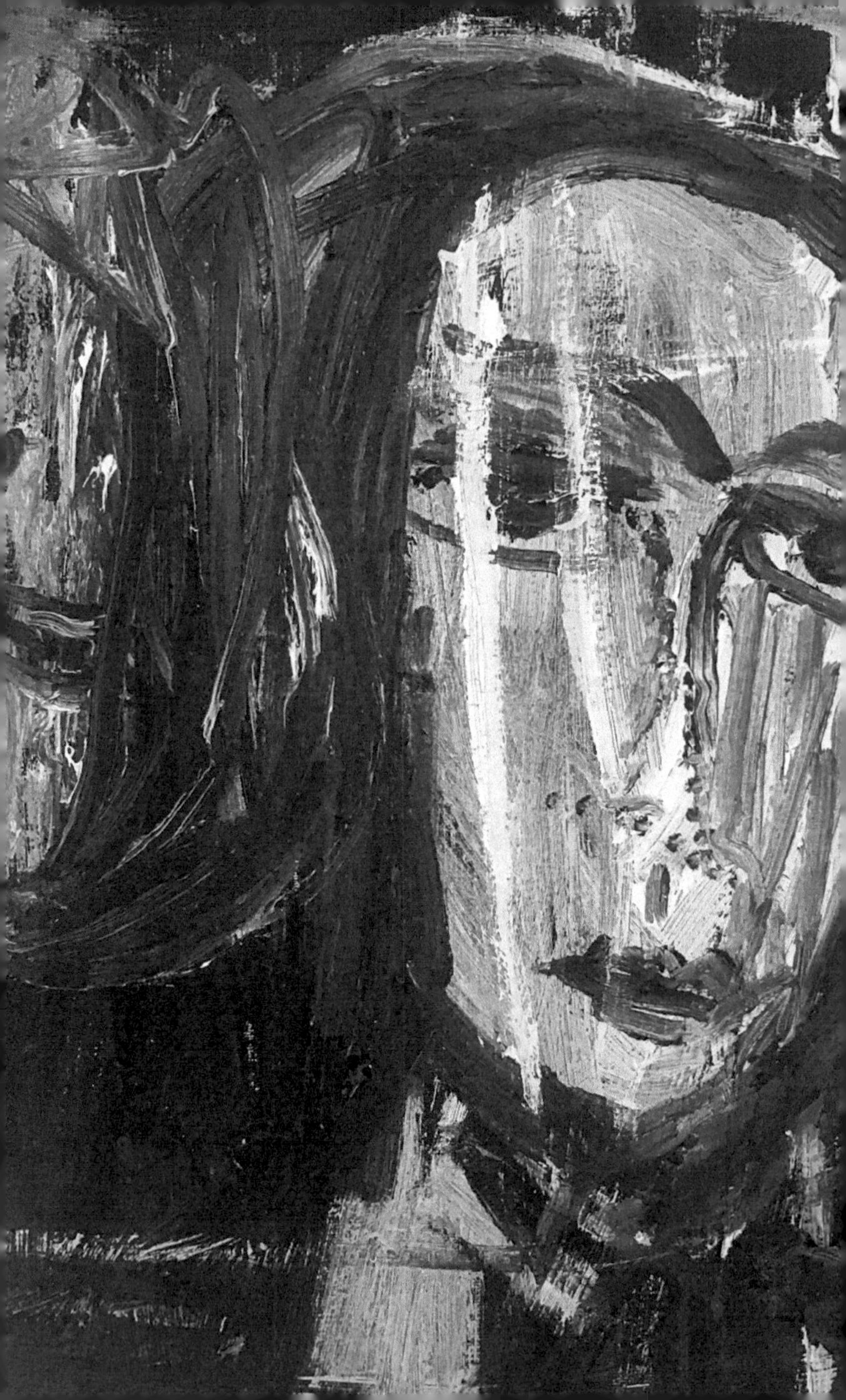

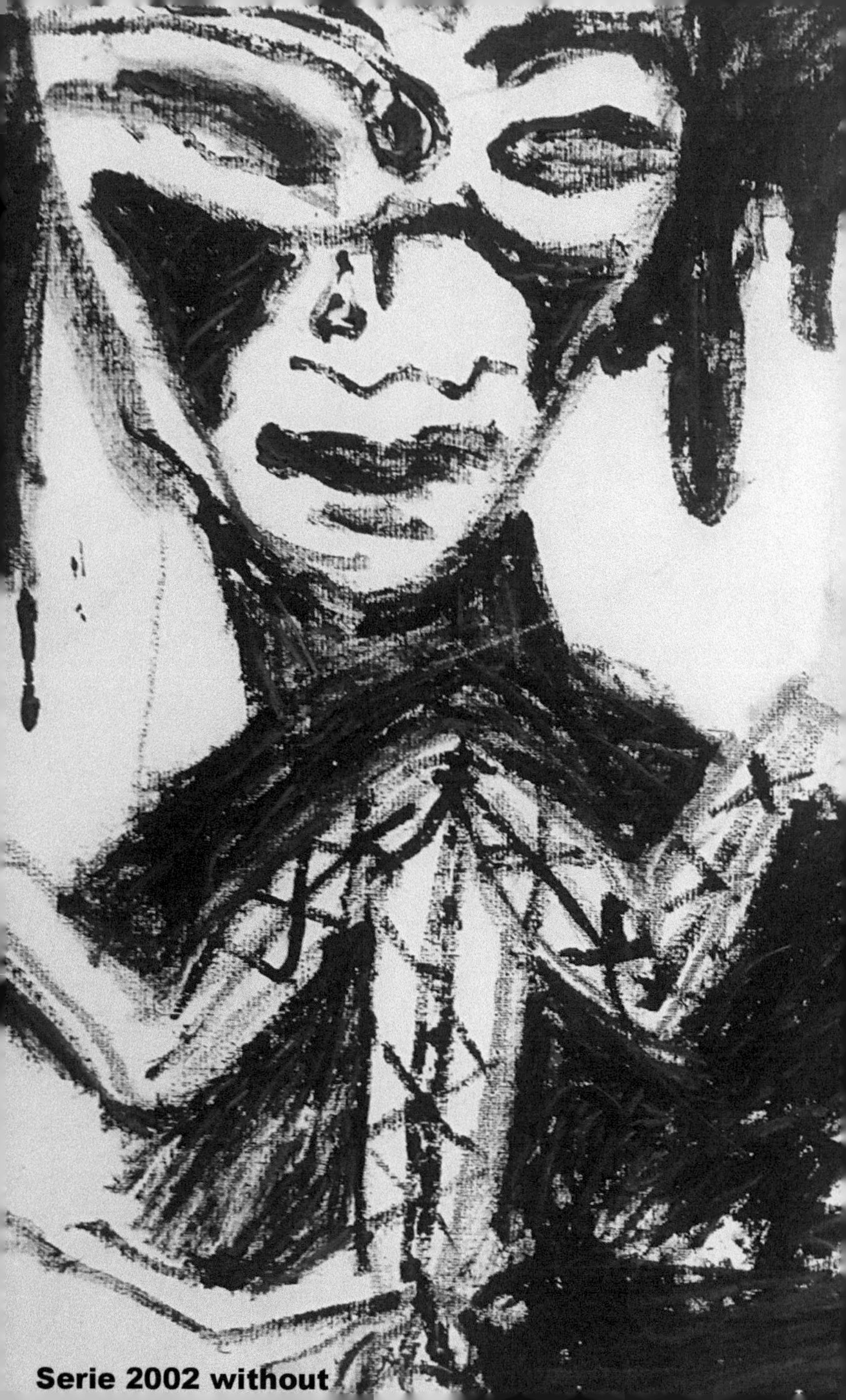

Serie 2002 without

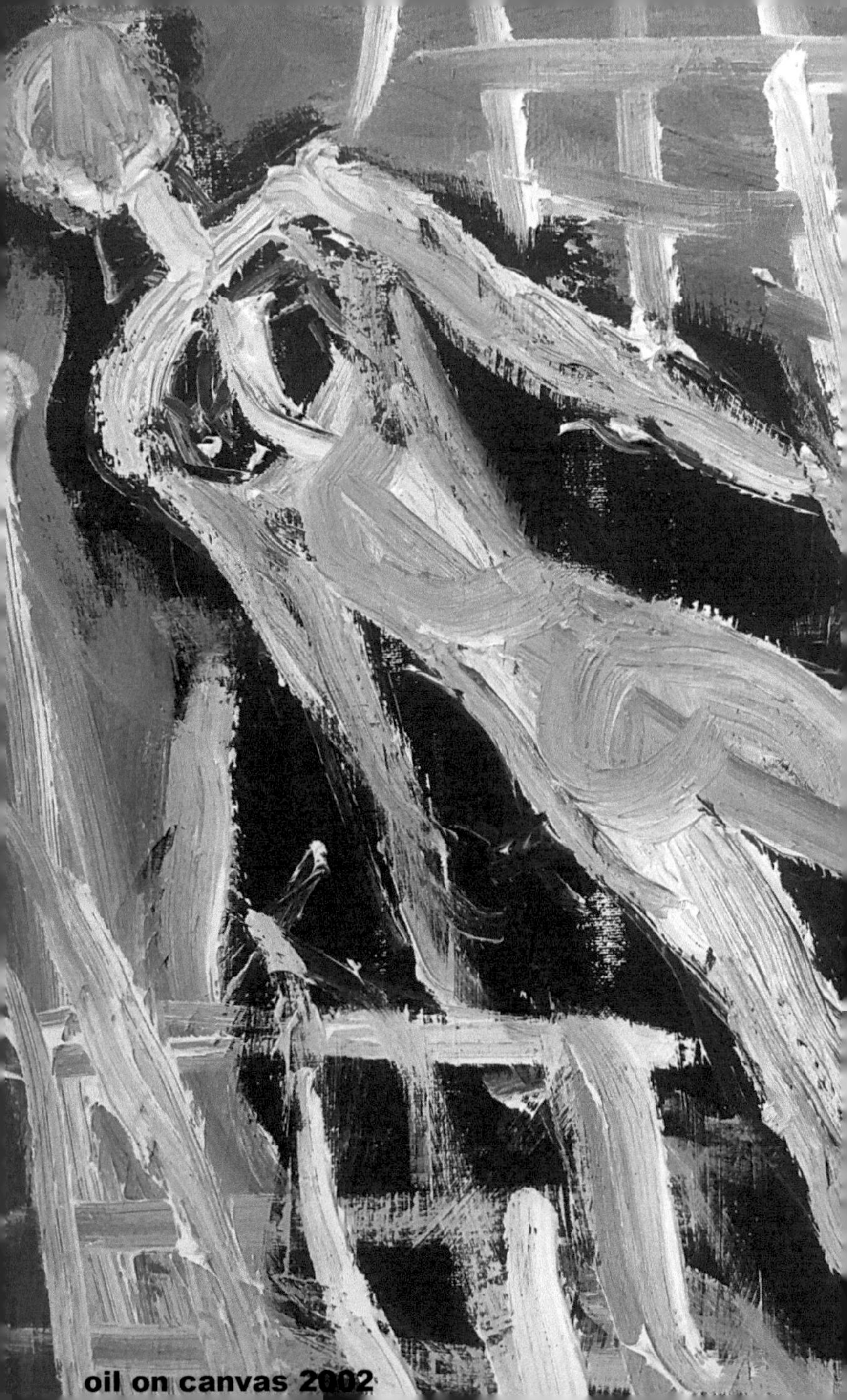

oil on canvas 2002

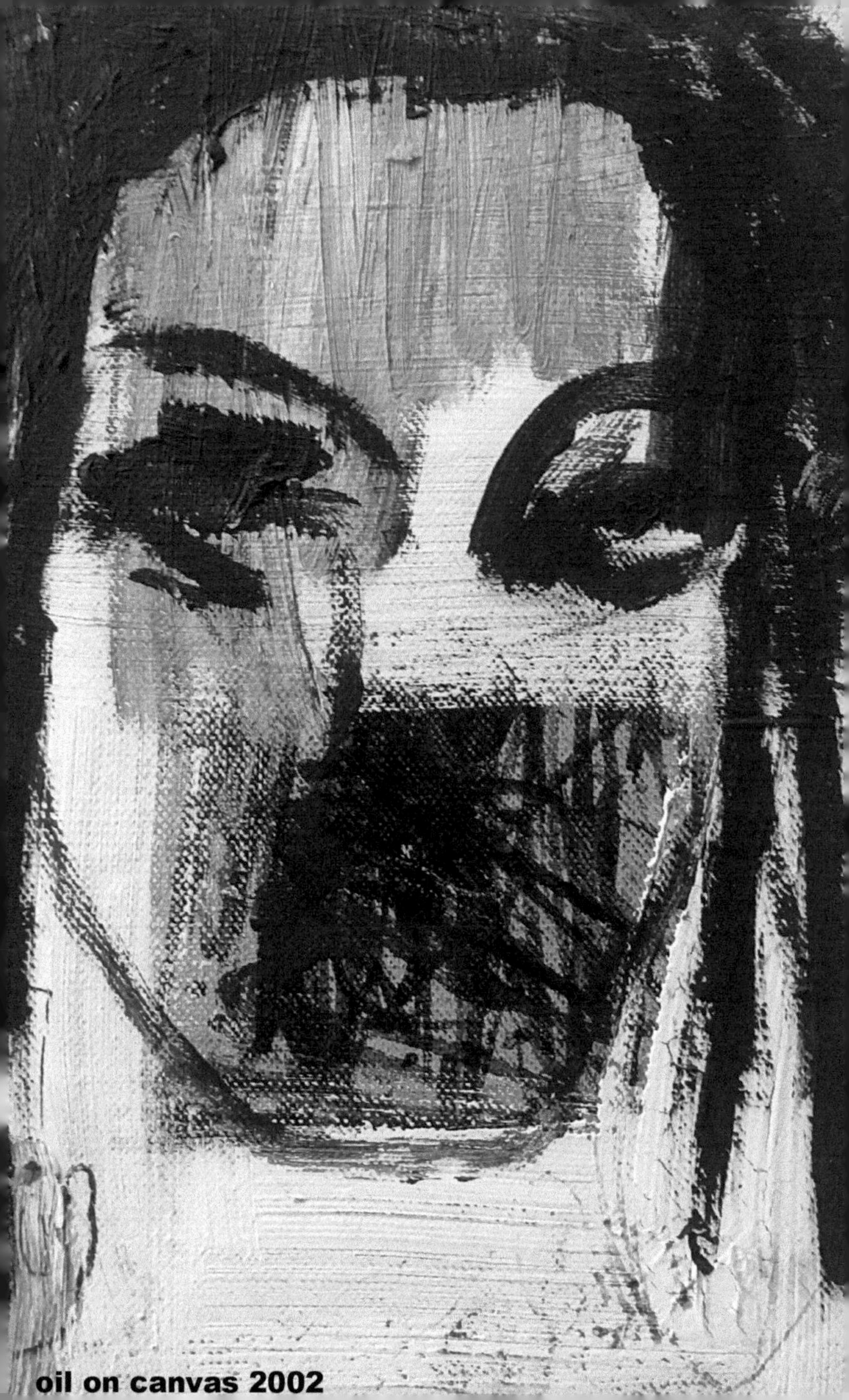

oil on canvas 2002

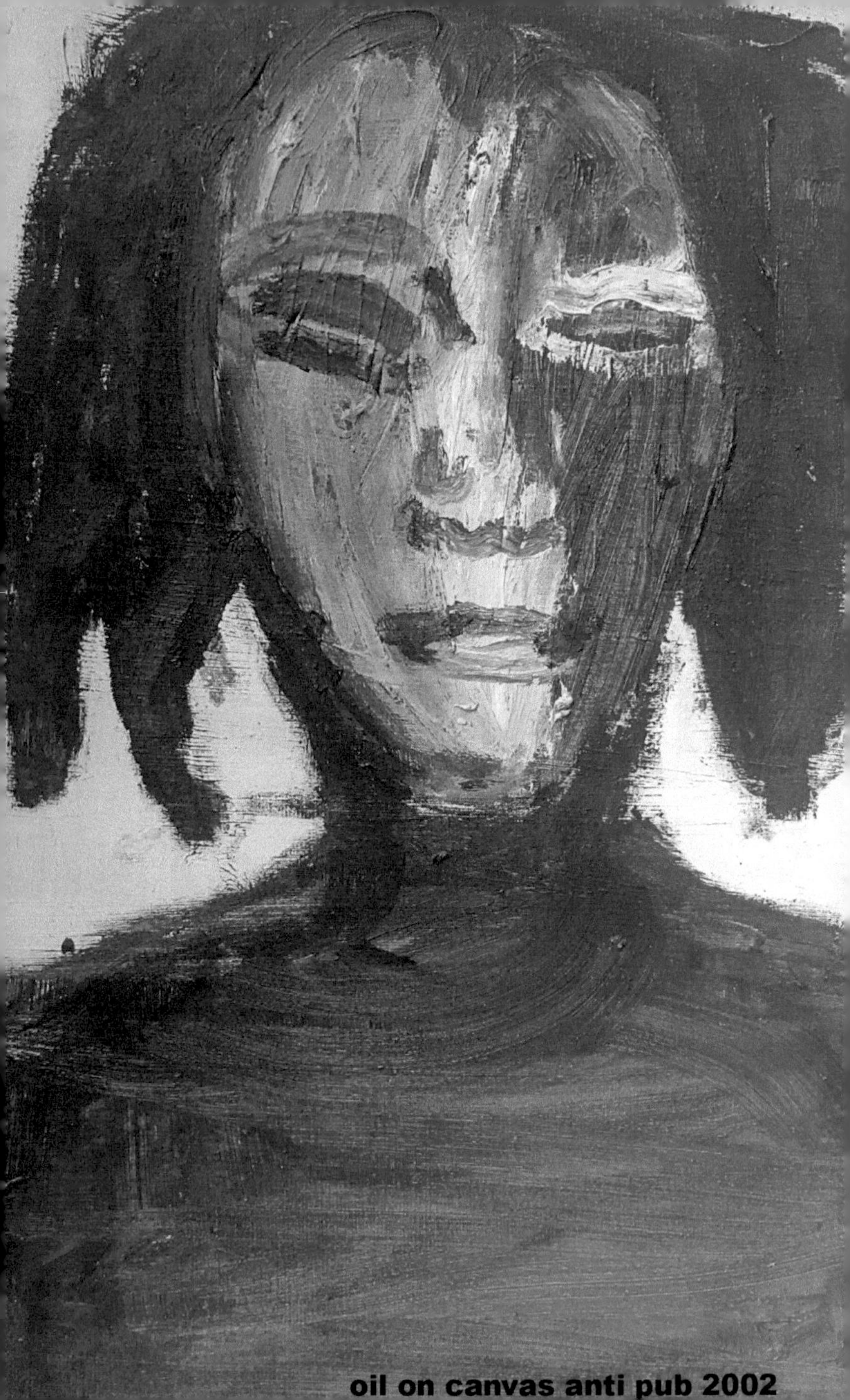
oil on canvas anti pub 2002

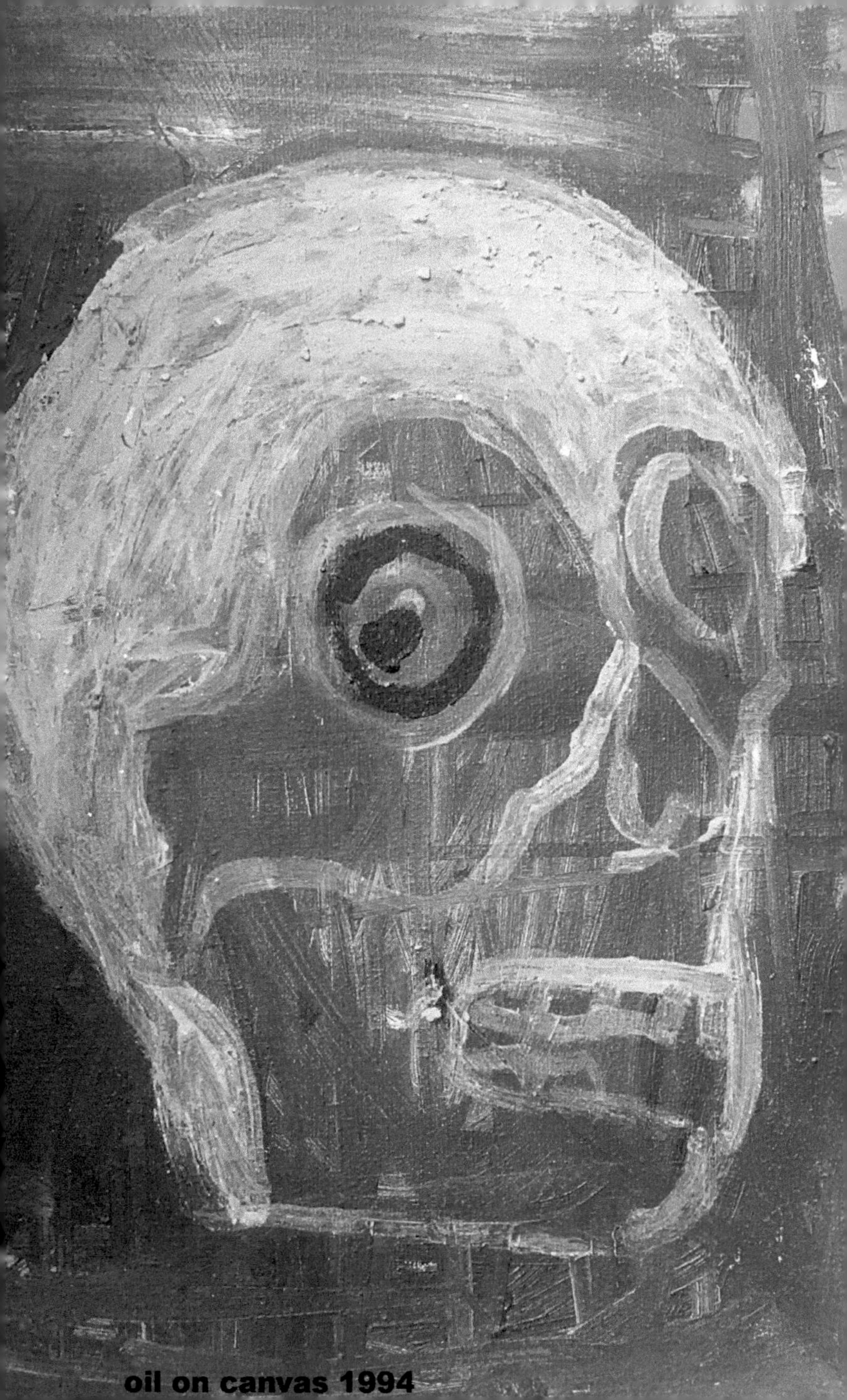

oil on canvas 1994

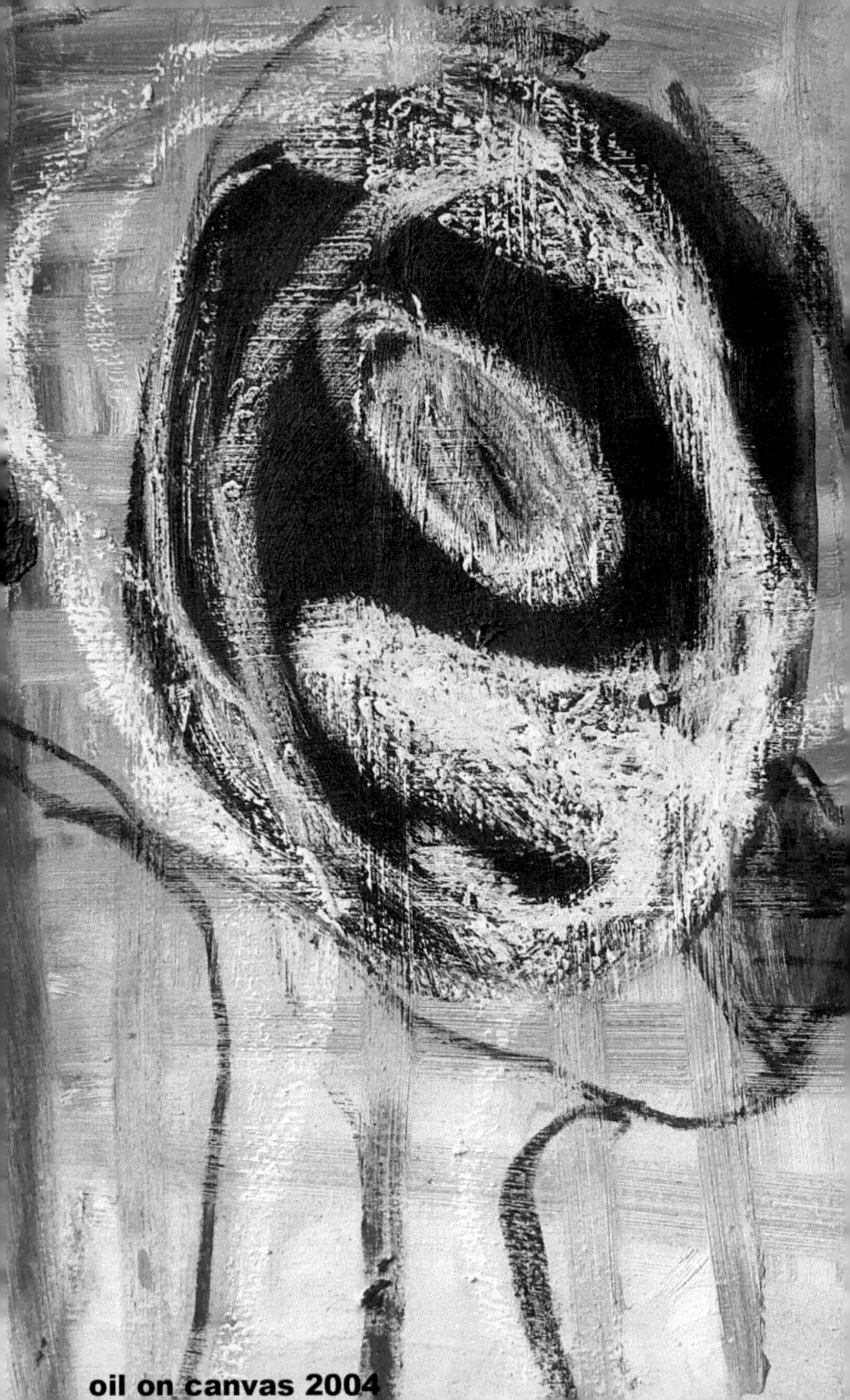
oil on canvas 2004

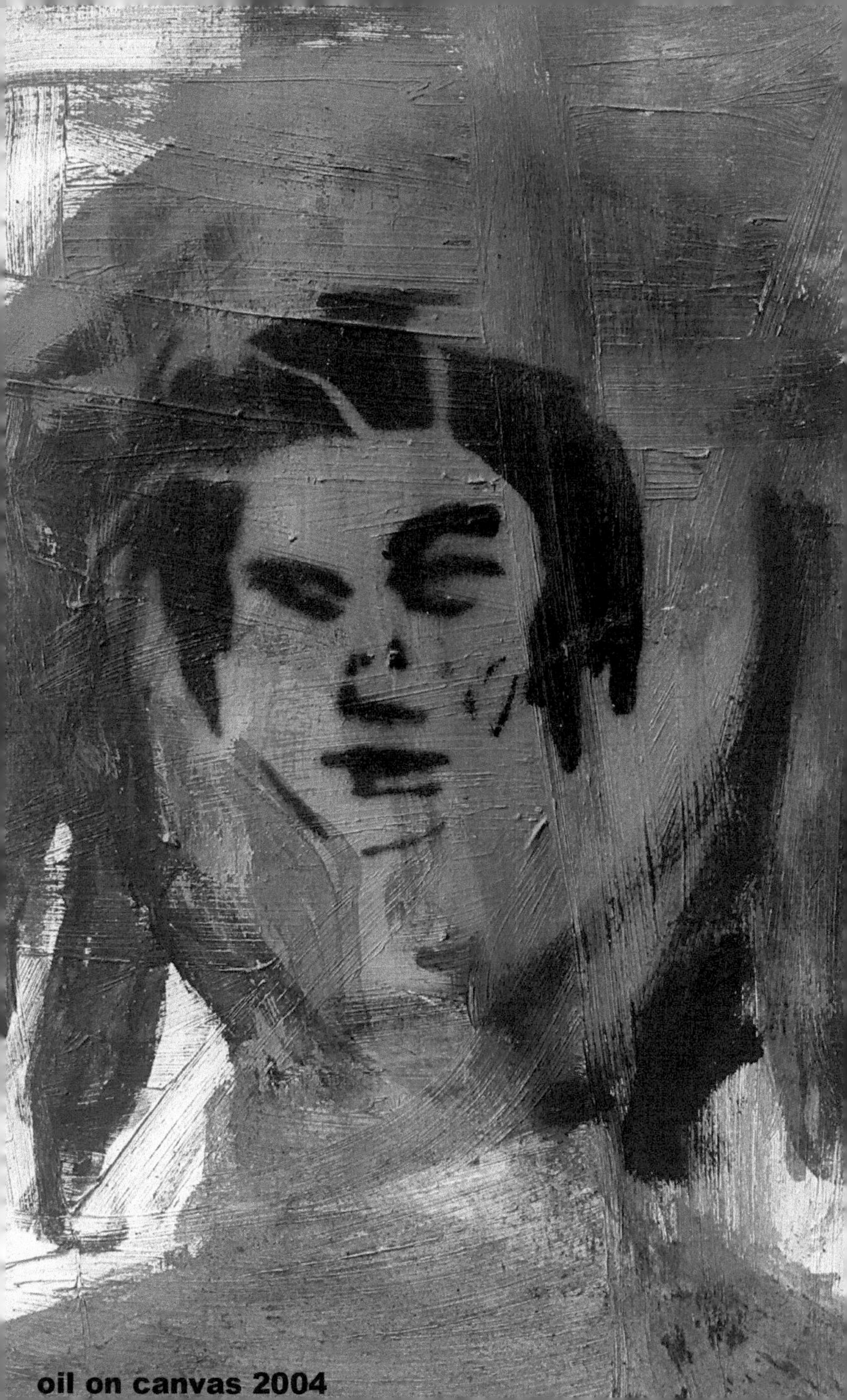
oil on canvas 2004

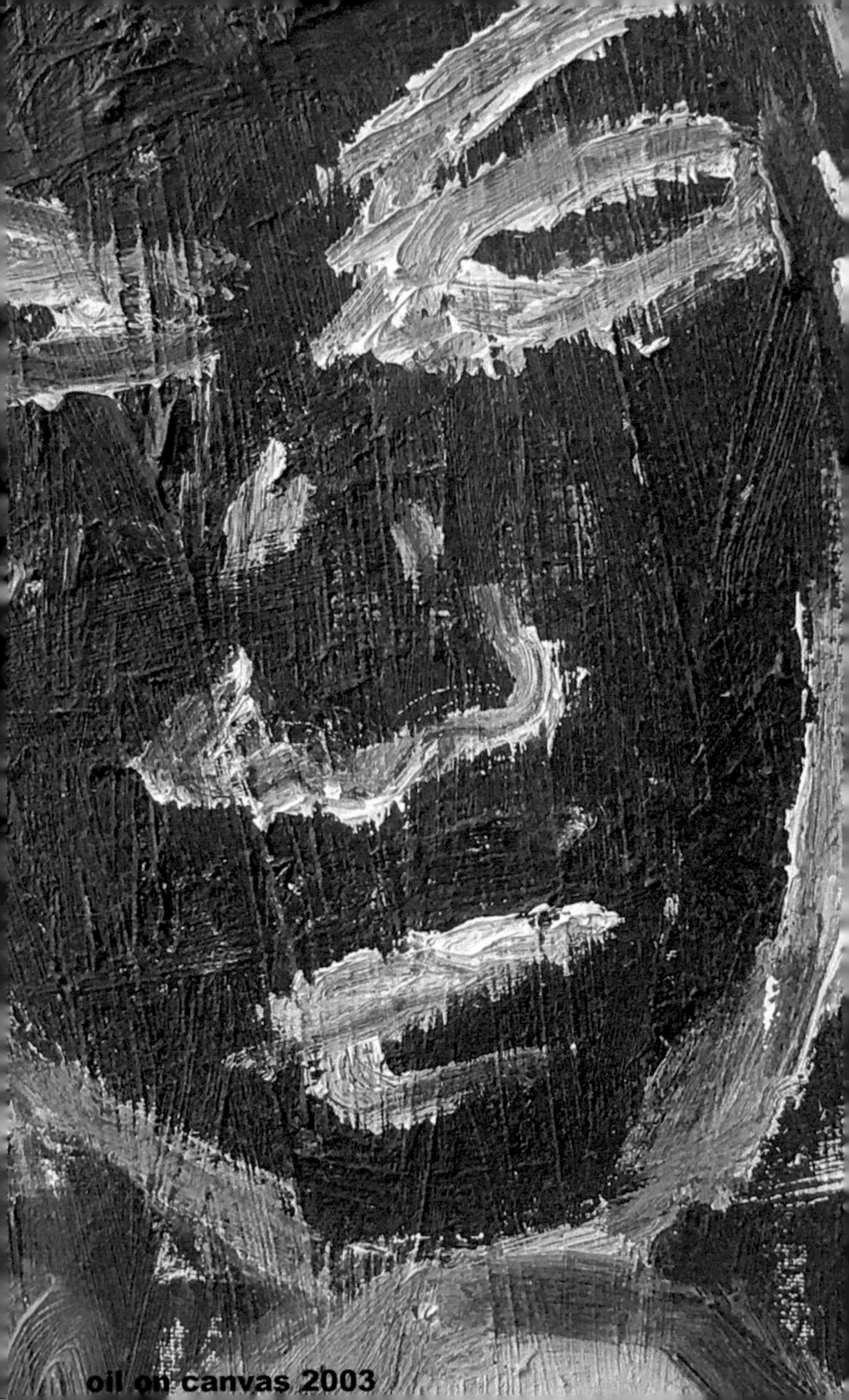
oil on canvas 2003

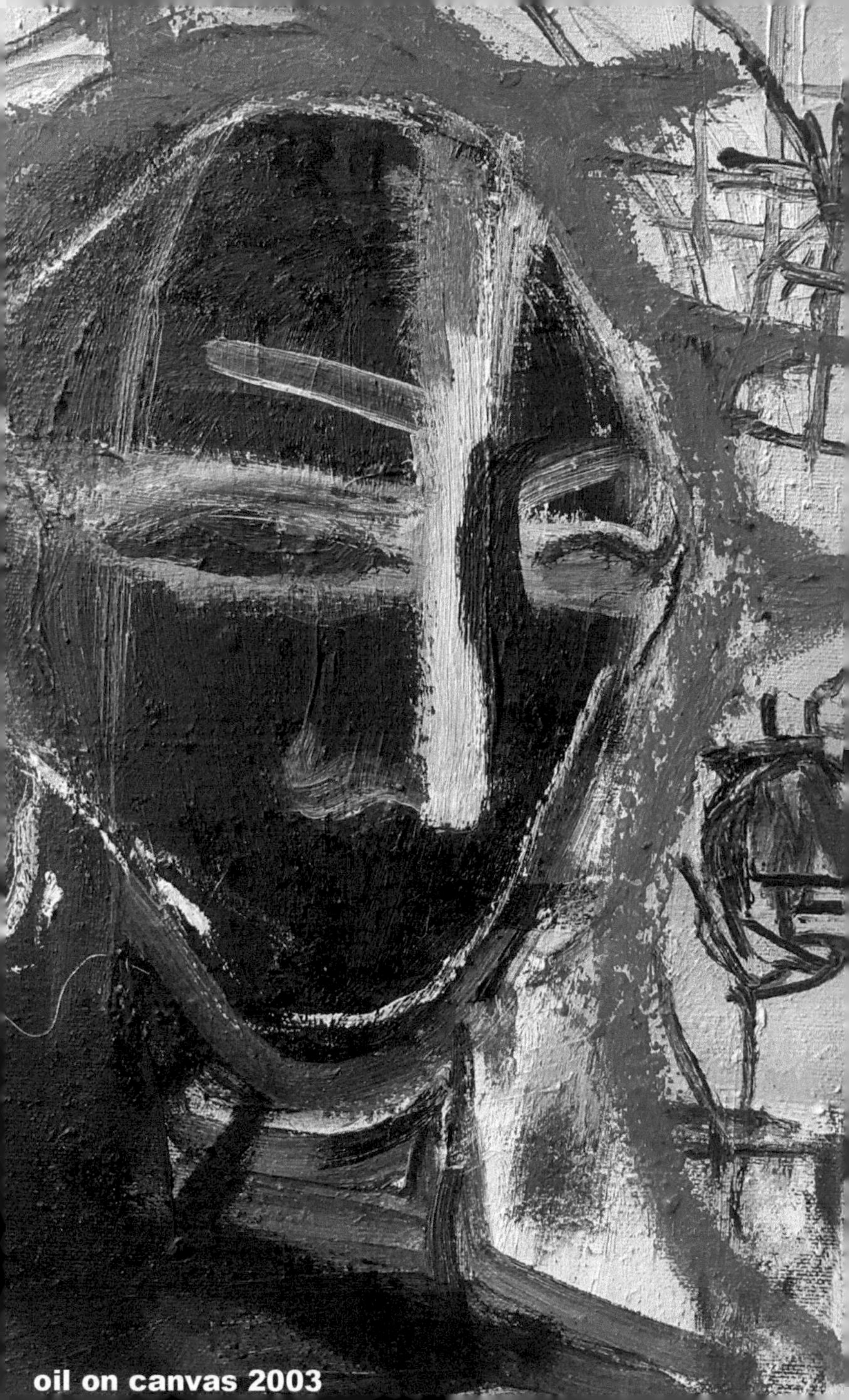

oil on canvas 2003

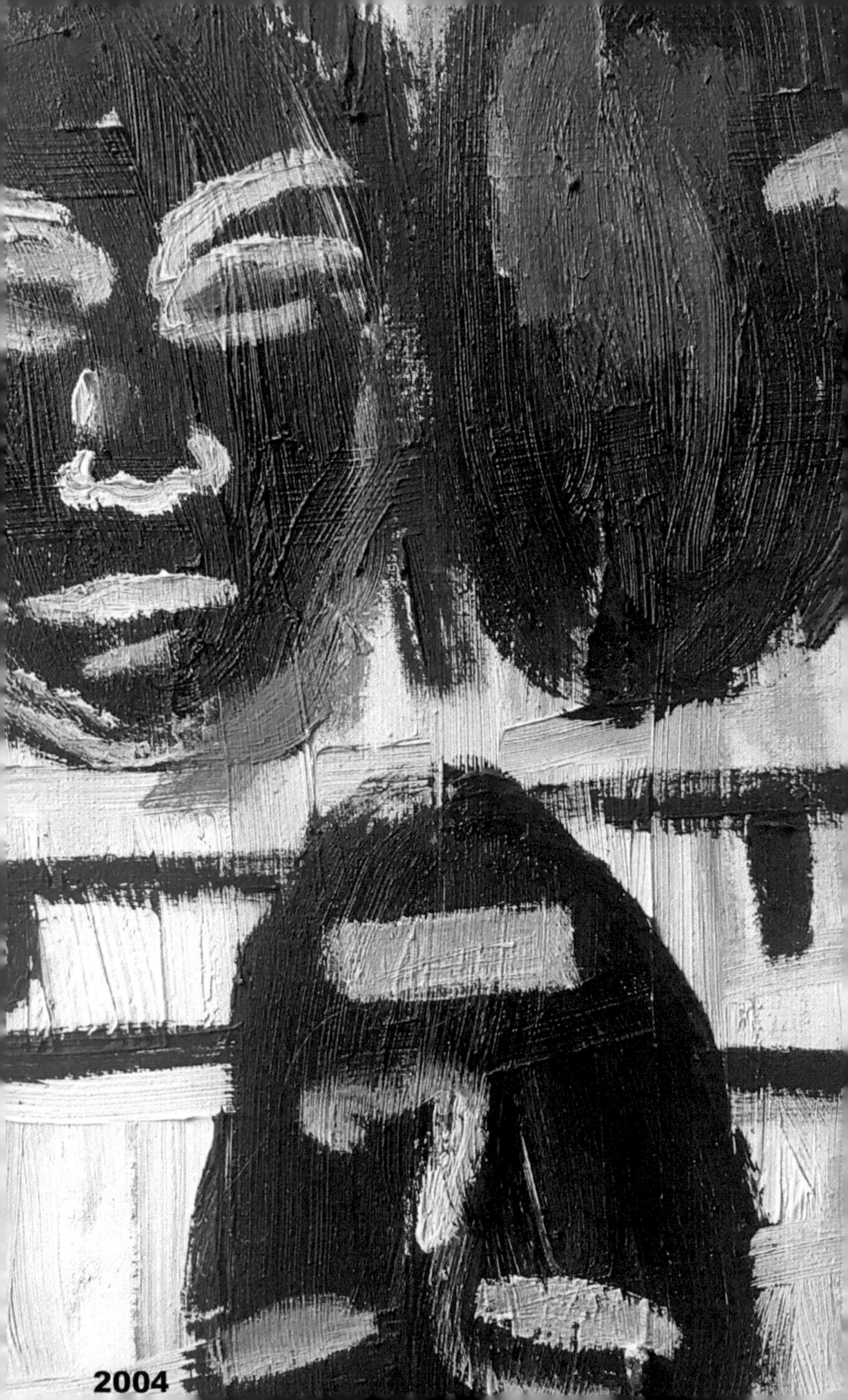
2004

2003

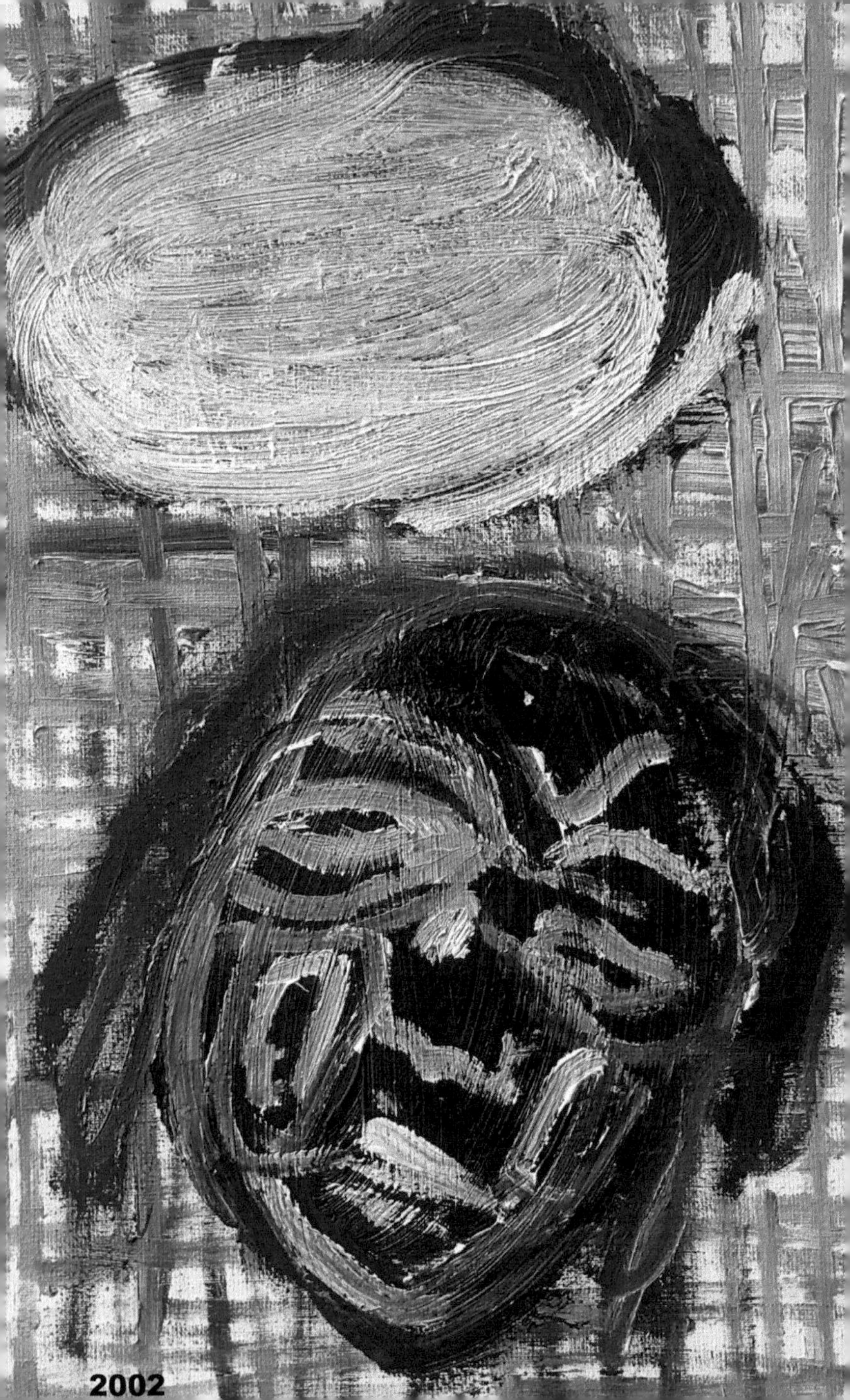
2002

2003

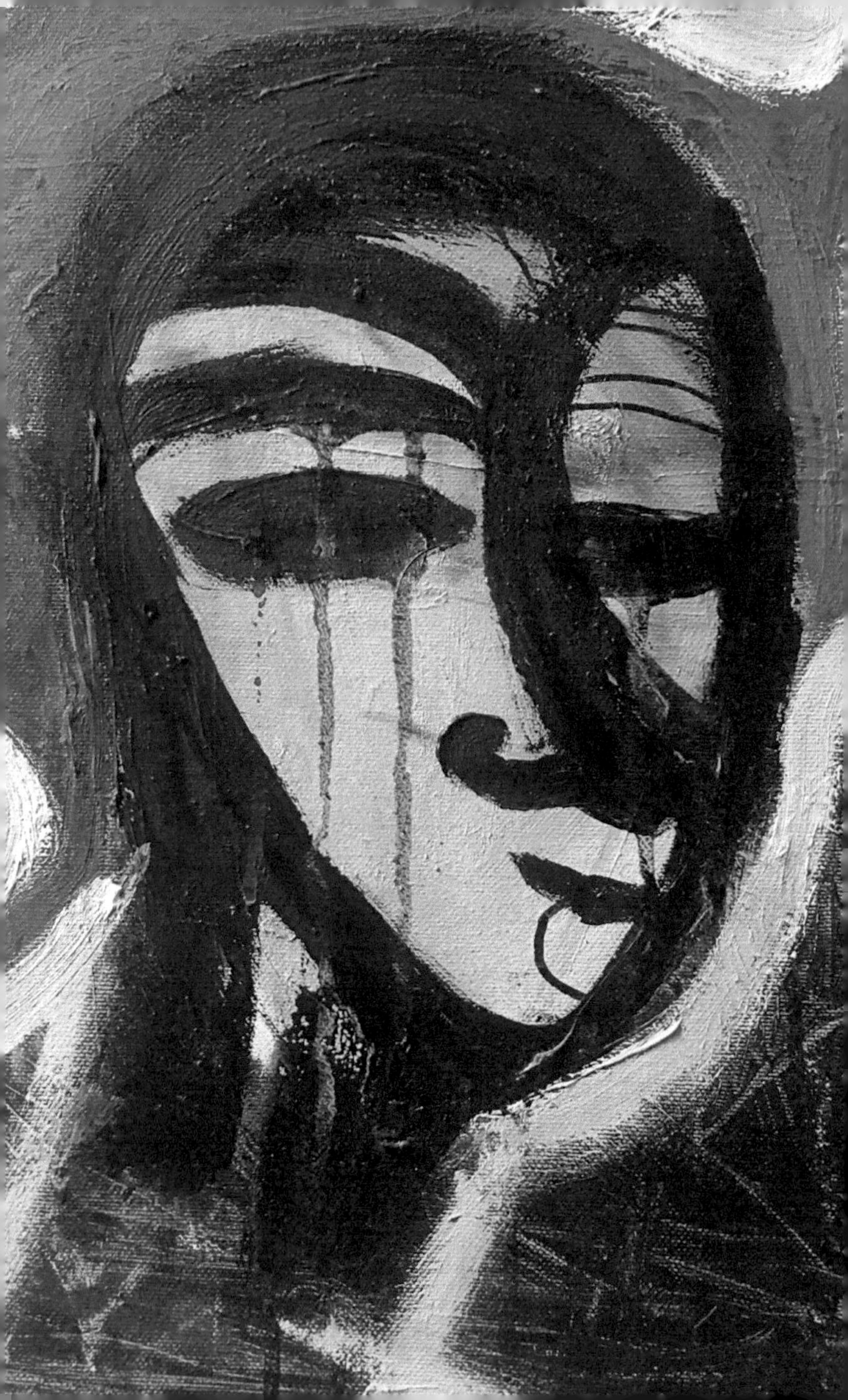

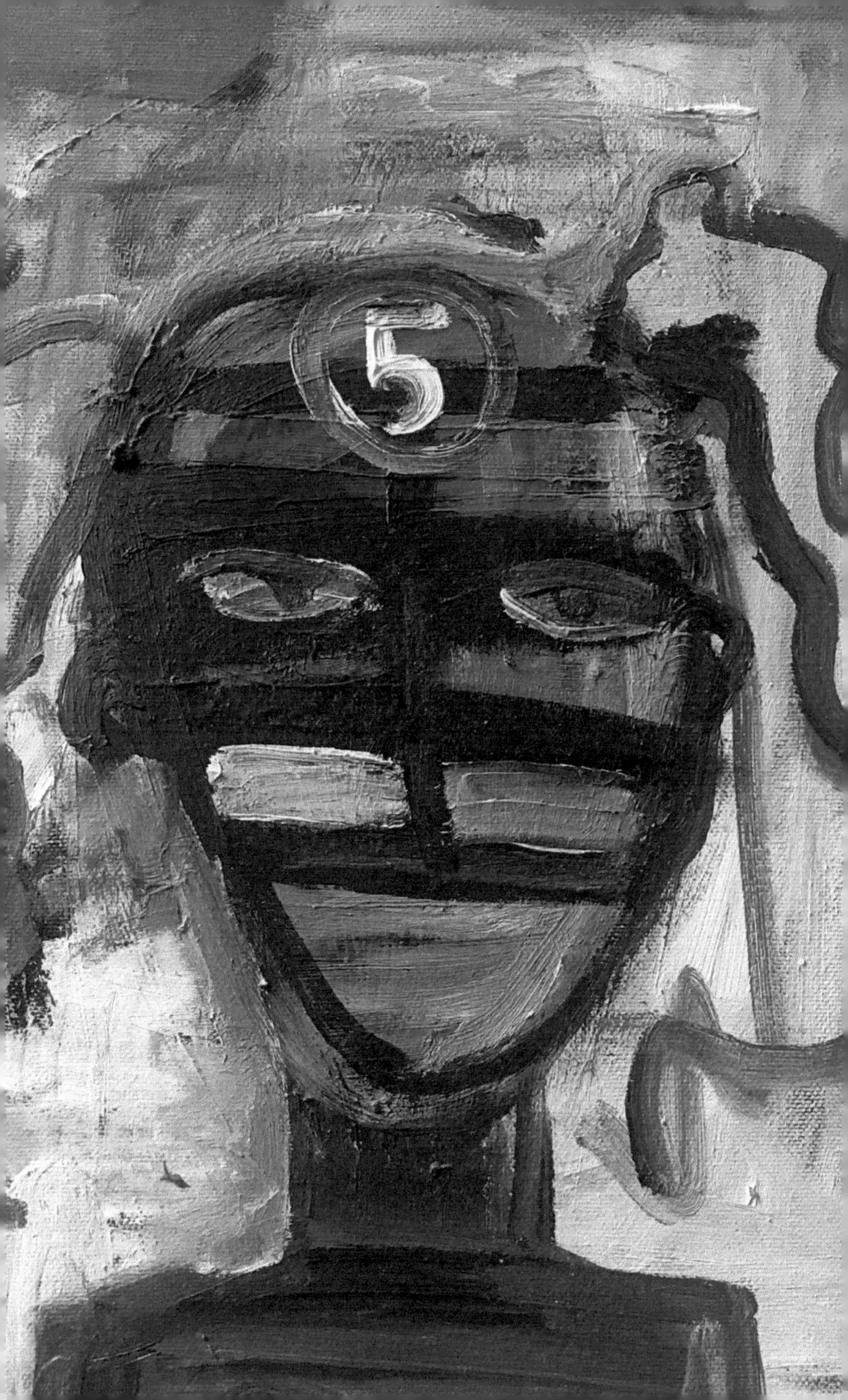

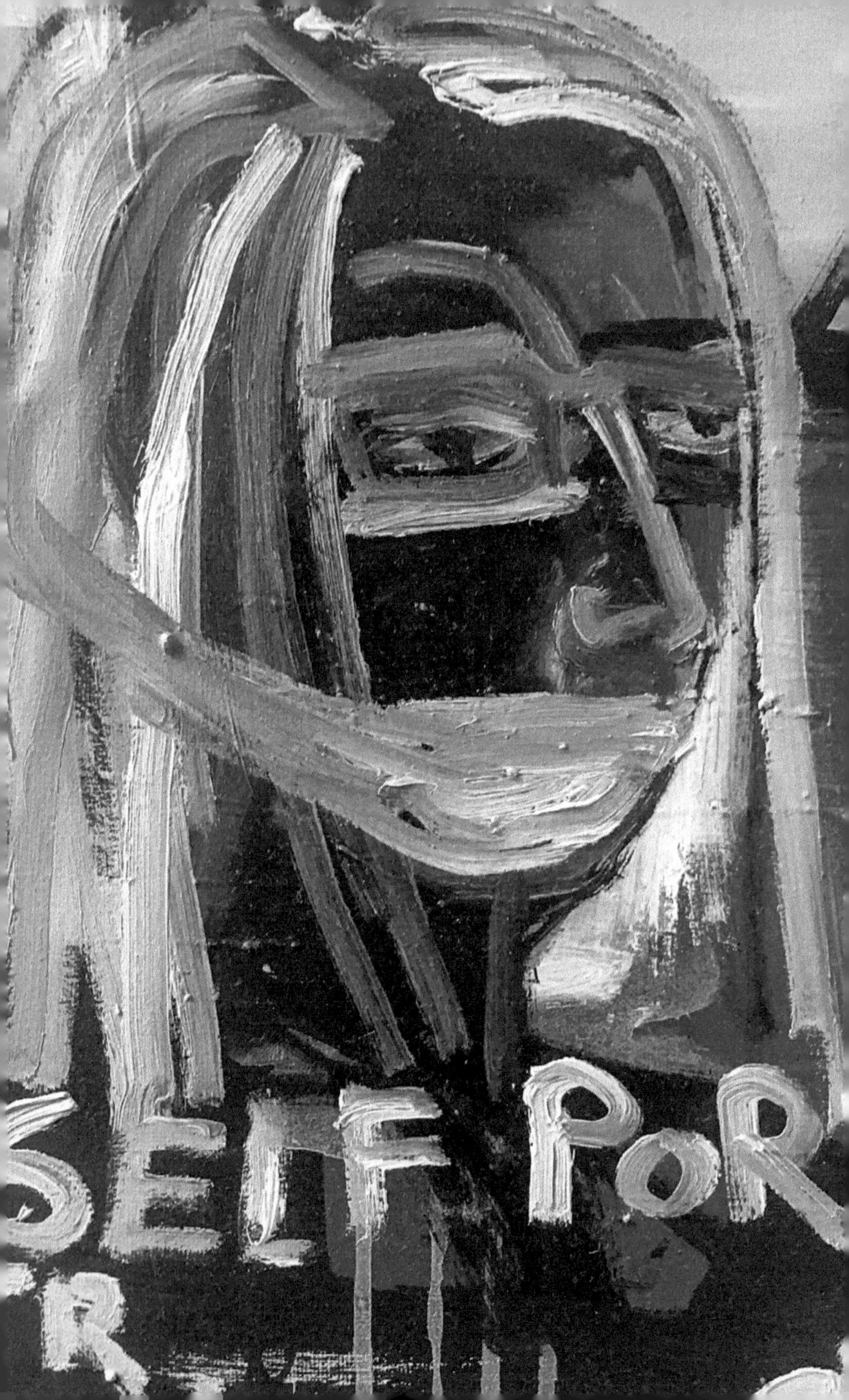

SE E POR
R

2003 Galerie Cllaude Dorval Paris

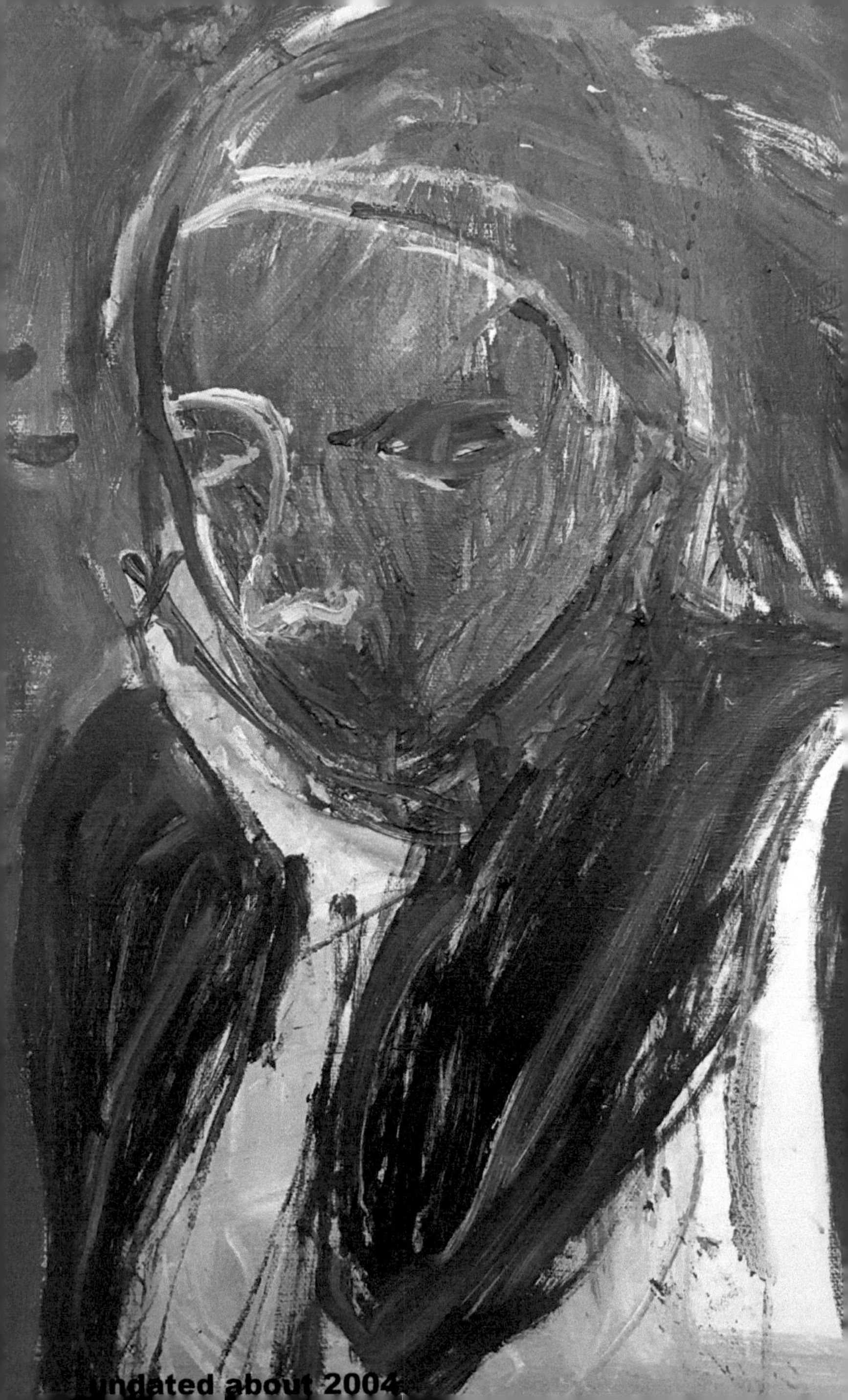

undated about 2004

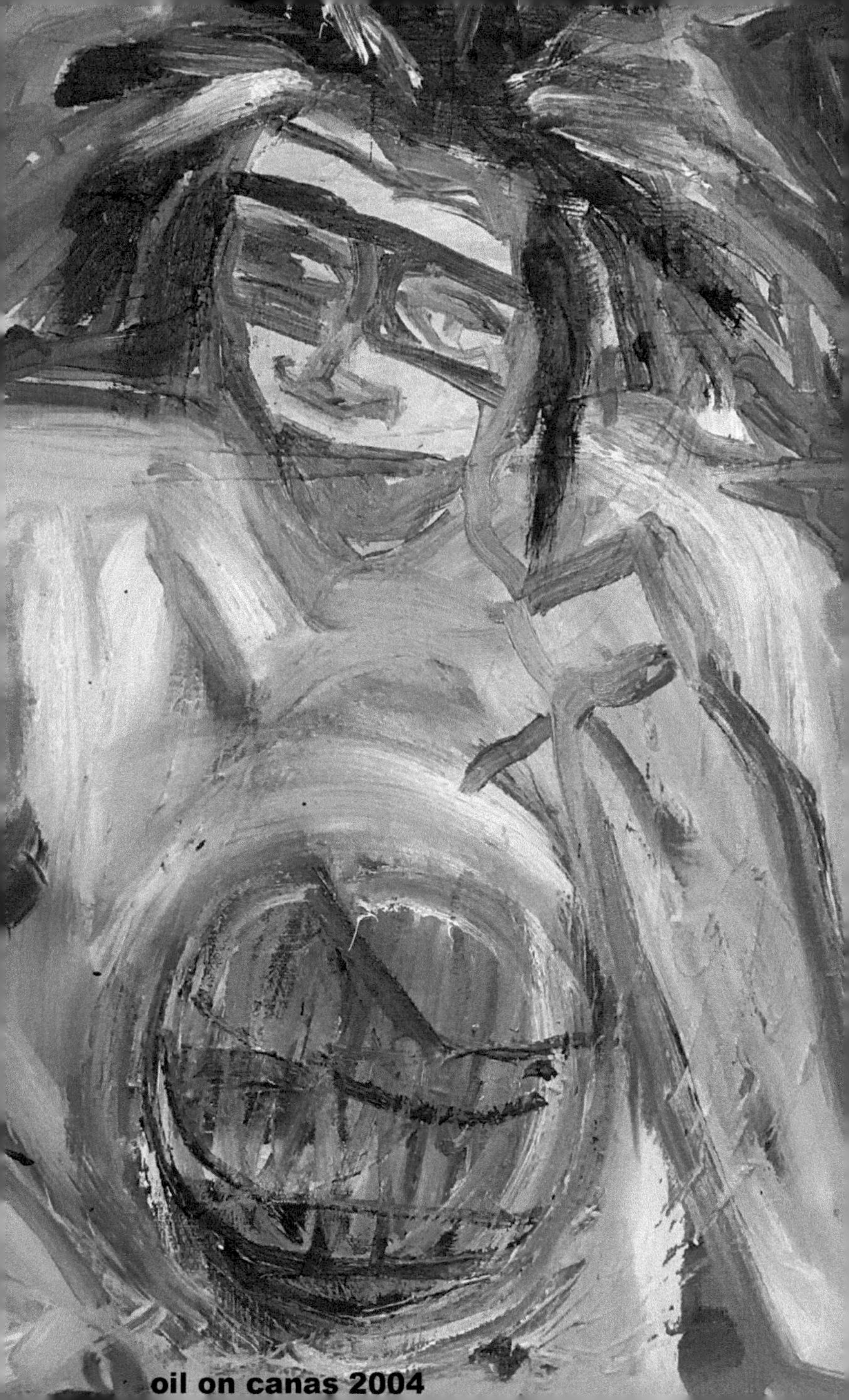

oil on canas 2004

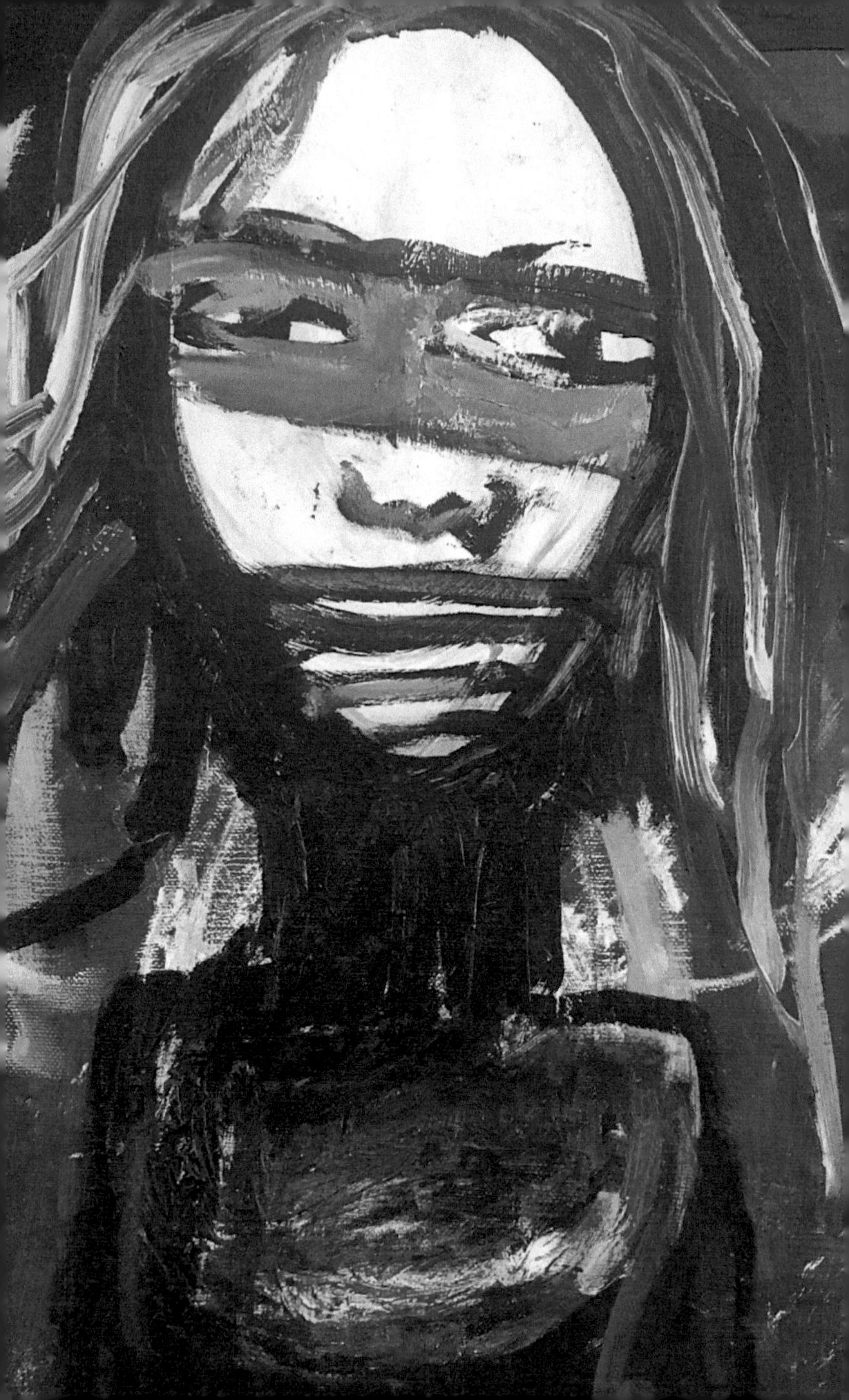

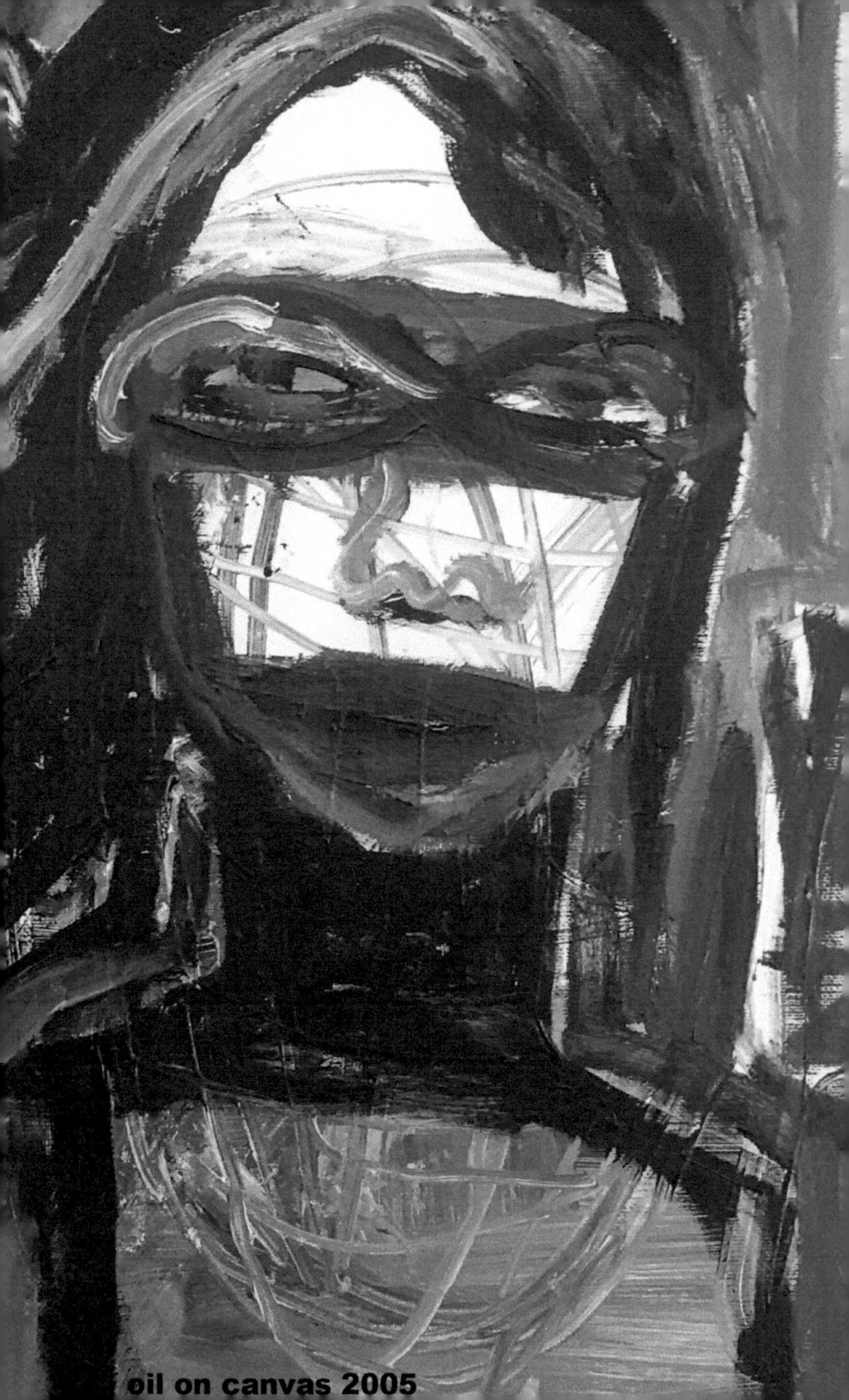
oil on canvas 2005

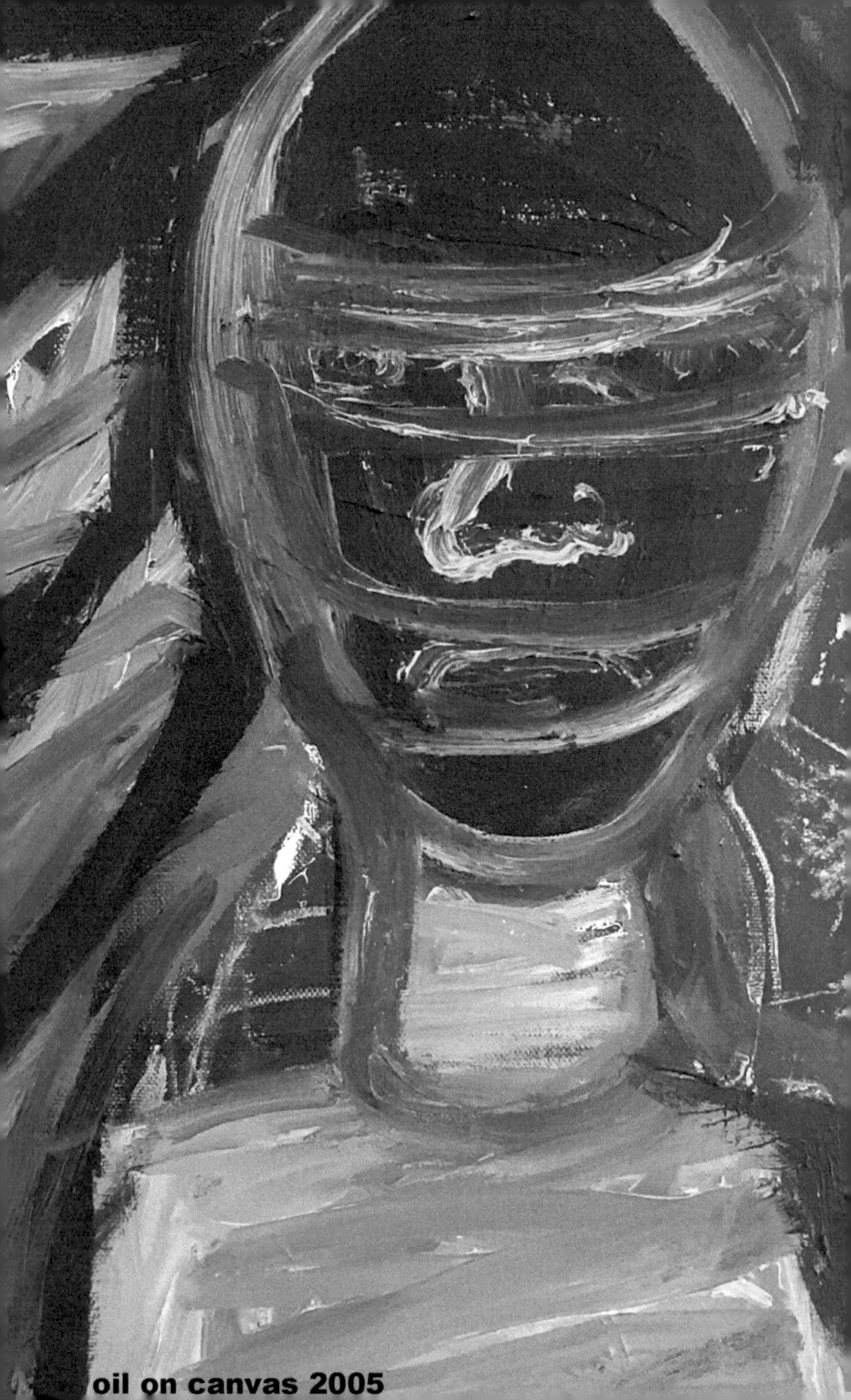
oil on canvas 2005

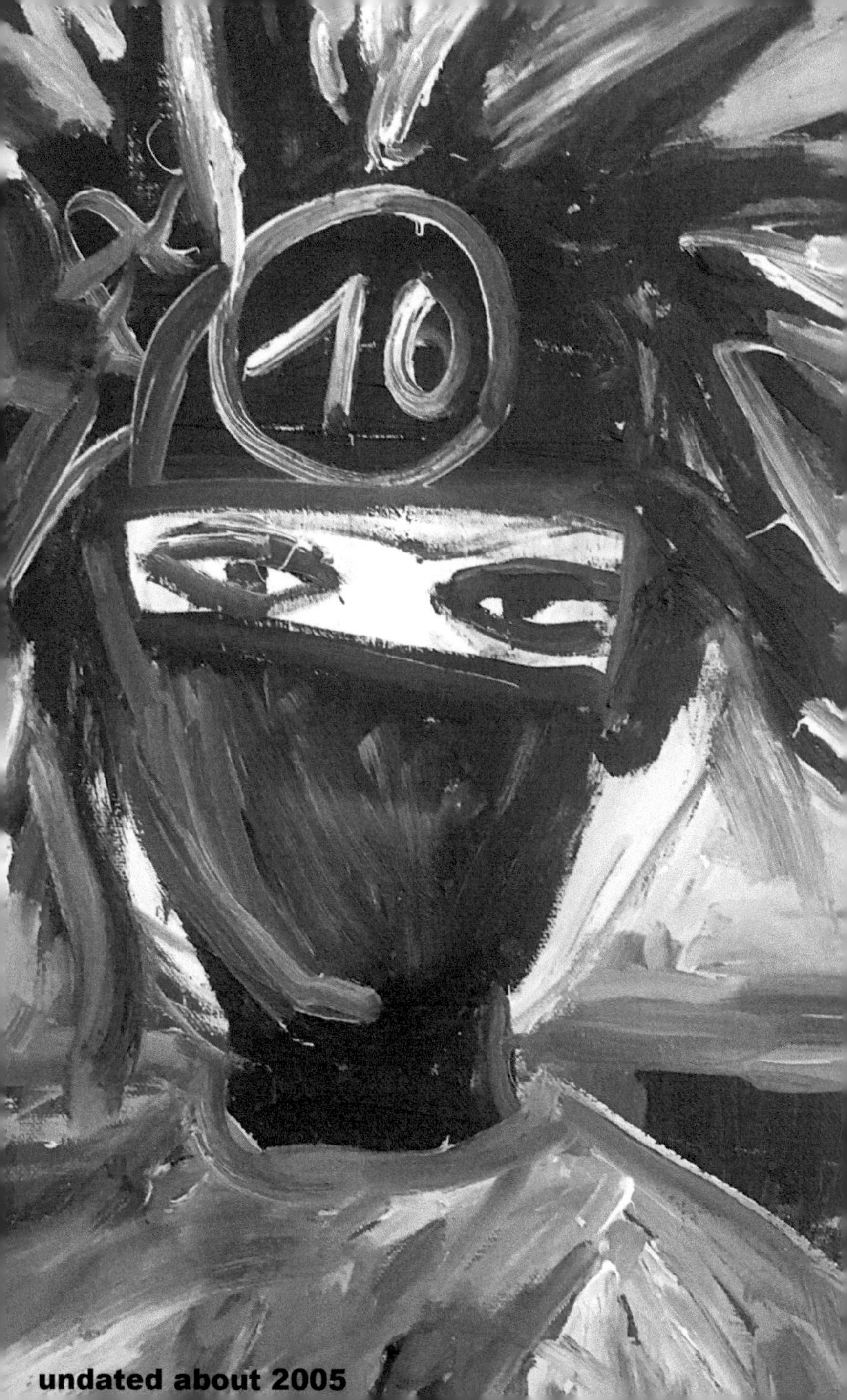

undated about 2005

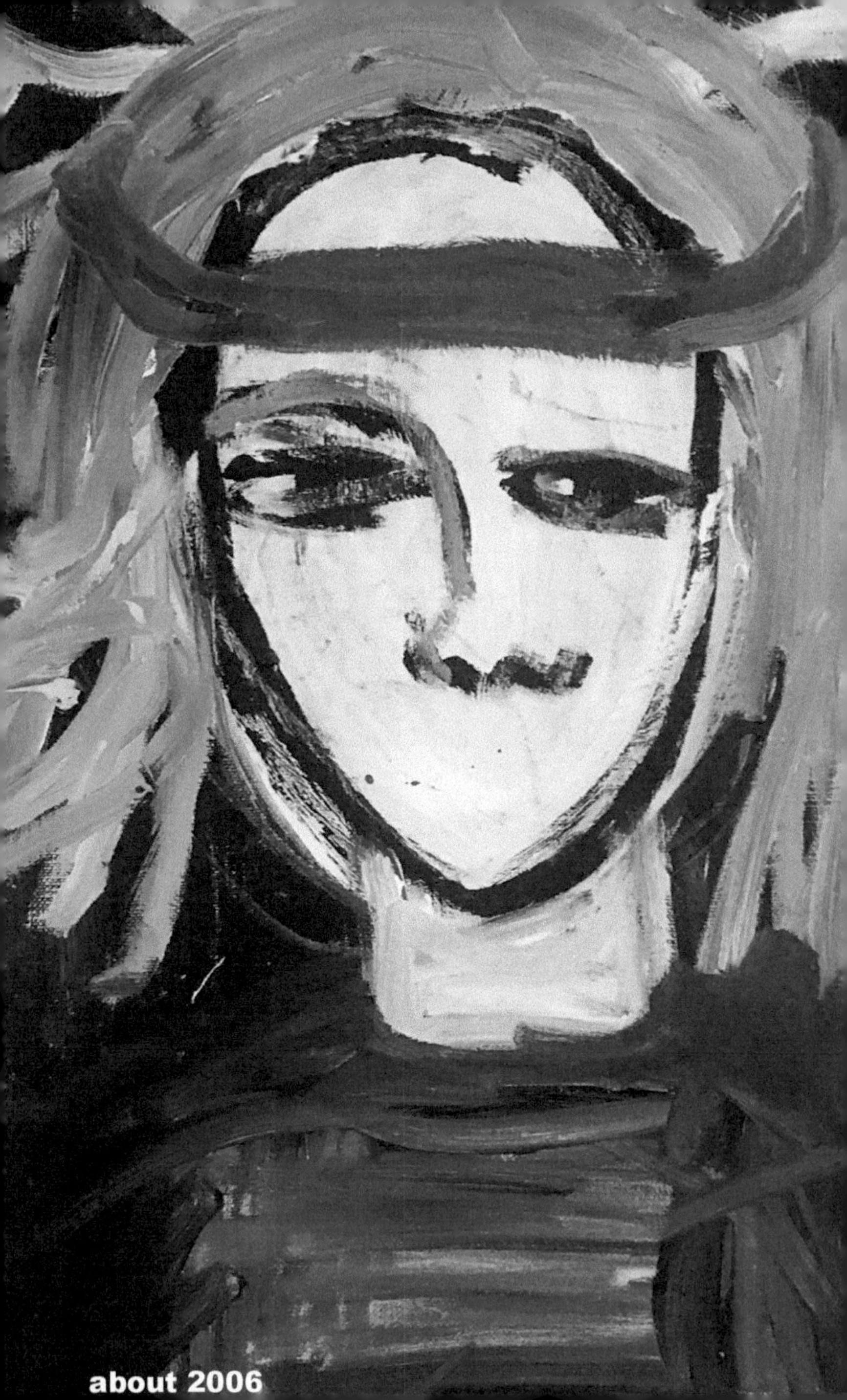

about 2006

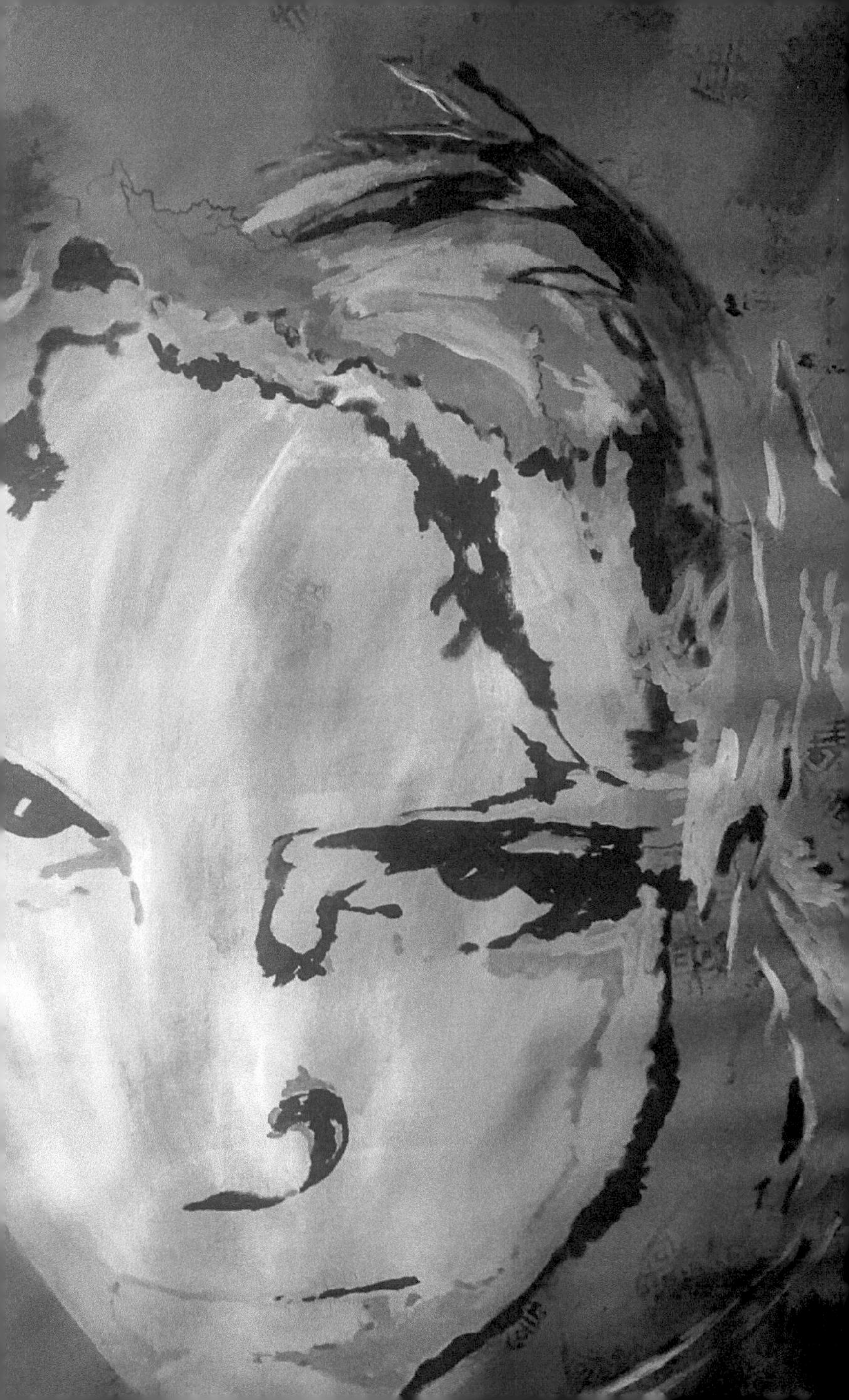

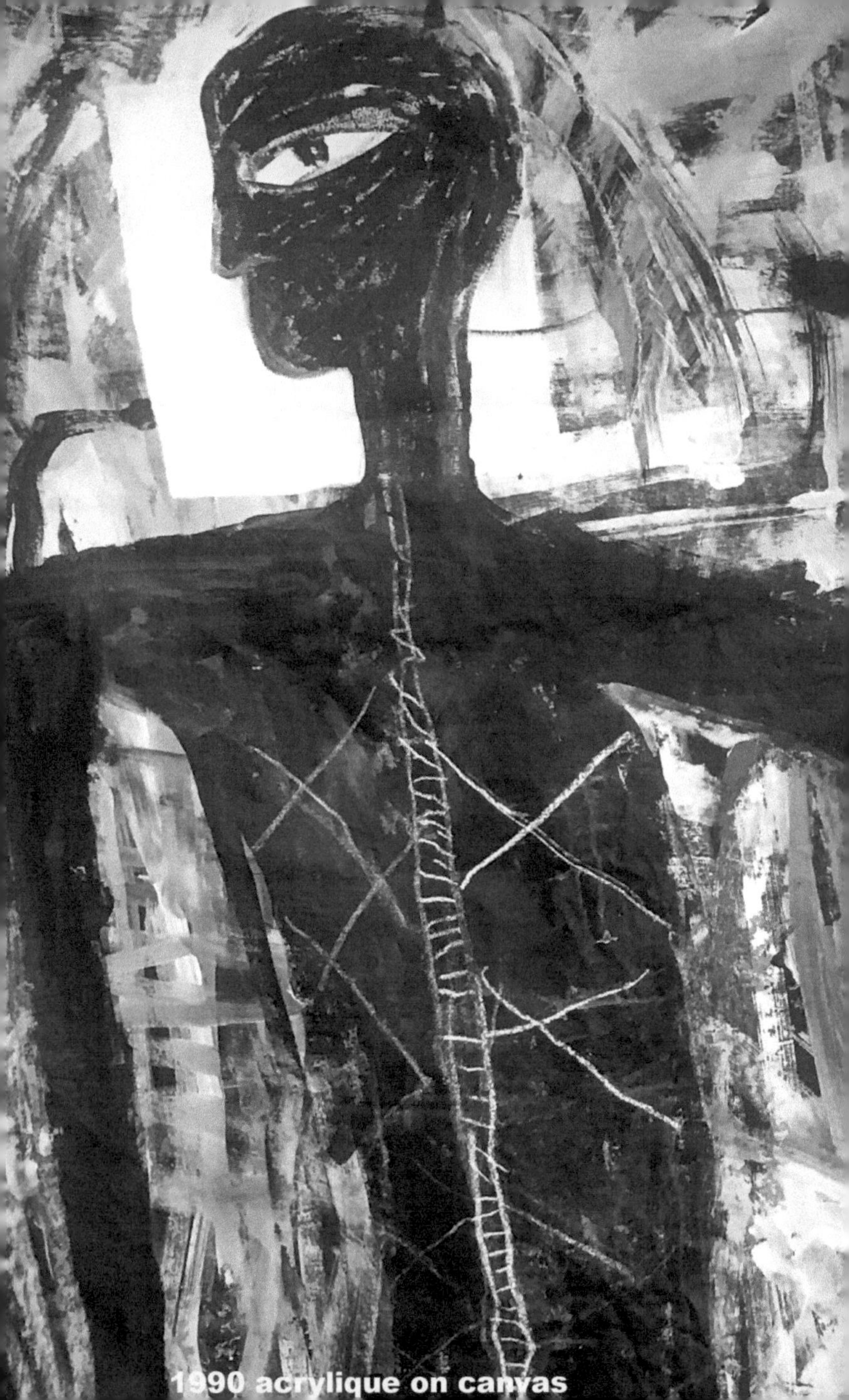

1990 acrylique on canvas

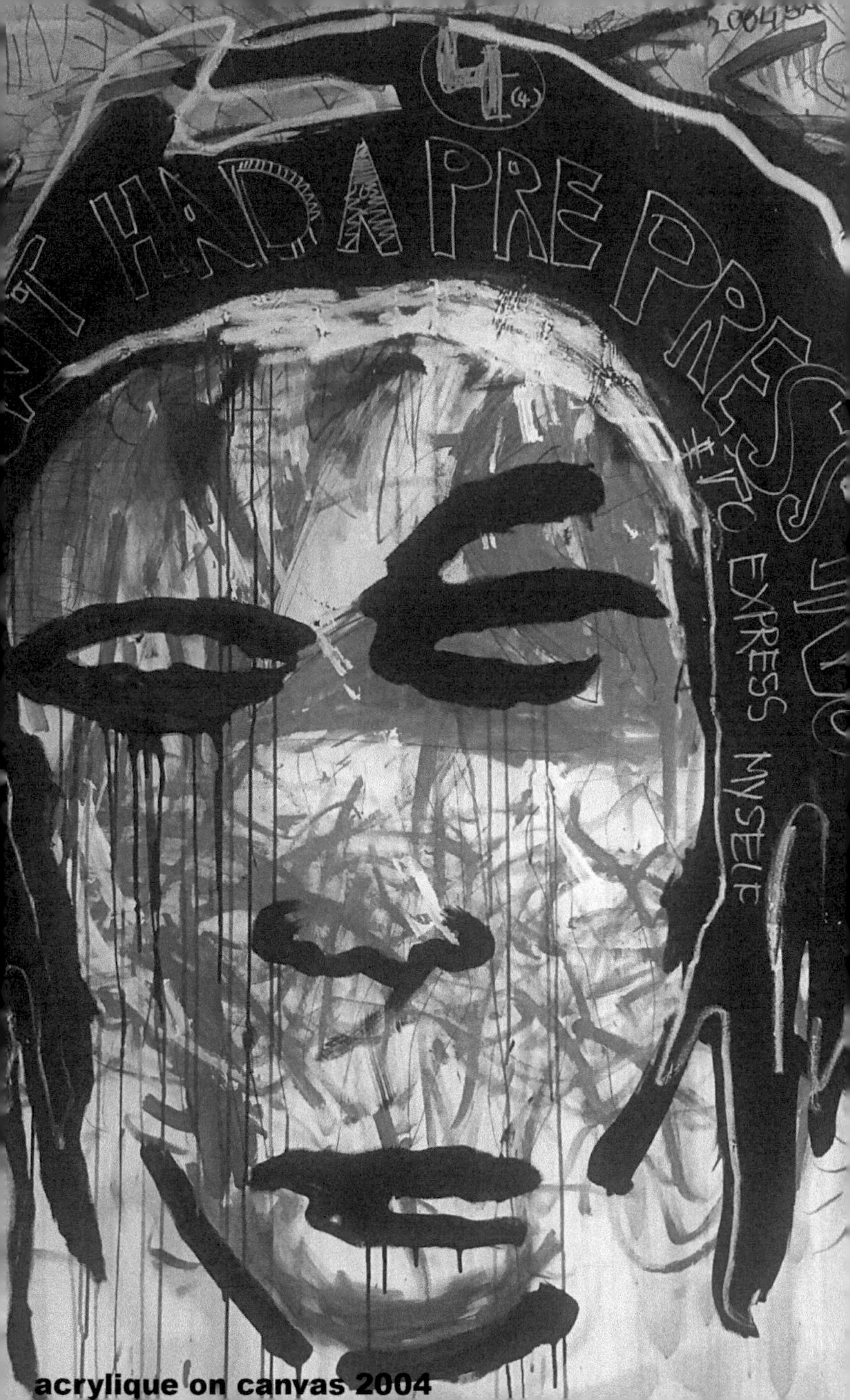
HAD A PRE PRESSION
4
(4)
2004
#TO EXPRESS MYSELF
acrylique on canvas 2004

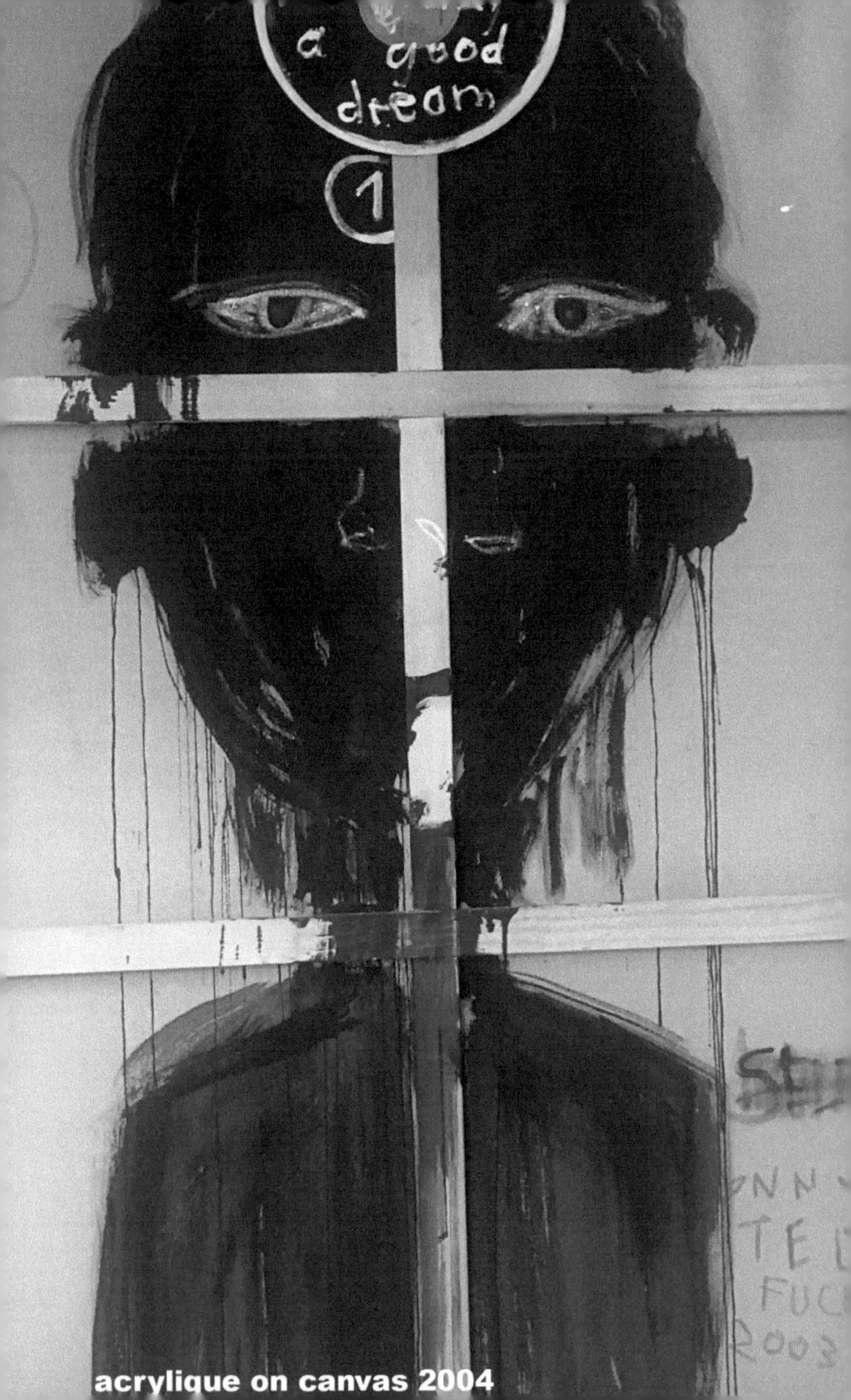

a good
dream
1
acrylique on canvas 2004

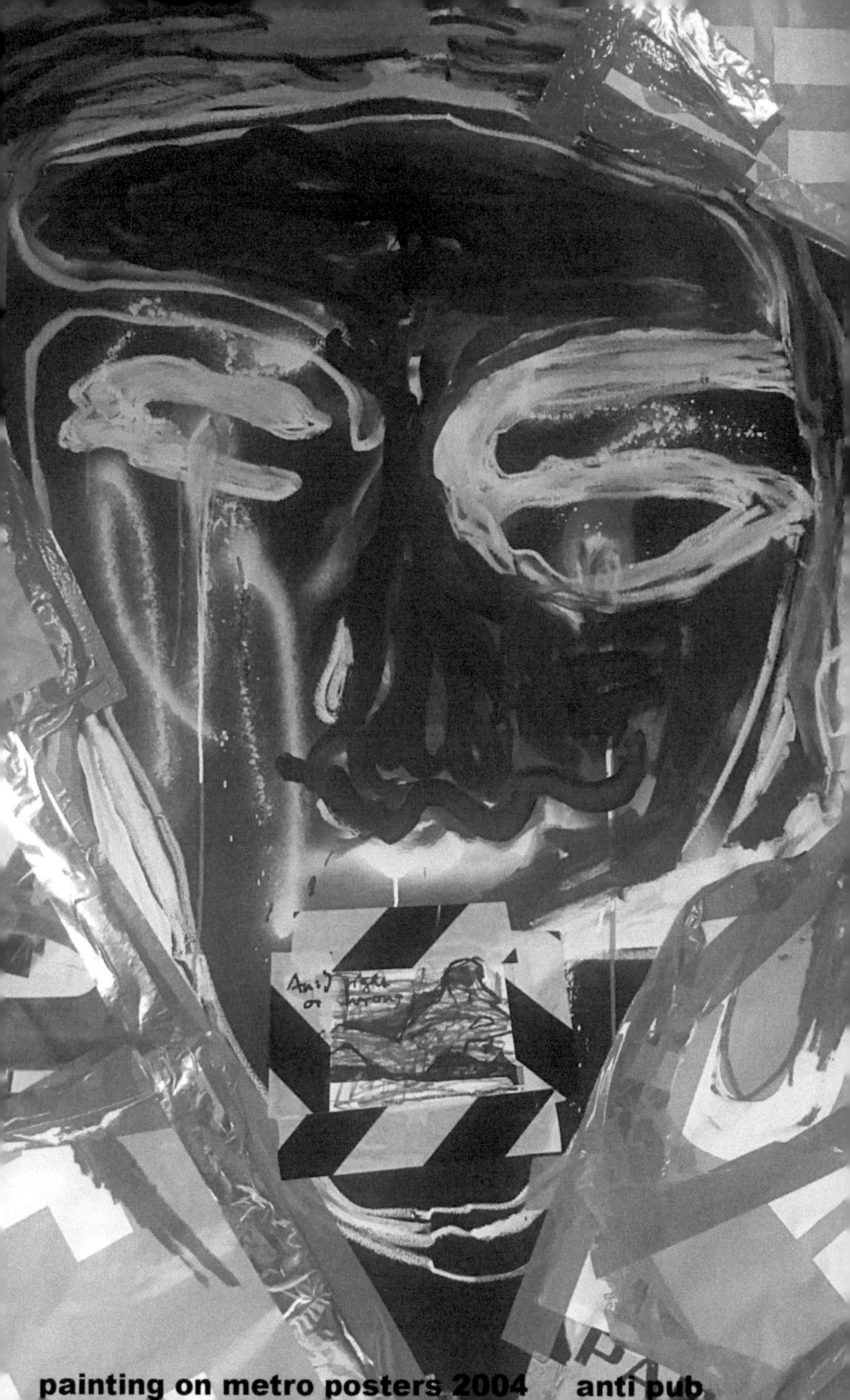

painting on metro posters 2004   anti pub

paintig on back side of canvas

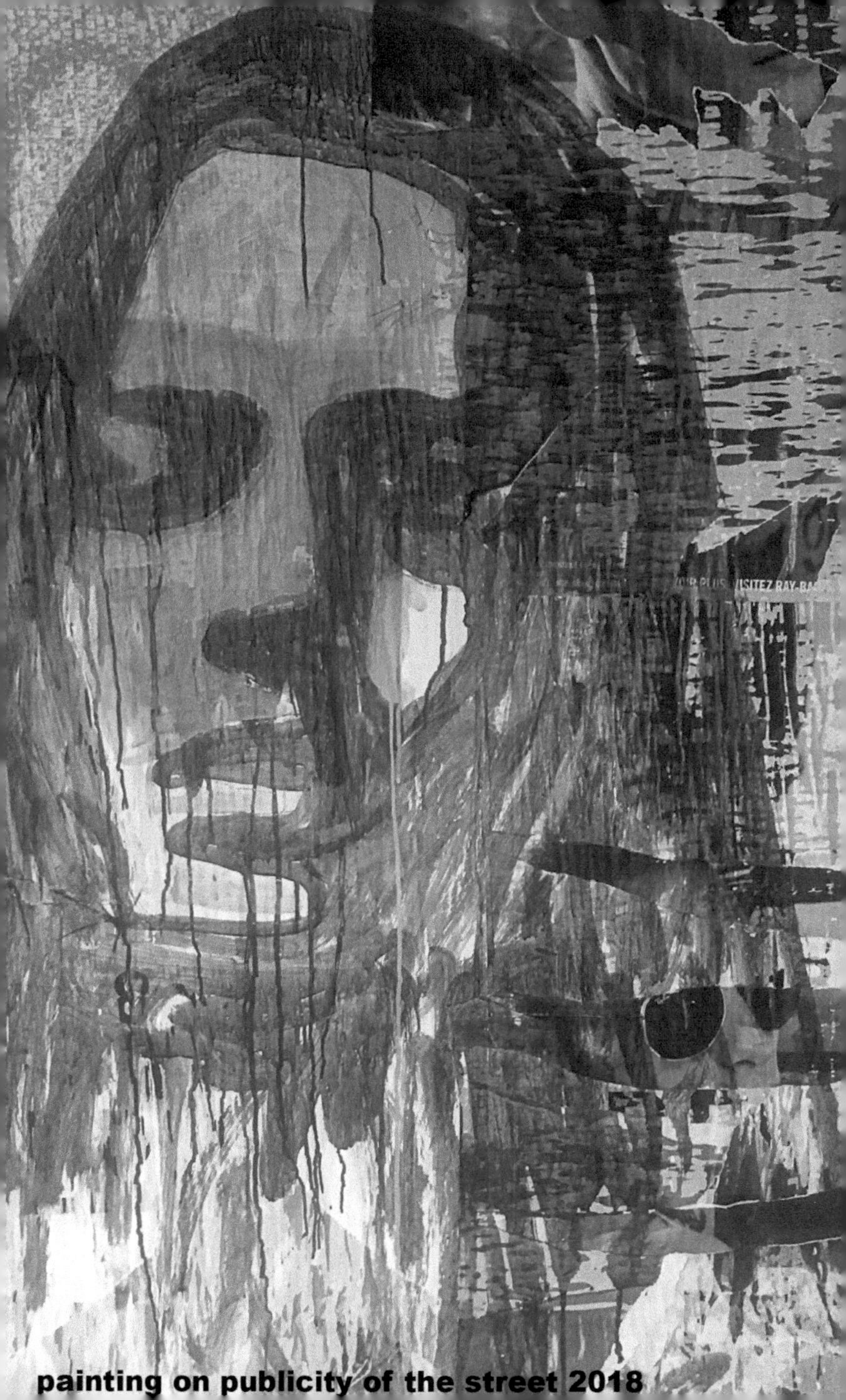

painting on publicity of the street 2018

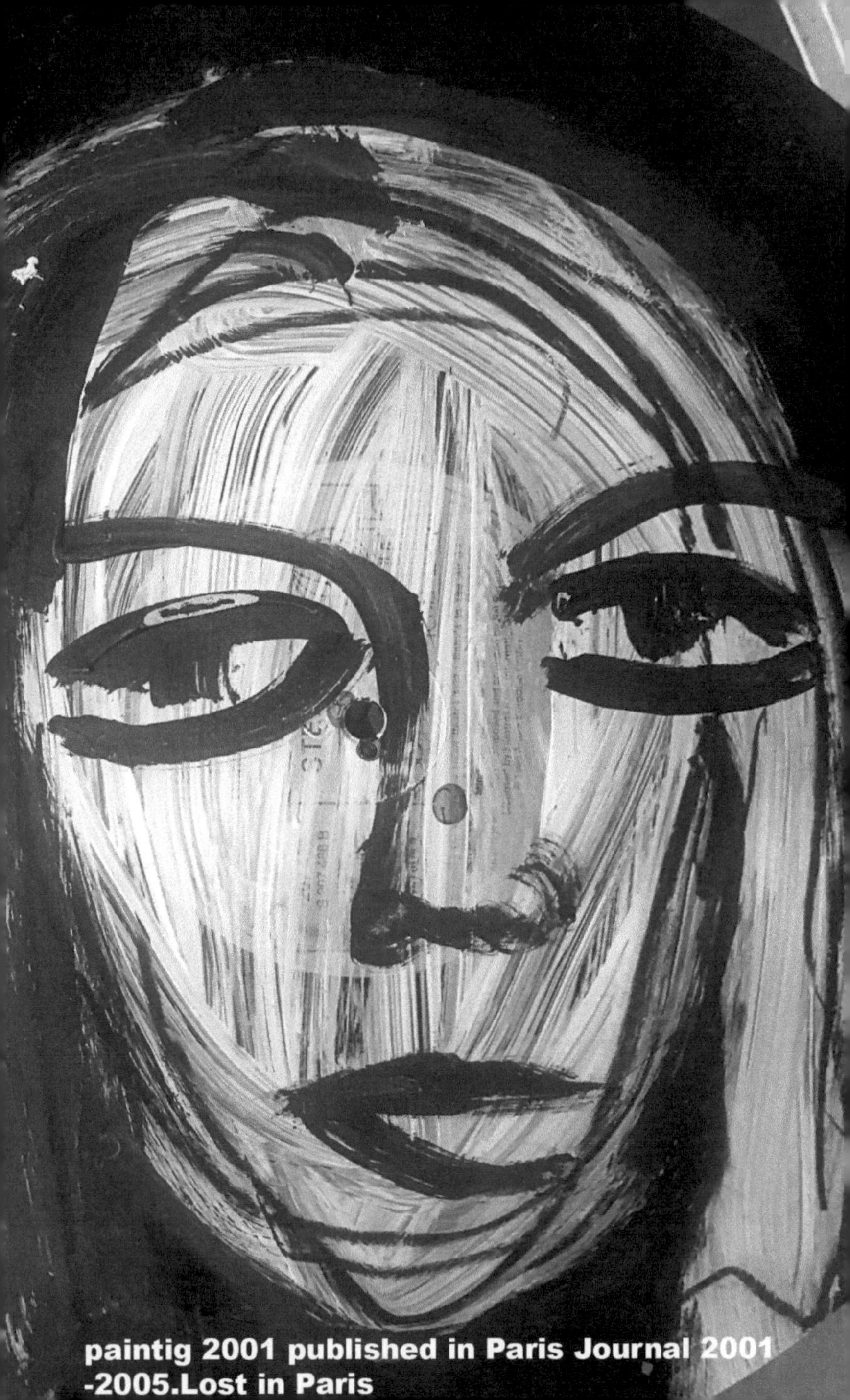
paintig 2001 published in Paris Journal 2001
-2005.Lost in Paris

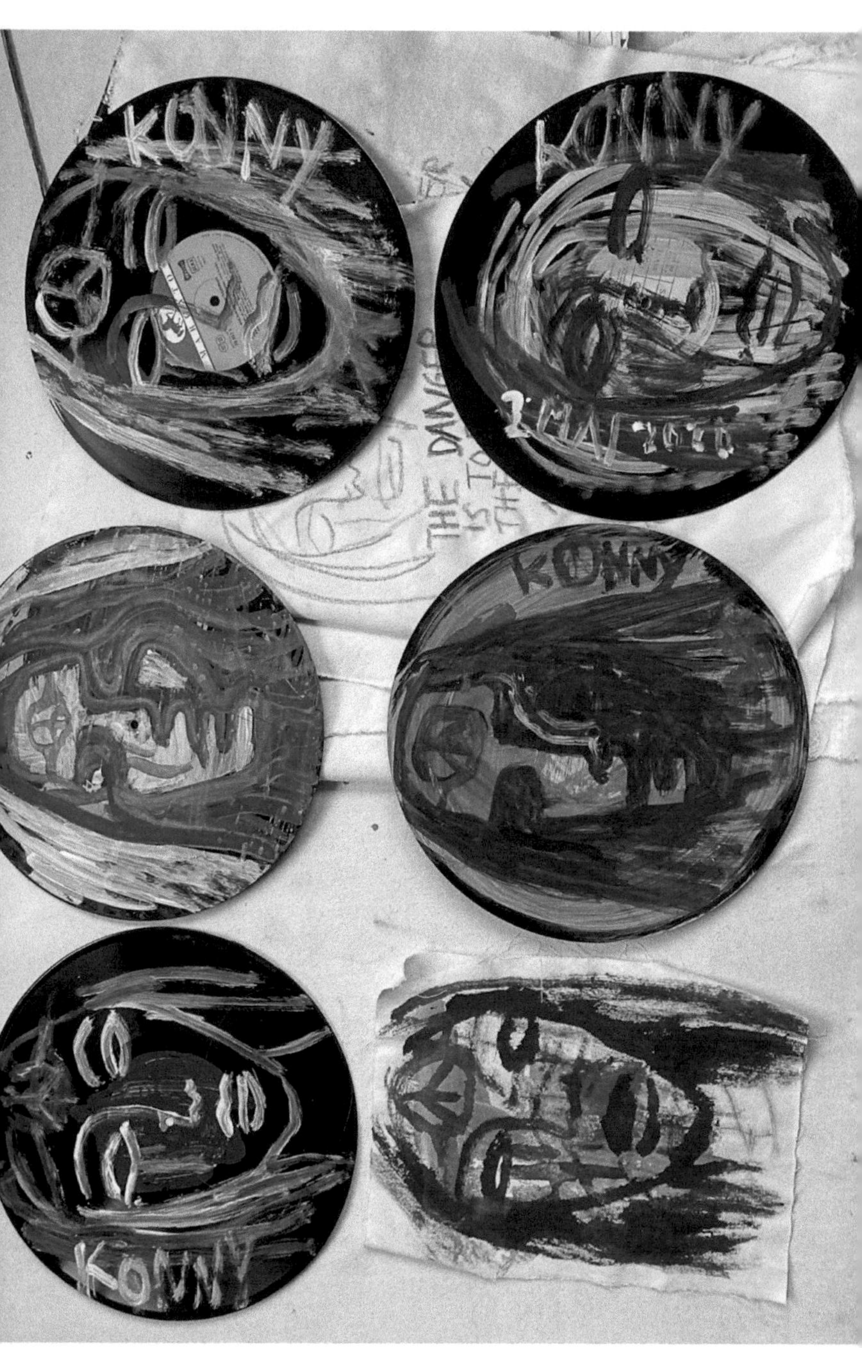

2020 painting on vinyl 2020

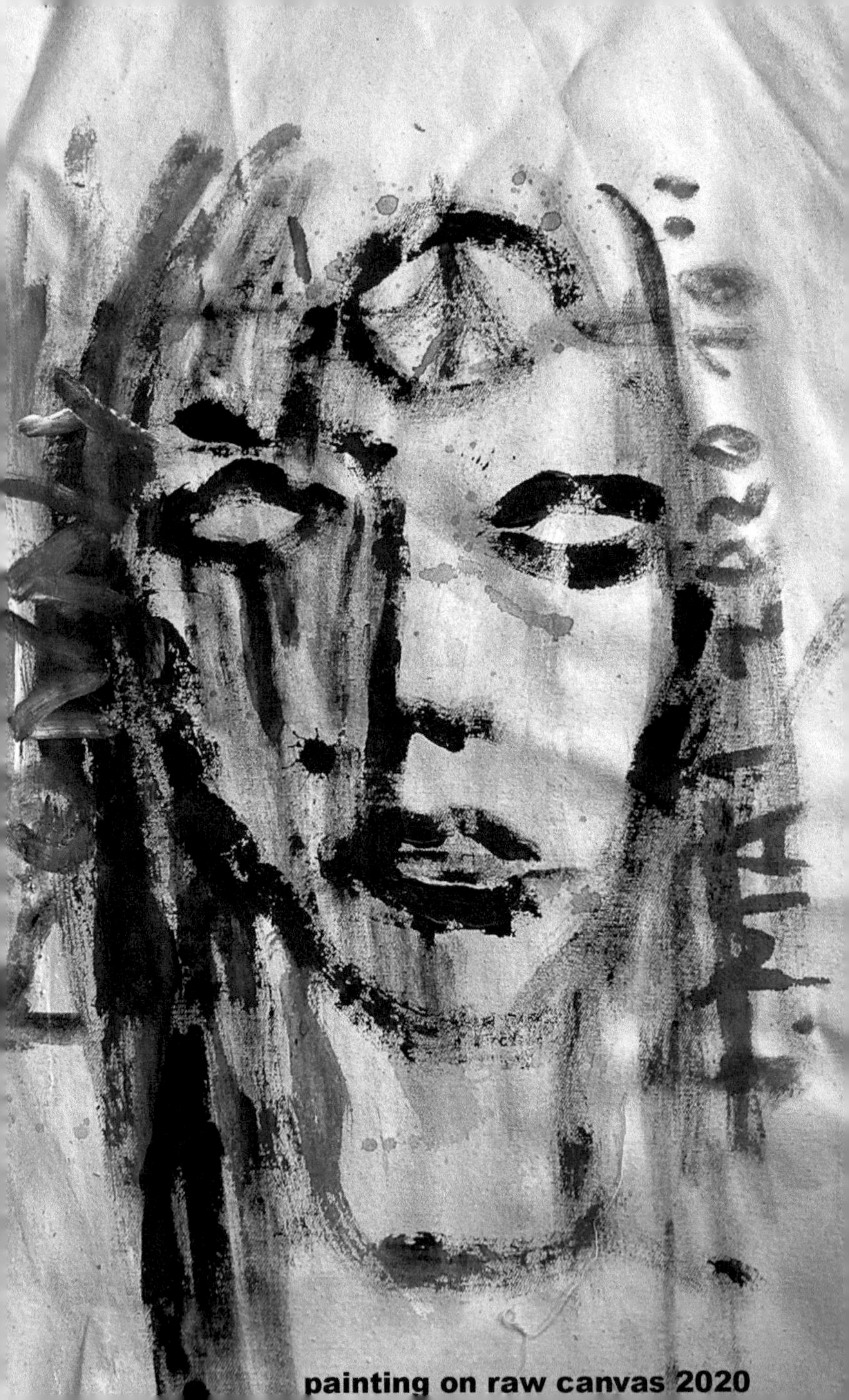

painting on raw canvas 2020

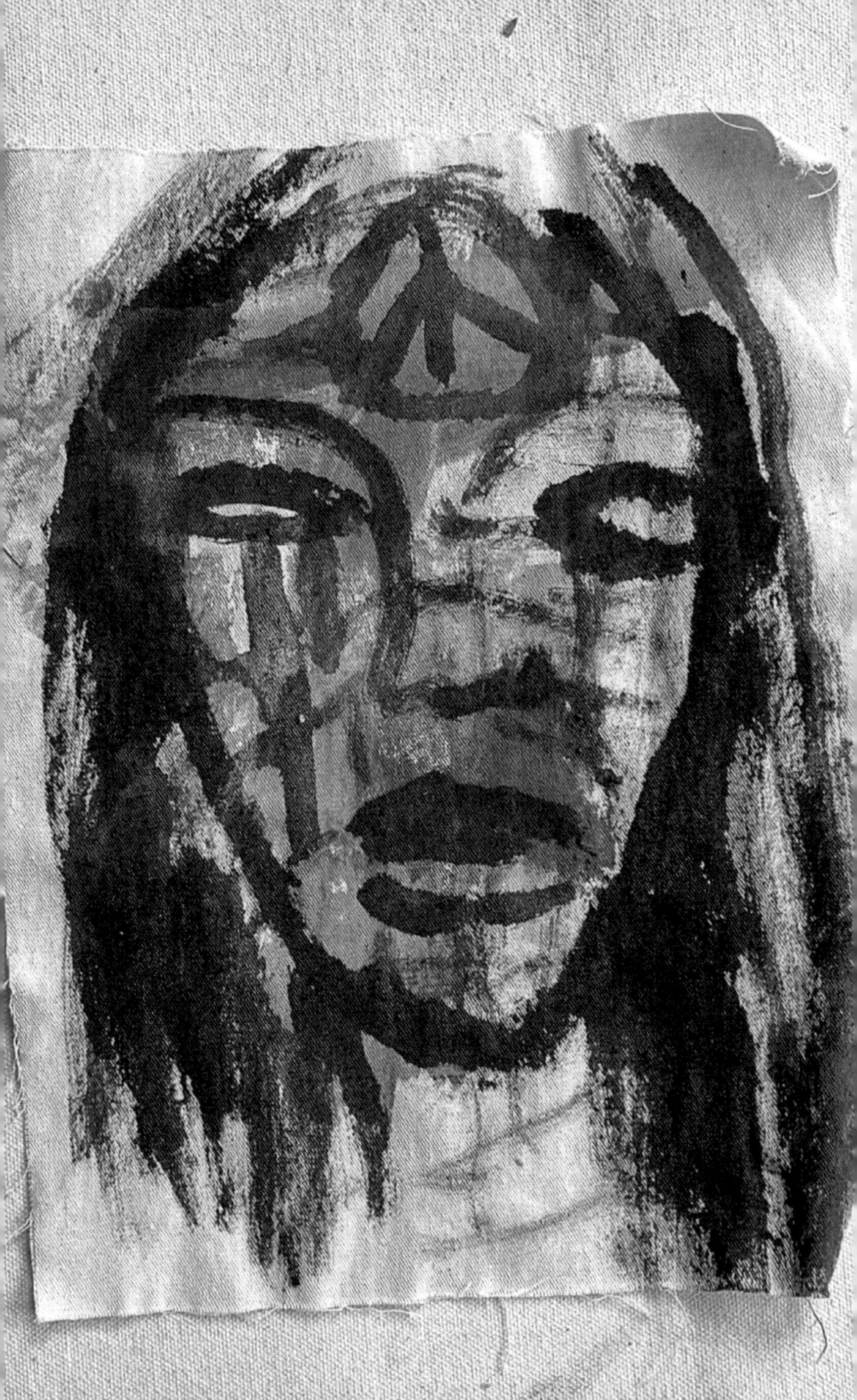

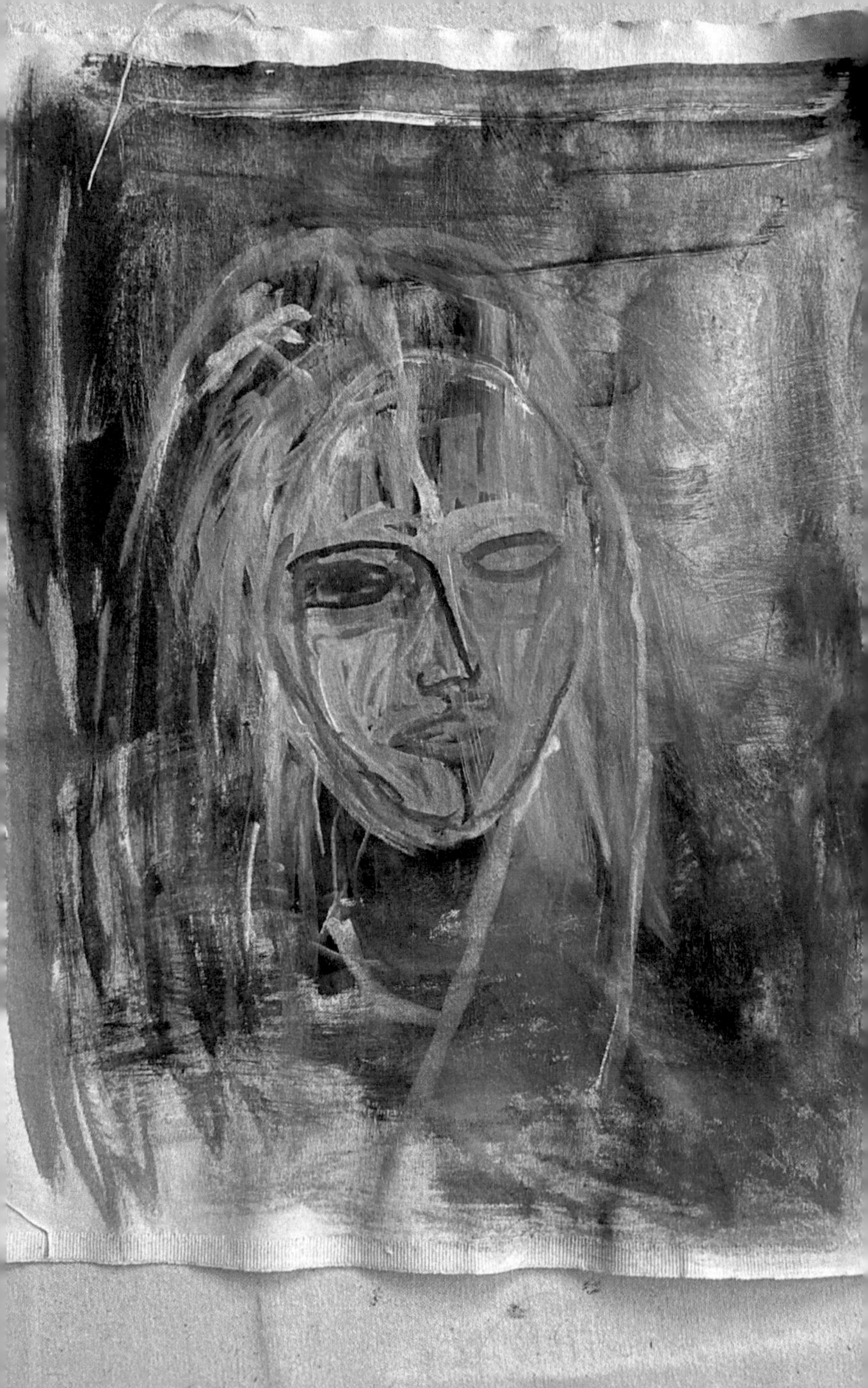

painting on raw canvas 2020

I am that TI painting on raw canas 2020

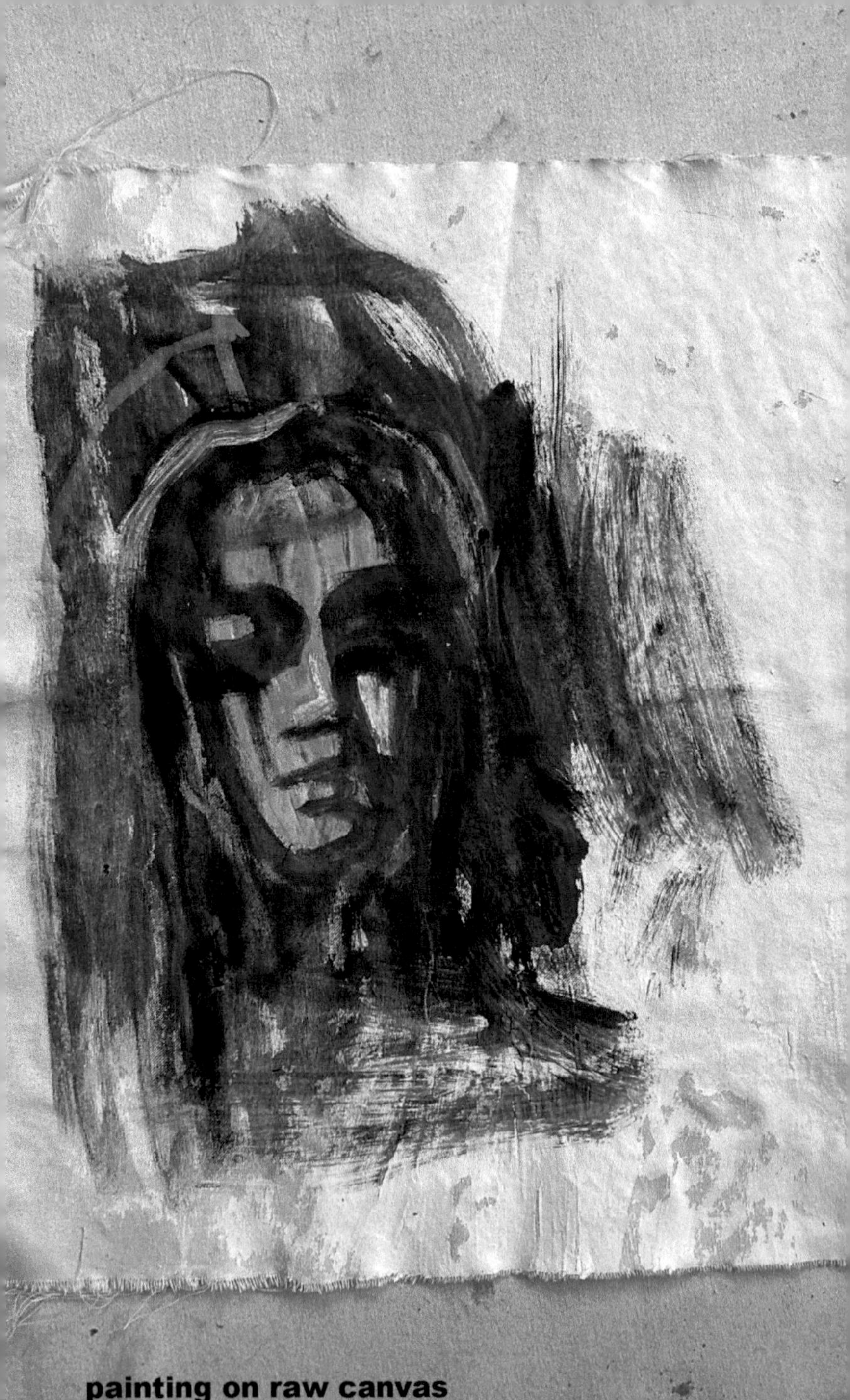

painting on raw canvas

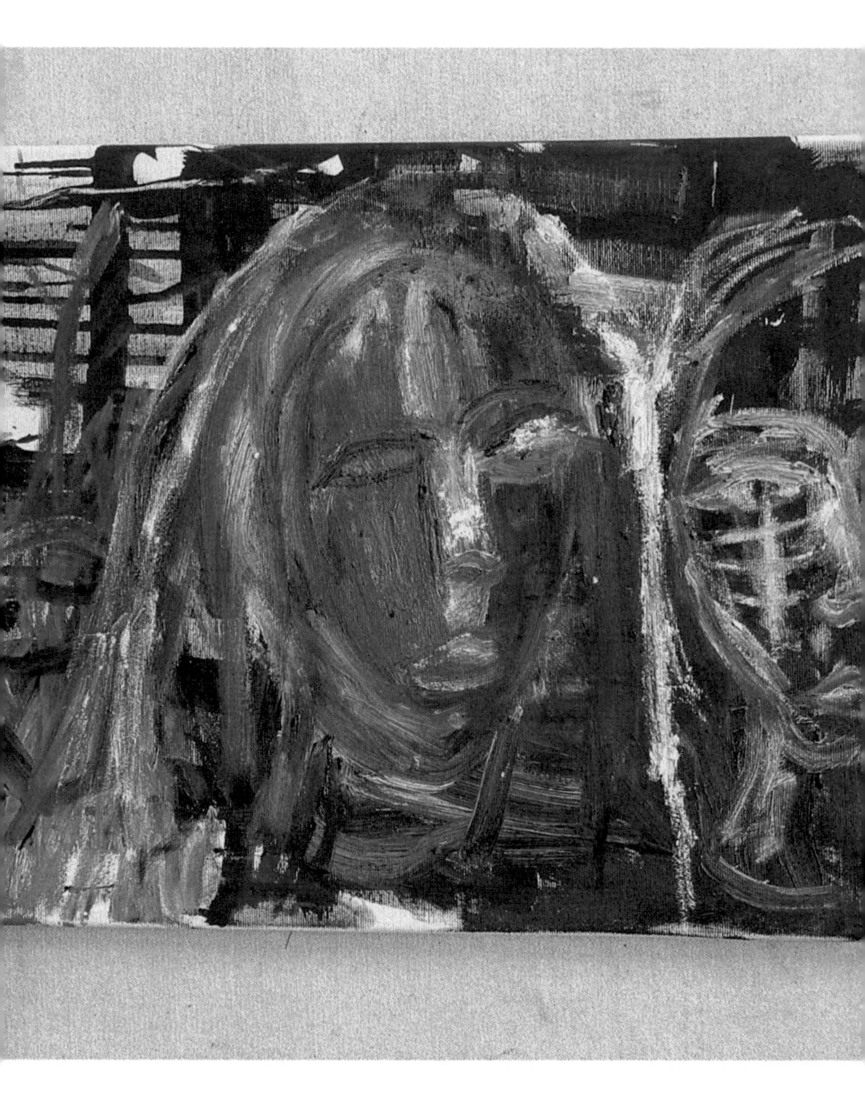

oil on canvas 2020

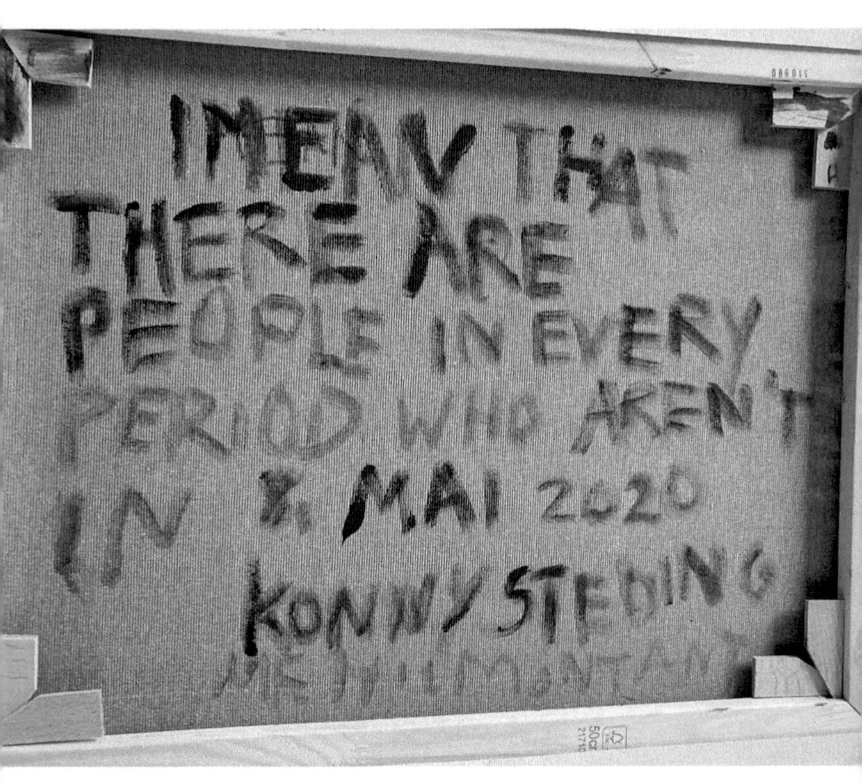

verso I mean that there are people in every
period who aren't in.

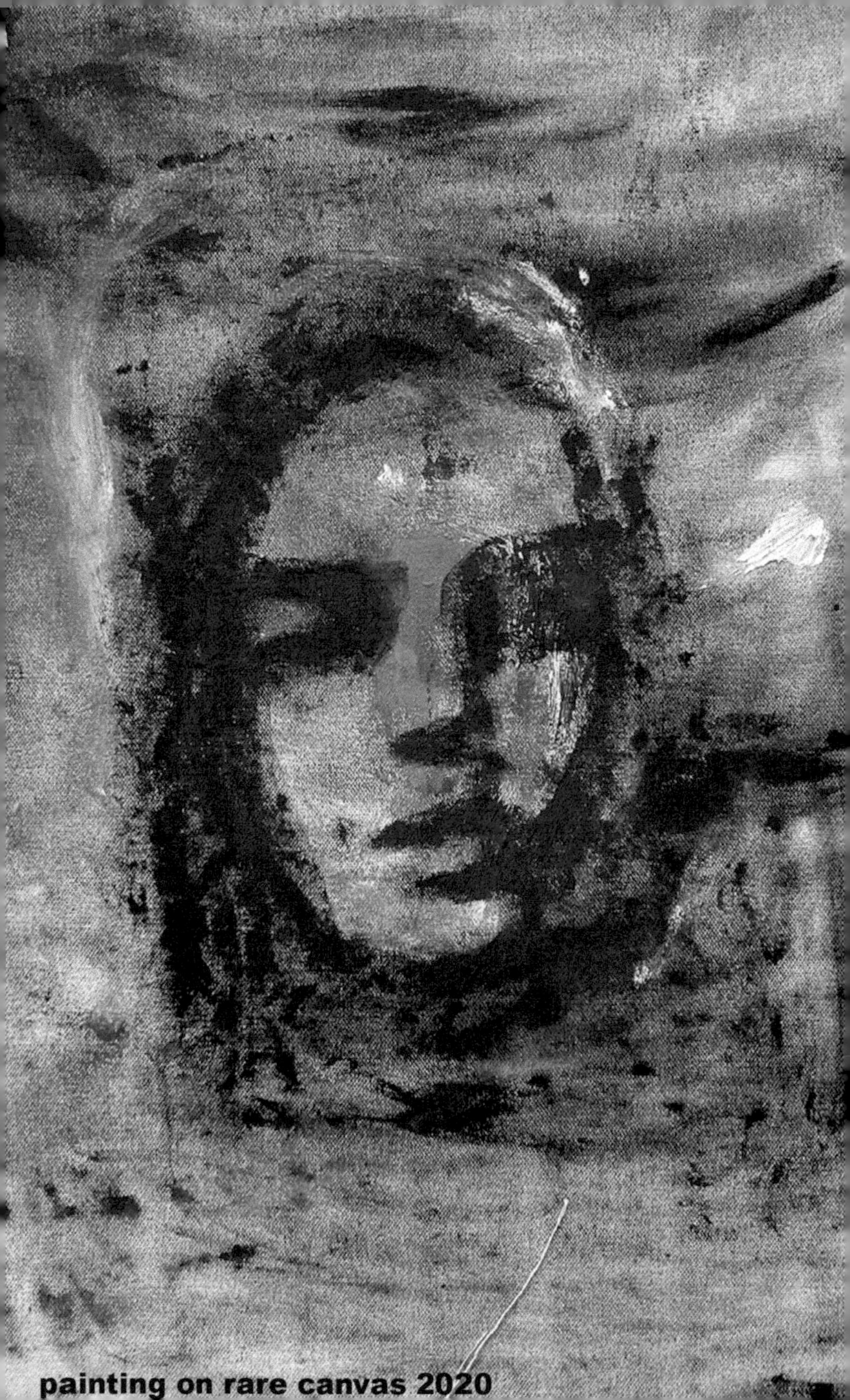

painting on rare canvas 2020

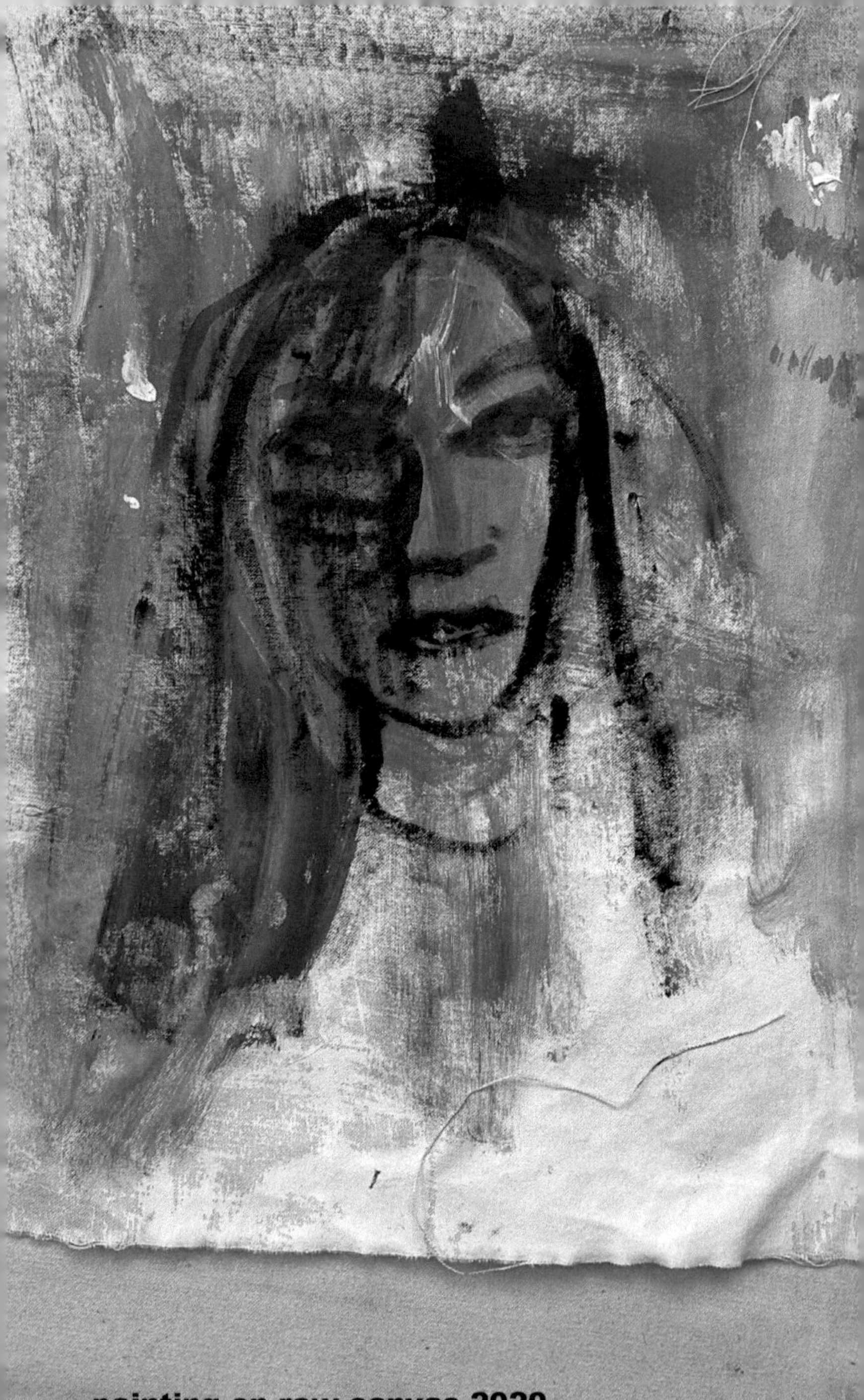

painting on raw canvas 2020

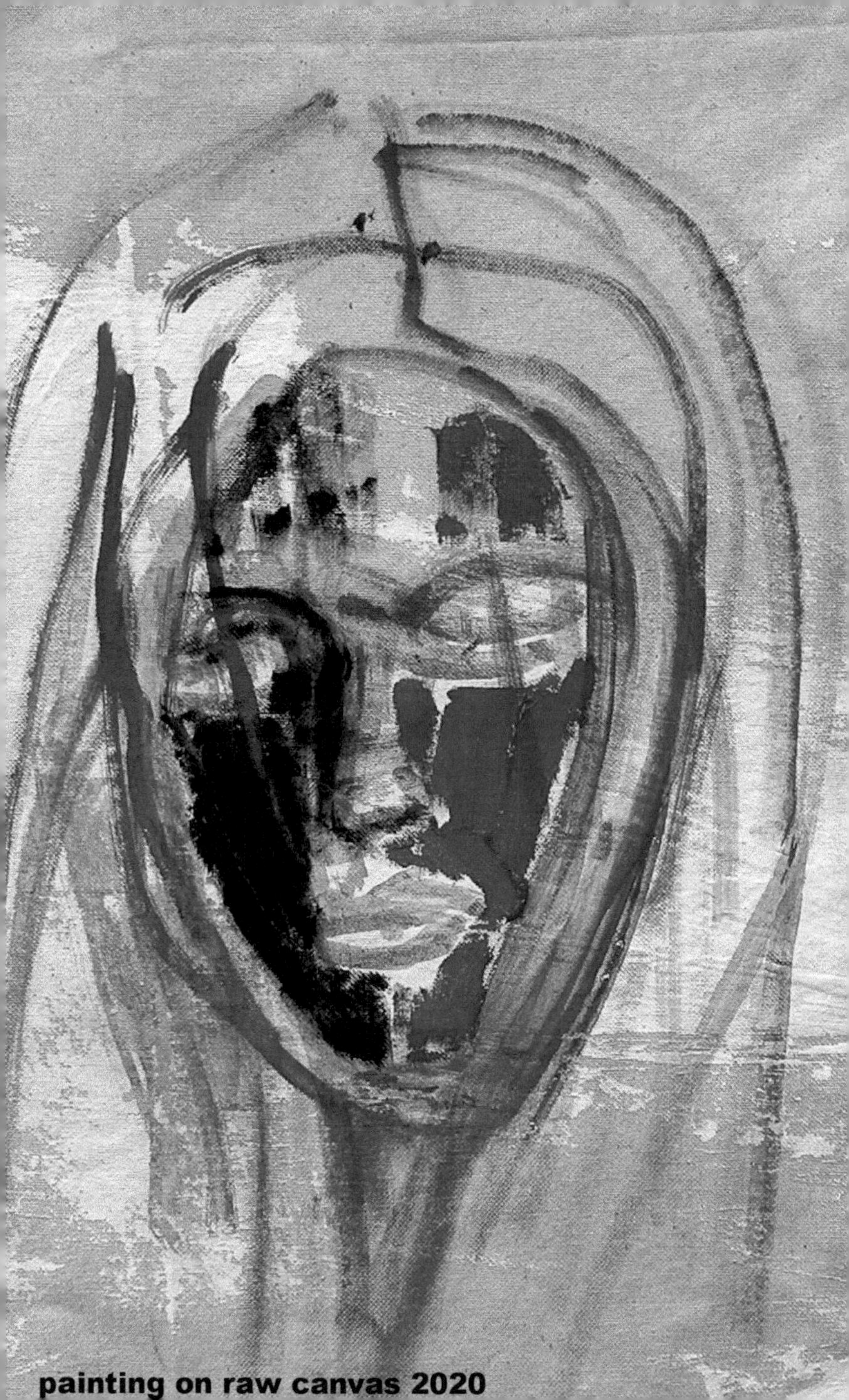

painting on raw canvas 2020

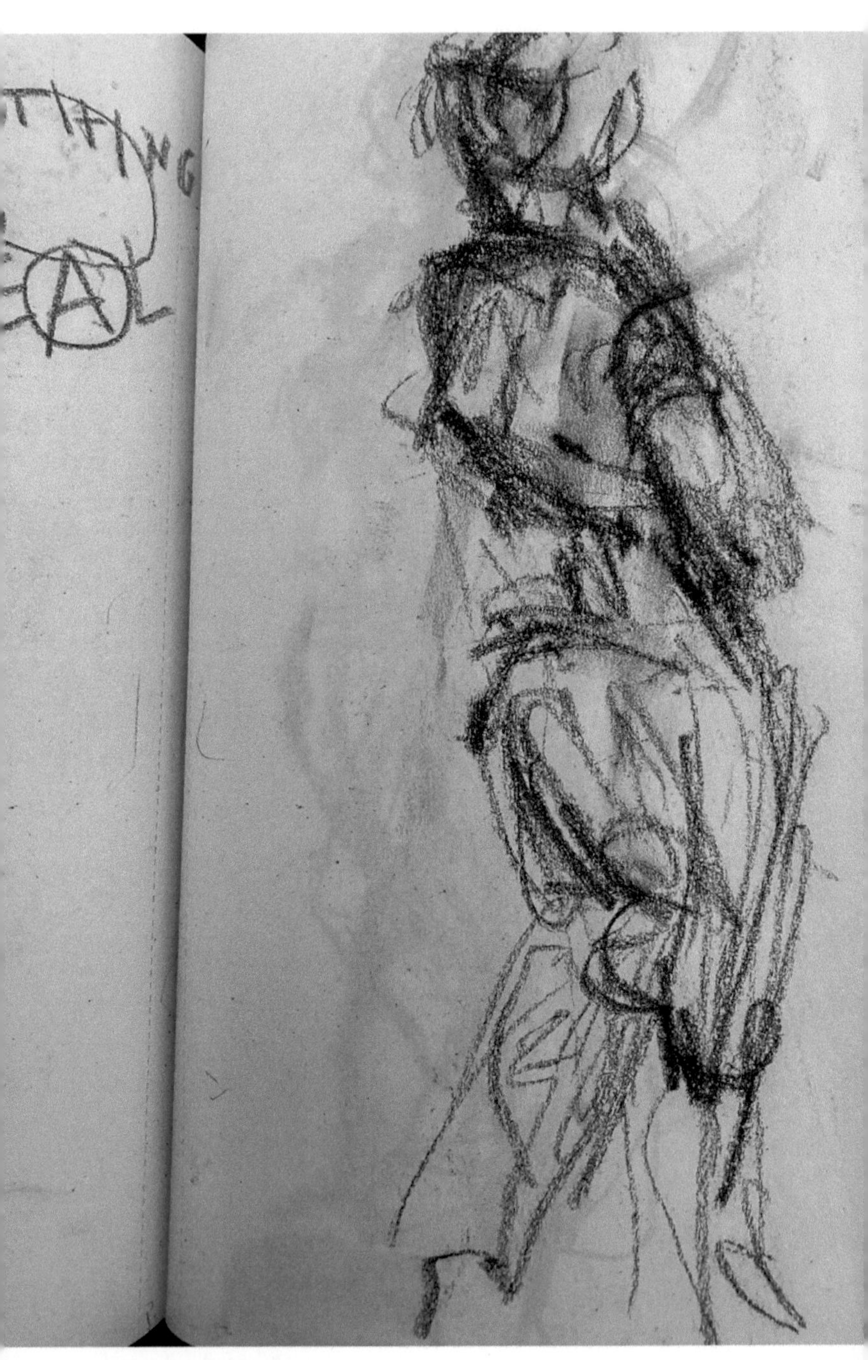

drawing 2020

and sat up all night burning holes with

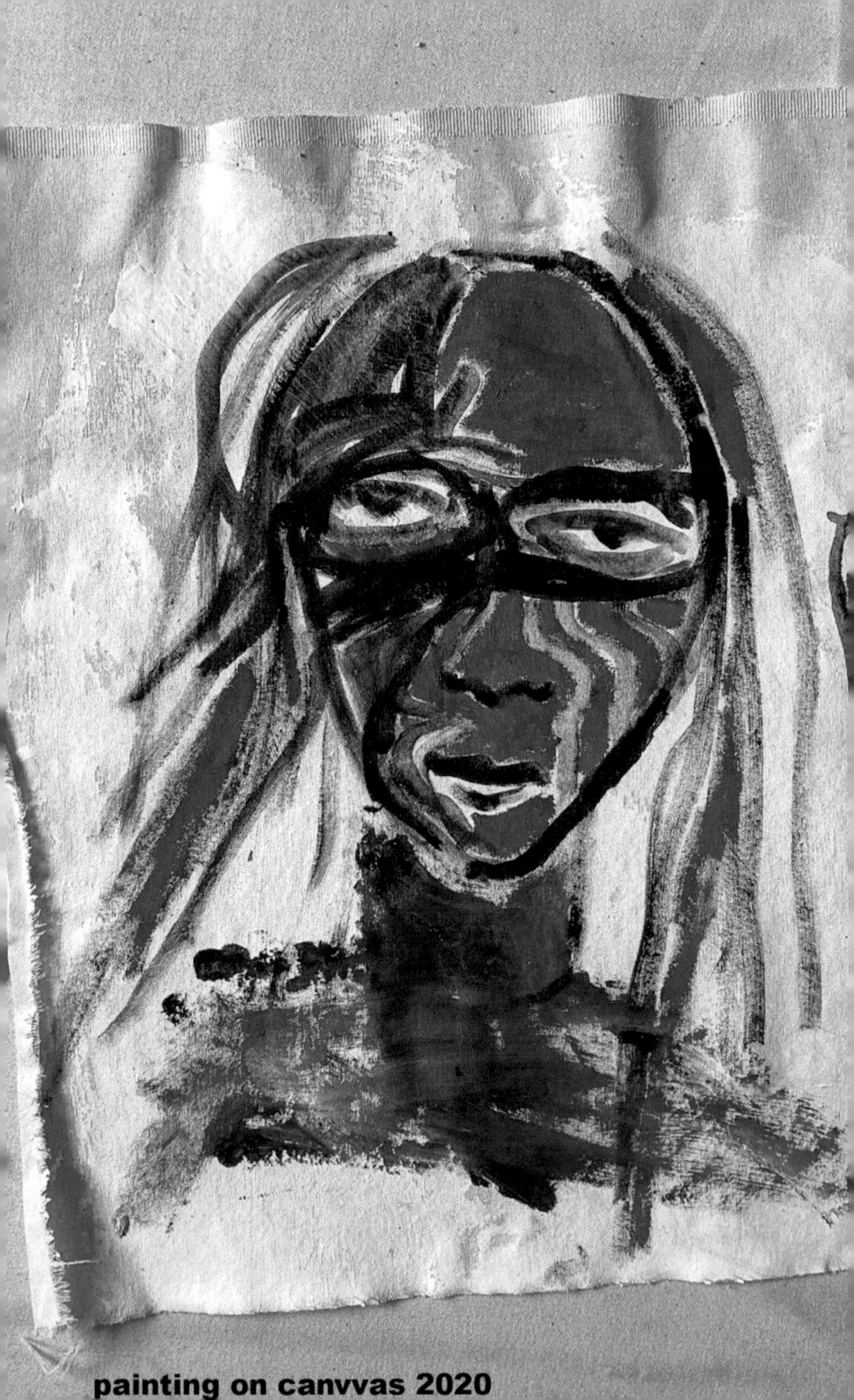

painting on canvvas 2020

"It took a few years to see that not talking was better than talking too much."

Marcel Duchamp
(in Cabanne, Pierre: Dialogues with Marcel Duchamp,
Da Capo Press, Inc. 1987)